False Colors:

Art, Design and Modern Camouflage

Roy R. Behrens

False Colors:
Art, Design and Modern Camouflage

OH GOD, as if we didn't have enough trouble! They send us artists!

— AMERICAN ARMY OFFICER, WORLD WAR I

Dedicated to MARY, RUSKIN,
FIONA, KEEKO, AND ZOOEY

False Colors:
Art, Design and Modern Camouflage

published by
Bobolink Books
2022 X Avenue
Dysart Iowa 52224-9767 USA
E-mail <ballast@netins.net>

◀ FRONTISPIECE
World War I American camouflaged sniper

First edition
ISBN 0-9713244-0-9

Printed in the United States of America

Portions of the earnings from this book will be used for student scholarships, *Ballast Quarterly Review*, and other educational projects.

WHOEVER OWNS two pairs of trousers ought to sell one and buy this book instead.

—GEORG CHRISTOPH LICHTENBERG

GLORY BE TO GOD for dappled things—
For skies of couple-color as a brinded cow;
For rose-moles all in stipple upon trout that
swim;
Fresh-firecoal chestnut-falls; finches' wings;
Landscape plotted and pieced—fold, fallow,
and plough;
And all trades, their gear and tackle and trim.

All things counter, original, spare, strange;
Whatever is fickle, freckled (who knows how?)
With swift, slow; sweet, sour; adazzle, dim;
He fathers-forth whose beauty is past change;
Praise him.

—GERARD MANLEY HOPKINS
"Pied Beauty"

FROM TIME IMMEMORIAL the philosophers and other scene painters have daubed the sky with dazzle paint.

—WALLACE STEVENS

I LEARNED from her and others like her that a first-rate soup is more creative than a second-rate painting, and that, generally, cooking or parenthood or making a home could be creative while poetry need not be; it could be uncreative.

—ABRAHAM MASLOW
Toward a Psychology of Being

THE ENEMIES of the esthetic are neither the practical nor the intellectual. They are the humdrum; slackness and loose ends; submission to convention in practice and intellectual procedure. Rigid abstinence, coerced submission, tightness on the one side and dissipation, incoherence and aimless indulgence on the other, are deviations in opposite directions from the unity of an experience.

—JOHN DEWEY
Art as Experience

I CAME to the conclusion many years ago that almost all crime is due to the repressed desire for esthetic expression.

—EVELYN WAUGH
Decline and Fall

Contents

LEGER WORE a checkered shirt, and the violent pattern of his clothes against the violent pattern of his paintings made him seem like a chameleon.

—ALEXANDER LIBERMAN
The Artist in His Studio

LEONARDO DA VINCI, a great artist and scientist, pointed out Nature's use of protective coloring before [Abbott H.] Thayer was born. Artists before and since have been fully aware of the principles of "countershading," "coincident pattern," "disruption," and "deflection," only they have been called in art schools since the time of Rembrandt such other names as "counterchange," "discord and harmony," "atmospheric and solid perspective." Indeed, it is impossible to paint a picture without using these principles.

—C.H. ROWE
"Camouflage in War-time"

THE ARTIST, with his understanding of the subtleties of color, tone, and texture and his ability to draw on visual memory, has probably contributed the most to military camouflage in all its forms.

—GUY HARTCUP
Camouflage: A History of Concealment and Deception in War

Prolegomenon

A PAINTING needs as much fraudulence, trickery and deception as the perpetration of a crime. Paint falsely, and then add a whiff of nature.

—EDGAR DEGAS

THE MAIN CHARACTER in Kurt Vonnegut's novel *Bluebeard* is Rabo Karebekian, a painter who served in a U.S. Army camouflage unit during World War II. All the soldiers in this troop were "artists of one sort or another in civilian life," Karebekian explains, because "it was the theory of someone in the Army that we [artists] would be especially good at camouflage."

According to Vonnegut, his novel is a "hoax autobiography" that is nonetheless based on a little-known fact: During World Wars I and II, there really were units of camouflage experts (called *camoufleurs*); and these units were largely made up of soldiers who in civilian life had been artists, architects and designers of one kind or another, including painters, sculptors, printmakers, graphic designers, illustrators, and theatre set designers. These camouflage units were organized not first or only by the Americans; instead, they were set up initially by the French, British, German, Italian, and Russian armies.

The belief that visual artists might be well-suited for camouflage was suggested in part by the publication in 1909 of a pioneering book about "protective coloration," the term that was commonly used at the time for camouflage in nature. Titled *Concealing Coloration in the Animal Kingdom*, it reported the findings not of a scientist but of an American painter, Abbott Handerson Thayer. Following that example, when the French Army established a few years later the first *section de camouflage* in military history, the person placed in its command was also an artist.

Someone got the bright idea [during World War I] that our division should have some camouflage men, so they started putting together a special squad of creative types who had some connection with painting. I'd been studying at Pratt Institute before I enlisted, so I volunteered.

—Henry Berry
Make the Kaiser Dance,
p. 206.

The primary purpose of this book is to describe very broadly the historic involvement in military and civilian camouflage of hundreds of artists, architects and designers during World Wars I and II, including such familiar names as Grant Wood, Jacques Villon, Thomas Hart Benton, Charles Burchfield, Arshile Gorky, and Ellsworth Kelly.

A second, more difficult goal is to talk sensibly about connections among art, design and camouflage in relation to perceptual psychology, esthetics, psychoanalysis, creativity, humor, sleight of hand, and so on.

More than two decades ago, I wrote a slim, effusive book titled *Art and Camouflage: Concealment and Deception in Nature, Art and War*. Long out of print and now impossible to find, it has become collectible, in spite of or maybe because of the fact that it is, as I've admitted elsewhere, "wildly inaccurate."

This new book revisits the scene of the crime. Looking back, there can be no doubt that I have aged; but my interest in camouflage has only intensified, and today I still daily discover some fact about the subject, while my thinking and writing continue to grow.

Art is always about turning two into three or three into two.

—Paul Feeley
quoted in Goossen,
p. 57.

I am indebted to the editors of *Gestalt Theory, Iowa Heritage Illustrated, Journal of Aesthetic Education, Leonardo, North American Review,* and PRINT, in which many of the ideas in this volume were published first in other forms. I am grateful to my colleagues (particularly Philip Fass, Osie Johnson, and Gary Kelley), to the brilliant and hard-working students I've taught at the University of Wisconsin-Milwaukee, Art Academy of Cincinnati, and University of Northern Iowa, and to the administrators who gave me research grants, awards, sabbaticals, and other forms of encouragement at those same schools.

For many years, I have benefited from both the pleasurable and agonizing aspects of being a classroom teacher; from editing *Ballast Quarterly Review*; and from years of writing letters to Guy Davenport, Rudolf Arnheim, Walter Hamady, and others.

More than anything else, however, I have gained from the love and support of my wife, artist Mary Snyder Behrens.

[Art] and camouflage are in reality obverse and reverse of a similar practice: the former makes nothing look like something, while the latter, as Humpty Dumpty might have said, makes something unlook like itself.

—Milton Fox
"Camouflage" (1942),
p. 137.

—Roy R. Behrens
June 27, 2001

Chapter One

Hundreds of Differences All Fitting In Together

Esthetics, Anesthetics and Gestalt Theory

IN 1923, MAX WERTHEIMER, one of the founders of Gestalt psychology, published an innovative paper titled "The Laws of Organization in Perceptual Forms."[1.1] Among his students at the Psychological Institute at the University of Berlin, it was nicknamed Wertheimer's *Punktarbeit* or "dot paper" because virtually all its examples were abstract patterns made of dots.

One of Wertheimer's graduate students was Rudolf Arnheim, a 19-year-old Jewish-German student who had grown up in Berlin and whose father owned a piano factory. Arnheim's major was in psychology, which was then a branch of philosophy, with a double minor in the histories of art and music. It was the interplay of these four academic disciplines—philosophy, psychology, art and music—that provided the groundwork for his subsequent trailblazing writings about the psychology of art.[1.2]

Art is the imposing of a pattern on experience, and our esthetic enjoyment is the recognition of that pattern.

—ALFRED NORTH WHITEHEAD
Dialogues, p. 228.

◀ **FIGURE I.A**
GARY KELLEY
Preparatory drawing for a pastel illustration titled *Aprés le Bain* (After the Bath).

Human speech is like a cracked kettle on which we tap out tunes that can make bears dance, when we would move the stars.

—GUSTAV FLAUBERT
Madame Bovary

[When asked about the beauty of stars in the night sky] Well, not bad, but there are decidedly too many of them, and they are not very well arranged. I would have done it differently.

—JAMES A.M.WHISTLER

We are all in the gutter, but some of us are looking at the stars.

—OSCAR WILDE

More than thirty years after Wertheimer's dot paper, Arnheim published *Art and Visual Perception: A Psychology of the Creative Eye*, a 500-page opus in which, in precise and exhaustive detail, he examined the visual arts through the filter of perceptual psychology. Arnheim's indebtedness to his teacher is shown by the fact that both documents (the dot paper and Arnheim's book) begin by affirming the very same point: We experience the world neither as an unbroken continuum nor as a mélange of disorderly blips. Rather, in the very act of perceiving it, we instinctively organize our experience (a process that Arnheim would later describe as "visual thinking"), with the result that we see it as being comprised (in the words of Paul Weiss) of "a patchwork of discrete fragments."[1.3]

Simply put, we see things in clusters or patterns or groups. In looking at the night sky, for example, we automatically see constellations, in which some stars are perceived as belonging together, others as belonging apart. Throughout human history, there has been a tendency to connect the seven stars of Ursa Major (the Big Dipper), despite the unfathomable physical space that separates, for example, the farthest star Alkaid (which is 210 light-years from the Earth) from Mizar, the one adjacent to it (the distance of which is 88 light-years).

The importance of this instinctive grouping process, which Gestaltist Fritz Heider called "unit forming,"[1.4] was described later by Arnheim in *Entropy and Art*, a succinct discussion of orderly form: "Order makes it possible to focus on what is alike and what is different," he wrote, "what belongs together and what is segregated. When nothing superfluous is included and nothing indispensible left out, one can understand the interrelation of the whole and its parts, as well as the hierarchic scale of importance and power by which some structural features are dominant, others subordinate."[1.5]

Units which resemble each other in shape, size, direction, color, brightness, or location will be seen together.

—Rudolf Arnheim
"Gestalt Psychology and Artistic Form"

Having established the inevitability of unit forming, both Arnheim* and Wertheimer go on to propose that there are certain conditions that make it more likely that some groupings will result rather than others. In Wertheimer's dot paper, he postulates four major "unit forming factors": *Similarity, proximity, continuity* and *closure*. Regarding the night sky (which features stars instead of dots), he is likely to claim that the stars in the Big Dipper (despite their phenomenal differences) coalesce into a constellation because, from our Earth-bound point of view, they appear similar in size, shape and brightness (similarity grouping); are comparatively close together (proximity grouping); and are more or less simply, consistently placed in ways that result in what Wertheimer called "good continuation" and "a good Gestalt."

★ Arnheim's books have influenced my writing and teaching since my undergraduate student days in the 1960s. I first wrote to him in 1971, when he was still teaching at Harvard, asking for advice about a proposed book on art and camouflage, which I had just begun to work on. As I write this sentence, he is 97 years old; we are still corresponding, and he is still actively publishing in scholarly journals.

It is now commonly assumed among artists that Wertheimer's unit forming factors provide confirmation of age-old rules of thumb in art. This is largely due to the writings of Arnheim, as well as an earlier widely-read book, titled *Language of Vision*, by the Hungarian-born painter György Kepes.

We tend to group units on the basis of proximity or of similarity—i.e., two shapes situated close to each other are seen together as a visual whole even though they may be dissimilar; but more insistent is the linking together of similar units, similar shapes or colors...

—MAURICE DE SAUSMAREZ
Basic Design

If your man says of some picture "Yes, but what does it mean?" ask him, and keep on asking him, what his carpet means, or the circular patterns on his rubber shoe-soles. Make him lift up his foot to look at them.

—STEPHEN POTTER
The Complete Upmanship, p. 202

In his book, Kepes demonstrates the "laws of visual organization" or unit-forming factors with neither stars nor dots, but with the arrangement of his own words. "We form the stars of the firmament into a variety of patterns, primarily because of their relative nearness to one another," he writes, and in the same way, "We read words as segregated wholes because their letters are closer to one another than are the last and the first letter of two words." Using proximity grouping, the letterforms in Kepes' book are spaced to support his intended reading, not to subvert it: "Spatial organization is the vital factor in an optical message," he asserts—not "Sp atialor gani zationalist hevital fa ctorin an optical message" nor "Spatial organizationis thevital fa ctorin an optical message."[1.6]

The same letterforms might also demonstrate the effects of similarity grouping. "The relative degree of similarity in a given perceptual pattern makes for a corresponding degree of connection or fusion," writes Arnheim.[1.7] As a result, in creating a typeface, a graphic designer must ensure that all the characters in the font are sufficiently similar that they appear to belong together, while different enough that one letter will not be mistaken for another. In designing a block of text, confusion—not fusion—can be the result if the difference among its elements is dramatically increased. Witness the playful disruptive effects of using a wider range of diverse elements: T**H E** REla Tiv**ede G**REe O si miLAR ITY InaG**IV enpeRC** EptUALP AtteR**NM** AKesfo racoRRESP**ONDIN gdegR**E o FCONNE **CTIO**NO r f**us i**ON.

From an esthetic standpoint, the oldest, most common description of "form" in the visual arts is unity-in-diversity, repetition with variation, strict wildness, or harmonious disarray. Few accounts of this intricate balancing act—a precarious interplay of continuity and disruption, of unit-forming and unit-breaking—are more vivid than a passage in *The Horse's Mouth*, the well-known novel by Joyce Cary, in which the main character, an artist named Gully Jimson,★ explains to his friend Cokey how to understand the pattern language of a painting, the score as distinct from the lyrics: "Don't look at it. Feel it with your eye," says Jimson. "And first you feel it in the round...Not as if it were a picture of anyone. But a colored and raised map. You feel all the rounds, the smooths, the sharp edges, the flats and the hollows, the lights and shades, the cools and warms. The colors and textures. There's hundreds of little differences all fitting in together."[1.8]

That the unit-forming strategies of literature

There are two morphological archetypes—expression of order, coherence, discipline, stability on the one hand; expression of chaos, movement, vitality, change on the other.

—György Kepes
The New Landscape in Art and Science

★ There is a delightful film version of *The Horse's Mouth*, in which Alec Guinness stars as Gully Jimson.

▶ **FIGURE 1.B**
RYAN MCADAM
Variations on a logo for the Dada Café, a hypothetical coffee shop, c. 1996. Courtesy the artist.

All art constantly aspires toward the condition of music.

—WALTER PATER
The Renaissance

and music are comparable to those of art, architecture and design was promoted by the American painter James A.M. Whistler, a leading figure in the Esthetic (or Aesthetic) Movement. "As music is the poetry of sound," wrote Whistler in 1878, "so is painting the poetry of sight, and the subject matter has nothing to do with harmony of sound or of color."[1.9] As a result, he insisted on calling his work "arrangements," "symphonies" "nocturnes," "harmonies" and "variations." In retrospect, it may be more accurate to say that painting is more often the prose of sight, while design and architecture are closer to poetry, in the sense that their patterns are often pronounced.

Reproduced here are five variations on the design of a corporate logo for a fictitious diner called the Dada Café (Fig 1.B), created by Ryan McAdam. While these are alternative solutions to the same problem, they all emphasize the same set of attributes: A restrained, medium-width geometric line; circles (appearing sometimes as ellipses); and a shallow s-shaped contour called the "Victorian scallop." This last element is also known as the "line of beauty," as proposed in 1753 by the British artist William Hogarth, whose book on *The Analysis of Beauty* (see Fig 1.C) was an early treatise on esthetic form.[1.10] One place in which that curve is found, said Hogarth, is the small of a woman's back, a statement that may have contributed to the popularity of tightly-laced corsets, garments that greatly constricted the waist, exaggerated the breasts and buttocks, and produced what is commonly known as the "hourglass figure."

In McAdam's logo variations, that shallow, scalloped form appears in four manifestations: As the steam that floats up from the coffee. As the black guitar-like shape that borders the side of the logos in the middle row. As an undulating tongue-like stripe that travels from mouth to the saucer. And as the s-shaped punctuation mark that underscores the letter A.

▲ FIGURE 1.C
William Hogarth
Detail from the title page of his *Analysis of Beauty* (1753), in which the Victorian scallop or "line of beauty" is framed within a pyramid.

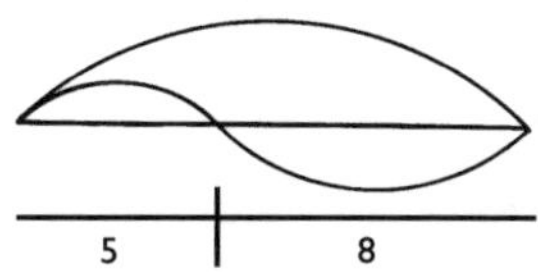

▲ FIGURE 1.D
Very likely Hogarth's "line of beauty" was inherited from the Golden Proportion (approximately 5 x 8), a relationship in which the smaller section has the same proportion to the larger section (5 to 8) as the larger section has to the whole (8 to 13).

McAdam's repetition of the Victorian scallop is far from accidental. Like the use of rhymes by writers in the construction of a poem, such parroting of attributes is both deliberate and purposeful, whether consciously planned or produced by intuitively "trying things out." Look closely, for example, at two stages of an illustration titled *Aprés le Bain* (After the Bath) by Gary Kelley: The first stage (FIG 1.A) is a pencil drawing, developed by the artist as a preliminary sketch for the project; while the second (FIG 1.E) is the completed pastel illustration. Comparing Kelley's drawing with the finished painting, it is clear that among its repeated motifs, just as in McAdam's logo, is Hogarth's line of beauty, the Victorian scallop: In the final version, it appears in the shape of the top of the screen in the background; in the mouth of the pitcher in the right foreground; in the right shoulder, the back of the head and the waves in the

▲ **FIGURE I.E**
GARY KELLEY
Pastel illustration titled *Aprés le Bain*. Courtesy the artist.

hair of the figure, in her neck, back and buttocks; and in the inclusion of a famous Victorian artifact, the Thonet bent wood café chair (Fig 1.F), which is often cited for its use of that same graceful curve. Recalling Wertheimer's dot paper, all these components are functioning as grouping attributes, as ways of promoting the unity of the composition.

The organizing factors that underlie Kelley's painting are the same devices that designers use in creating a typeface, composing a block of text, designing a logo, or laying out a printed page or a Web site. Further evidence of this is supplied by an intricate, well-designed ad from the Oxford University Press (Fig 1.G), in which Wertheimer's laws of organization are all being used to influence the way in which a human perceiver is likely to interpret—to configure, group or constellate—the various parts of the layout.

▲ **FIGURE 1.F**
Michael Thonet
Bent wood café side chair, c. 1855.

This ad first appeared in print about 1997. It uses the marketing slogan "looking at art history from a fresh perspective" to announce a new series of art history textbooks titled *The Oxford History of Art*. Reproduced are the covers of five books from the series, each of which features the same ingredients, consisting of a pictorial detail, the title and the author's name, and a small, square series logo in the upper left corner (which is always in full intensity orange on the covers). The layout of

A funny thing about a
Chair:
You hardly ever think it's
there.

—Theodore Roethke

the ad mimics that of the book covers, in the sense that they share the proportion of 5 by 7, and because the series logo is used in the upper left corner of the advertisement.

Throughout the ad, typographic similarities (e.g., size, weight, slant and style of font) are used in combination with proximity (or nearness) to make certain elements appear to belong together, while the use of differences makes others appear to be disconnected. Not infrequently, components are purposely made to connect by one grouping tendency and, at the same time, to separate by another. In this case, it is especially true of the typographic handling of the slogan—*looking at art history from a fresh perspective*—which reads as a single continuous phrase while still enabling the critical aspect of *a fresh perspective* to stand out distinctly.

As shown in the accompanying diagram, the photographs and text blocks in this ad have been purposely lined up with a network of upright and lateral lines called a "grid system." As a result, the edges of the photographs line up with the blocks of type, just like the indentations for paragraphs on a typewritten page. The most delightful use of this tactic is the single upright line that stands between *looking at art history from* and *a fresh perspective*, and which is set up to quietly also align with the back leg of a famous chair by Alvar Aalto.

...the nonesthetic lies within two limits. At one pole is the loose succession that does not begin at any particular place and that ends—in the sense of ceasing—at no particular place. At the other pole is arrest, constriction, proceeding from parts having only a mechanical connection with one another...

—JOHN DEWEY
Art as Experience

[Esthetic form might be described] as a kind of stylistic "mean" lying between the extremes of chaotic overdifferentiation and primordial homogeneity.

—LEONARD MEYER
Emotion and Meaning in Music, p. 161.

IN THE ORIGINAL GREEK, the word *esthetic* was the antonym of *anesthetic*. An esthetic experience was "perceptible": It was provocative, striking and stirringly felt, whereas anesthetic

◀ **FIGURE 1.G**
Printed advertisement and grid analysis (above) for the Oxford History of Art textbook series, c. 1997. Courtesy of Oxford University Press.

structures were benumbing or stupefying. Esthetic quality was not a question of prettiness nor pleasantness, but of vividness and cogency. Through esthetic form, it becomes possible (to repeat Arnheim) "to focus on what is alike and what is different, what belongs together and what is segregated," with the result that "one can understand the interrelation of the whole and its parts, as

At one of the annual conventions of the American Society of Aesthetics much confusion arose when the Society for Anesthetics met at the same time in the same hotel.

—RUDOLF ARNHEIM
Parables of Sun Light

well as the hierarchic scale of importance and power by which some structural features are dominant, others subordinate."[1.11]

Since the 18th century, the meaning of the word has strayed. Now, the majority of philosophers, along with nearly everyone else, regard esthetics as the study of beauty. Since beauty is "in the eye of the beholder," there is no reliable critical gauge, and formal issues have drifted, in the vapor of what is derided as "taste." To complicate matters, esthetics is also devalued because beauty, while it may be comforting, is widely regarded as nonessential to the prosaic, pragmatic utility of "the real world."

In organic architecture then, it is quite impossible to consider the building as one thing, its furnishings another and its setting and environment still another. The spirit in which these buildings are conceived sees all these together at work as one thing...The very chairs and tables, cabinets, and even musical instruments, wherever practicable, are of the building itself, never fixtures on it.

—FRANK LLOYD WRIGHT
Introduction to *Ausgeführte Bauten und Entwürfe von Frank Lloyd Wright* (1910).

The American architect Frank Lloyd Wright would disagree. He taught that esthetics and function are one, that esthetic quality is far more than merely a matter of taste. Born a half century before the publication of Wertheimer's dot paper, Wright anticipated Gestalt theory in the sense that he also believed that a whole and its component parts are interdependent (as the Gestaltists put it, "the whole is greater than [or at least different from] the sum of its parts"), and that patterns are seen as coherent because of the same unit forming factors that were described later by Wertheimer.

In characterizing his own work, Wright preferred the term "organic" architecture, which means that all parts of a building should have the same functional duality as parts of the body, words in a sentence, or members of society. Each part should function as a whole, a discrete fragment, while at the same time contributing to a larger unit, a patchwork. This governed his view of esthetics as well: "Every house worth considering as a work of art must have a grammar of its own," he said; a grammar in which "everything has a related articulation in relation to the whole and all belongs together; looks well together because all together are speaking the same language."[1.12]

He [Frank Lloyd Wright] was like a painter—touching every square inch of his building, inside and out.

—Vincent Sully
Foreword to Hanks, p. xiv.

For example, when Wright designed the Martin House in Buffalo, New York, in 1904, he "used one kind of brick outside, so he used the same brick on the inside." And, "In keeping with the grammar, the tile on the floor of the exterior porch was the same as the tile on the floor inside. He used only one kind of plaster. And only one kind of wood: oak. The chairs and tables were oak and so was all the wood trim." Like nearly all of Wright's buildings, the Martin House was a *Gesamtkunstwerk* (German for "total work of art"), in which the style of the entire house "was of one stripe, from the overall plan down to the furniture, the door jambs, and the window frames."[1.13]

One Saturday evening, the [German] architect Erich Mendelsohn was our guest [at Taliesin West]...He was a bit late in arriving at dinner and when he hurried to get into his seat he hit his knee against a sharp corner of the table. He said to Mr. [Frank Lloyd] Wright, "You and your organic architecture." We all laughed, including Mr. Wright.

—Mansinh Rana
in Tafel (1993),
pp. 175-176.

Wright believed, as did the Shakers, that "every force evolves a form," that form and function are inseparable. The elongated Gothic rectangular shape is a recurring element in his architecture. It is especially evident in the dining room chairs for the Robie House, which he designed in 1908. The chair backs are extended uprights, made to look even more vertical by the use of thin, protracted strips. More typical of Wright, however—and the Robie House is a prime example—is his practice of using elongated shapes in a horizontal direction. As other writers have noted, while Wright inherited the elongated upright of the Gothic cathedral, he radically changed it by making it rhyme with the flat, boundless horizon of the Midwestern prairie.[1.14] Unlike Gothic cathedrals, Wright's early buildings do not reach skyward. Called "Prairie Style," they reach but they reach for the prairie instead. It is as if his buildings say (as he himself said many times) that "God is Nature with a capital N"[1.15]—that God is not just in the clouds, but everywhere, in everything and everyone, in all of creation. Consistent with that, he once said that a house should never be built *on* a hill; it should instead be *of* a hill. He anticipated ecology, which says that a man should not live *on* the earth—but should instead live *of* the earth.

> Ornament is a crime.
>
> —ADOLF LOOS

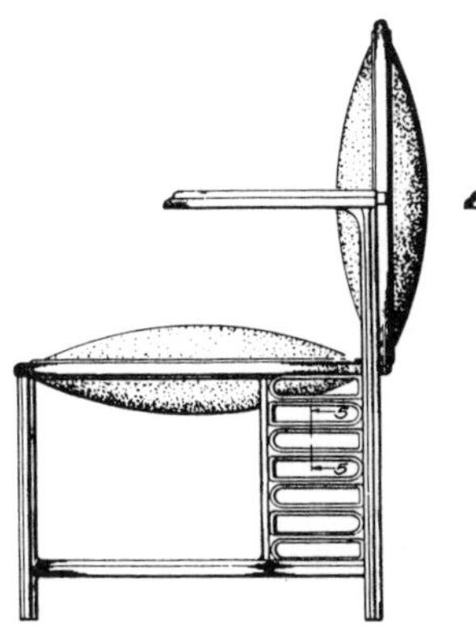

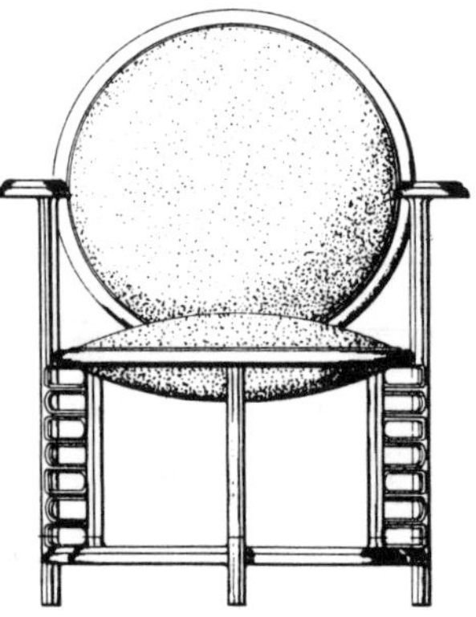

▲ **FIGURE I.H**
FRANK LLOYD WRIGHT
Patent drawings for office chairs in the Johnson Wax Office building in Racine, Wisconsin (1938).

As elongated horizontals, some of Wright's Prairie Style houses are reminiscent of wide-brimmed Shaker farmer's hats. So shaped, they function to provide natural cooling and heating: In the hot Midwestern summer, when the sun is overhead and high, the overhanging roof provides shade for the house, in the way that a hat brim may shelter the face. In the winter, when the sun is low and on the south, sunlight shines through walls of glass and provides solar heating. What better example is there of the indivisibility of esthetics and utility—an attitude Wright had inherited from his teacher, the Chicago architect Louis H. Sullivan, who insisted that "form follows function."

I have been black and blue in some spot, somewhere, almost all my life from too intimate contacts with my own furniture.

—Frank Lloyd Wright
"Prairie Architecture" in Kaufmann and Raeburn

Without instruction, as Whistler forewarned, surprisingly few people (artists among them) can see the forest instead of the trees—can focus on the implicit pattern language of an artwork instead of the greater attraction of explicit subject matter. Among those who can, there are those who oppose abstract seeing, especially when politics, religion and other social causes are at issue, for fear that, as some have contended, it may encourage "indifference to cultural meaning."[1.16]

The most notorious example of an artistic tradition in which its practitioners purposely made nonesthetic (or anesthetic) forms was the anti-art movement called Dada, which began during World War I in Switzerland. Founded in Zurich in 1916 by Hugo Ball, a German writer and pacifist, and his mistress Emmy Hennings, a café singer, this small but obstreperous circle began at the Cabarat

...some of the greatest music is great precisely because the composer has not feared to let his music tremble on the brink of chaos, thus inspiring the lister's awe, apprehension, and anxiety and, at the same time, exciting his emotions and his intellect.

—Leonard Meyer
Emotion and Meaning in Music, p. 161.

A truth about art is the company it keeps with the slightly askew, the fly in the woodpile of symmetry.

—Stanley Elkin

Voltaire, a makeshift café chantant at Spiegelgasse No. 1, diagonally opposite No. 12, where the well-behaved Vladimir Lenin was housed.

These writers and artists protested the ghastliness of trench warfare (engaged in by "rational" nations) and the complacency of the middle class, by performing in nightly theatrical pranks that were openly rude and outrageous, and nearly always based on chance. Even the movement's name was chosen haphazardly, by pointing while blindfolded to a page in a French-German dictionary. A fortuitous enigma, Dada might be English baby talk for "father," French for "hobby-horse," Rumanian for "yes-yes," or German for "there-there."

As nihilists, the goal of the Dadaists was to repudiate everything that made sense, not just literature and art. Their only program, wrote Hans Richter, "was to have no program...to unfold in all directions, free of esthetic or social constraints."[1.17] But in truth, they were never outside of constraints, since to sidestep a tradition is another way of being driven by it. To be genuinely unreliable, to create effective anti-art, the Dadaists had to rely on the same organizing principles—the unit forming factors—that were later explicitly targeted in Wertheimer's dot paper.

To produce anesthetic annoyances, the Dadaists used two old sabotage techniques: Extreme repetitiveness or HUMDRUM (which results in monotony and boredom), and

Ladies and jellyspoons:
I come before you
To stand behind you
To tell you something
I know nothing about.
Last Thursday
Which was Good Friday
There will be a mothers' meeting
For fathers only.
Wear your best clothes
If you haven't any,
And if you can come,
Please stay at home.
Admission is free
So pay at the door
Pull up a chair
And sit on the floor.
It makes no difference
Where you sit
The man in the gallery
Is sure to spit.
We thank you for your unkind attention.
The next meeting will be held
At the four corners of the round table.

—ANON
Children's nonsense verse

extreme variation or HODGEPODGE (which produces chaotic disorder and confusion). Not by coincidence, these mirror exactly the ways to create visual mayhem and indecipherability—better known as camouflage—through *blending* (high similarity) and *dazzle* (high difference).

Thus, typical Dada productions include Tristan Tzara's rant called "Roar," which consists of 147 repetitions of the same word; Richard Huelsenbeck's "Fantastic Prayer" (read aloud to the rhythmic swishing of a riding crop), which begins "This is how flat the world is / The bladder of the swine / Vermillion and cinnabar / Cru cru cru"; and the chance-made nonsense verse of Ball, the most famous of which commences with "gadji beri bimba glandridi laula lonni cadori."[1.18]

In their visual art, the Dadaists frequently opposed one unit forming factor to another, most often by placing dissimilar things in the same space. Among their forerunners was the 19th-century French poet Isidore Ducasse, better known as Comte de Lautréamont, who provided the classic example of "the chance encounter of a sewing machine and an umbrella on a dissecting table,"[1.19] or, as Max Ernst paraphrased it, "the exploitation of the chance meeting on a nonsuitable plane of two mutually distant realities."[1.20]

To bring things together with little if any regard for their compatibility is called *radical juxtaposition* or "the collage principle." Dada

Automatic poetry springs directly from the poet's guts or any other organs which have stored up usable reserves...The poet croaks, swears, signs, stammers, yodels, just as he feels like it. His poems are like nature: they laugh, rhyme, stink like nature. Trivialities, or what are commonly called trivial things, are as valuable to him as elevated histrionics; for in nature an atom is as lovely and important as a star, and only men have the temerity to decide what is beautiful and what ugly.

—Hans Arp
"Dadaland" in Raabe,
pp. 176-177.

[Gertrude Stein was] the mama of Dada.

—Clifton Fadiman

artist Meret Oppenheim, for example, covered the surfaces of a cup, saucer and spoon with a prurient fur pelt; Man Ray glued a row of tacks to the flat, smooth undersurface of an iron; and Joan Miro produced what he termed a "poetic object" by combining such disparate elements as a stuffed parrot on a perch, a doll's leg, a map, a hat, a ball, and a hollowed out wooden slab.

Salle and her boyfriend, who is a surrealist, staged a weird performance in Hyde Park [in June 1939, at the outset of World War II], reading bits out of *Alice in Wonderland* and the telephone directory, but the police thought it was some sort of code and took it all down.

—JOAN WYNDHAM
Love Lessons: A Wartime Diary, p. 79.

In 1922, one year before Wertheimer's paper appeared, the Dadaists' nonsense strategies (e.g., radical juxtaposition, automatic writing and the exquisite corpse) were coupled with Sigmund Freud's "talking cure," the psychoanalytic technique of *free association* (to say aloud while lying on a couch whatever comes to one's mind), to beget a fresh art and literature called Surrealism. Under that banner, artists continued to experiment with paired incompatibles and disturbing dreamlike visual puns, such as butter-soft watches and blazing giraffes.

The simplest surrealist act consists of going down into the streets revolver in hand, and shooting at random.

—ANDRÉ BRETON
Manifestoes of Surrealism

Surrealism: An archaic term. Formerly an art movement. No longer distinguishable from everyday life.

—BRAD HOLLAND
"Express Yourself—It's Later Than You Think"

A riddle asks: How many Surrealists does it take to screw in a light bulb? And the answer is: Two. One to hold the giraffe and the other to fill the bathtub with brightly colored machine tools. Salvador Dali defined Surrealism as "the systemization of confusion"; both Dada and it were attempts to create disorder.[1.21]

To again echo Arnheim, it may be a fitting description to say that, on a conceptual level, both Dada and Surrealism made it difficult, almost impossible, "to focus on what is alike and what is different, what belongs together and what is segregated."[1.22] They extolled the superfluous and dispensed with the indispensible to curtail the clear-cut and too effortless grasp of the interrelation of the whole and its components.

Reproduced here are two similar but distinct phenomena: The first is a Dada experiment with chance (which anyone can easily replicate); the other a demonstration of *closure*, one of Max Wertheimer's organizing principles.

The Dada experiment (Fig 1.I) was made by tearing up scraps of paper, dropping them through the air onto a sheet of paper, and gluing them down wherever they fall. The Gestalt diagram (Fig 1.J) is a fragmented silhouette (or constellation), which, however incomplete, can still be recognized as the image of a rider on a horse.

The "central experience" of Dada, said Richter—the aspect that sets it apart from all preceding art movements—is the use of chance "as a new stimulus to artistic creation."[1.23] Chance was essential to the Dadaists because it enabled them to create accidental forms, instead of rehashing conventional thought.

But it also does one other thing, and it is this that explains its relation to the principle of closure: It shifts much of the responsibility

▲ **FIGURE 1.I**
Chance-based Dada pattern made by dropping scraps of paper onto a blank page, then gluing them down wherever they fall.

▲ **FIGURE 1.J** (bottom)
Gestalt demonstration of closure, showing a horse and a rider.

The better the book the more room for the reader.

—HOLBROOK JACKSON

for interpretation away from the artist toward the viewer. It proffers a maze of suggestions as indeterminate as the night sky, then forces the viewer to make sense of it all—to configure, group or constellate.

"The most basic fact of esthetic experience," writes E.H. Gombrich, is "that delight lies somewhere between boredom and confusion"[1.24]; while Arnheim has said that "Complexity without order produces confusion" and "order without complexity produces boredom."[1.25] Such comments suggest that esthetics is linked to what Mihaly Csikszentmihalyi calls *flow* (a term that Dewey used as well in *Art as Experience*), an effect that "appears at the boundary between boredom and anxiety, when the challenges are just balanced with the person's capacity to act."[1.26] Also called "optimal experience," it requires a constant adjustment between the incompleteness of an image and the viewer's capacity to complete it.

▲ **FIGURE 1.K**
ROBERT GIBBINGS
Wood engraved portrait of William Walcot (1921), in which various contours are suggested, but not actually drawn in. From the Dover Pictorial Archives.

Csikszentmihalyi provides a vivid example of that adjustment in a story about his dog Hussar, who loved to run circles around him during their walks together, daring his master to catch him. "Occasionally I would take a lunge," writes Csikzentmihalyi, "and if I was lucky I got to touch him. Now the interesting part is that whenever I was tired, and moved halfheartedly, Hussar would run much tighter circles, making it relatively easy for me to

...as the designer you wind the spring, and it is released in the mind of the viewer.

—ABRAM GAMES

Dwn wth vwls.

—RUTH OLLINS

catch him; on the other hand, if I was in good shape and willing to extend myself, he would enlarge the diameter of his circle. In this way, the difficulty of the game was kept constant."[1.27]

Likewise, the arts can be games of adjustment in which artists are forever "running circles" around their viewers. "But the audience has a tendency to become more sophisticated with time," Arthur Koestler has noted, and "once it has mastered all the tricks [of a style or tradition], the excitement goes out of the game; so the message must be made more implicit, more tightly folded."[1.28]

The technique of triggering closure through incompleteness was investigated in 1927 by a graduate student of the Gestalt psychologists at the Berlin Psychological Institute. In her experiment, Bluma Zeigarnik asked 164 subjects to engage in various manual tasks, requesting that these be completed both accurately and quickly. In half the instances, she interrupted them, leaving their work unfinished, while, in the other half, they were allowed to proceed unimpeded. Afterwards, by interviewing the subjects, she concluded that, by an overwhelming margin, the unfinished tasks were remembered far more vividly than the completed ones.[1.29]

One may infer from "Zeigarnik's effect" that the finest, most lasting examples of art combine clarity with implicitness: They provoke

The classical tradition of striptease offers a valid metaphor for the activity of reading. The dancer teases the audience, as the text teases its readers, with the promise of an ultimate revelation that is infinitely postponed. Veil after veil, garment after garment, is removed, but it is the delay in the stripping that makes it exciting, not the stripping itself; because no sooner has one secret been revealed than we lose interest in it and crave another...To read is to surrender oneself to an endless displacement of curiosity and desire from one sentence to another, from one action to another, from one level of the text to another. The text unveils itself before us, but never allows itself to be possessed; and instead of striving to possess it, we should take pleasure in its teasing.

—David Lodge
Small World

Less is more.

—Ludwig Mies van der Rohe

closure and provide what Gombrich once described as "the beholder's share" of esthetic interpretation.[1.30]

He that uses many words for the explaining any subject, doth, like the cuttle fish, hide himself for the most part in his own ink.

—John Ray
On the Creation (1691)

The purpose of "infolding" (which is not brevity, but implicitness), writes Koestler, "is not to obscure the message, but to make it more luminous by compelling the recipient to work it out by himself—to re-create it." As he explains, unity in diversity in esthetics really means unity *implied* or suggested in diversity: "If a work of art strikes one as hopelessly dated, it is not because its particular idiom dates from a remote period, but because it is spelled out in a too obvious, explicit manner."[1.31]

It is no less important in art to *leave out* as to *put in*. It is in this sense—as well as the knowledge of how to make use of Wertheimer's unit-forming factors—that a great number of artists, designers and architects have daily experiences in camouflage, since distorting, withholding and hiding are indispensible ingredients of all genuine art making. ✂

A CAMOUFLAGE TIMELINE

1896 Abbott H. Thayer publishes "The Law Which Underlies Protective Coloration."

1907 Pablo Picasso completes *Les Demoiselles d'Avignon*, the first major Cubist painting.

1909 Gerald H. Thayer publishes *Concealing Coloration in the Animal Kingdom*.

1910 Gestalt perceptual psychologists meet in Frankfort, Germany.

1914-18 WORLD WAR I

1915 As proposed by Guirand de Scevola, an artist and infantryman, the French Army establishes the first *section de camouflage*. Other camoufleurs include Jacques Villon, Jean-Louis Forain, Dunoyer de Segonzac, Othon Friez, Jean Puy, and Charles Camoin.

1917 American Camouflage Corps is organized, commanded by Homer Saint-Gaudens. Others include Grant Wood, Barry Faulkner, Sherry Fry, Robert Lawton, Richard Meryman, Kimon Nicolaides, and Charles Burchfield. British painter Norman Wilkinson initiates the use of "dazzle painting" for naval camouflage.

1918 American Camouflage Corps deployed to France. U.S. begins camouflage of merchant ships, as directed by artist Everett L. Warner, with contributions by Frederic Waugh, Thomas Hart Benton, Louis Bouché, and others.

1939-45 WORLD WAR II

1940 Hugh B. Cott publishes *Adaptive Coloration in Animals*.

1941 Bauhaus designer and photographer Laszlo Moholy-Nagy appointed to mayor's commission to disguise Chicago shoreline.

1942 Various camouflage courses are taught at art schools and universities throughout the U.S., including the New Bauhaus (taught by György Kepes), Grand Central School of Art (Arshile Gorky), Pratt Institute, Kansas City Art Institute, and Ohio State University.

Among artists, designers and architects, contributors to military or civilian camouflage include Eric Sloane, Ellsworth Kelly, Jon Gnagy, Oskar Schlemmer, Bill Blass, Norman Bel Geddes, Jay Doblin, Donald Oenslager, Jo Mielziner, Noel Martin, Oliver Messel, Hans Erni, Victor Papenek, Roland Penrose, William Stanley Hayter, and many others. ✂

Chapter Two

The Meaning of the White Undersides of Animals

Abbott H. Thayer and the Laws of Disguise

In 1932, a psychologist named Angeline Myra Keen published an article on "Protective Coloration in the Light of Gestalt Theory," in which she discussed the axioms of Gestalt psychology in relation to the writings of Abbott H. Thayer, a turn-of-the-century American painter.

In Keen's brief paper, she compares Max Wertheimer's unit-forming factors with the "laws of disguise" that were introduced by Thayer in 1909 in a book titled *Concealing Coloration in the Animal Kingdom: An Exposition of the Laws of Disguise Through Color and Pattern: Being a Summary of Abbott H. Thayer's Discoveries*.

Keen writes that she finds it remarkable that "Thayer's account, written from the standpoint of an artist, parallels so closely, in the field of figure and ground perception, the conclusions drawn after prolonged, careful experimentation by such Gestalt psychologists

When people see the camouflaged uniforms for jungle warfare, or elaborate concealments for installations, few realize that the technique for all this was "pioneered" by a New England artist in the woods of Dublin, New Hampshire.

—Nancy Douglas Bowditch
George de Forest Brush, p. 187.

◀ **FIGURE 2.A**
During World War I, a camouflaged American soldier emerges from a foxhole.

as [Edgar] Rubin, Köhler, Koffka, and [Harry] Helson."[2.1]

...the concealing coats of animals that hunt or are hunted are now the models for the armies' camouflage corps...

—ABBOTT H. THAYER
"Camouflage"

While Thayer's findings predate those of Gestalt psychology, she does not suggest that one was derived from the other, or that the two parties were even aware of each another. Rather, she only expresses surprise that Thayer, working far in advance of Wertheimer and relying only on his artistic training, "enunciated a principle which is basically very like the findings of the Gestalter's laboratory—an unexpected confirmation of the Gestalt doctrine."[2.2]

The French, with their natural alertness to the uses of science, saw in the protective coloration of birds and animals a solution to [the camouflage of artillery]...With this in mind the camoufleurs darkened the highlights along the top of a gun barrel and lightened its under surfaces, using for their paint colors that were agreeable to the existing surroundings.

—J. ANDRÉ SMITH
"Notes on Camouflage,"
p. 474.

ABBOTT HANDERSON THAYER was born in southwestern New Hampshire in 1849, and grew up near Keene, at the foot of Mount Monadnock. Early in his life, he became interested in ornithology, hunting, trapping, and taxidermy. He became, in his words, "bird crazy," and his aptness for art was initially shown through watercolor paintings of these and other animals.

At age 18, Thayer moved to New York, where he studied painting at the Brooklyn School of Art and the National Academy of Design. It was there he also met his wife, Kate Bloede. In 1875, a week after their wedding, the Thayers moved to Paris, where he studied painting at the École des Beaux-Arts with the painter Jean-Léon Gerome, the legendary master of the French Academy. While living in Paris for four years, Thayer's closest friend was

George de Forest Brush, an American artist who later played a minor role in American military camouflage.

Moving back to New York, Thayer shared a studio with Daniel Chester French, the sculptor whose familiar works include the Minuteman statue and the seated Abraham Lincoln in the Lincoln Memorial. Thayer became active in the New York art world, serving for several years as Vice-President, then President, of the Society of American Artists. However, both he and his wife were devastated by the unexpected deaths of two of their children in 1880 and 1881. For the next six years, the family moved from place to place, until 1887, when they began to spend part of the year in Dublin, New Hampshire, not far from the home in which Thayer was raised.

Thayer had begun to attract a small following of apprentices when his wife's father died. Soon after, she began to exhibit the symptoms of severe depression, described then as an "attack of melancholia," which eventually led to her being confined, first in an asylum, then a sanatorium. Her health continued to decline, both emotionally and physically, and she died of a lung infection in 1891.

Five months later, Thayer married Emma Beach, whose father owned the *New York Sun*, who was a long-time family friend, with whom he remained for the rest of his life. They settled permanently in the woods of New Hampshire, where Thayer "became more and more

There was nothing more interesting in the nineteenth century than little by little realizing the detail of natural selection in insects flowers and birds and butterflies and comparing things and animals and noticing protective coloring...

—GERTRUDE STEIN
Wars I Have Seen,
p. 17.

This hybrid art [of camouflage], at its best, spans many fields, amongst them art, photography, architecture, biology and nature study, physics, chemistry, psychology, and aviation. Obviously, then, thorough training for camouflage is no matter for art classes alone. But equally obvious, camouflage is the manipulation, in one way or another, of visual effects and appeals to vision. And the basic preparation for such manipulation is to be found in the training of perception and the powers of observation such as one should expect in art classes.

—MILTON S. FOX
"Camouflage" (1943)

hermit-like in his habits, his communion with nature for long hours expressing itself in his growing interest in the coloration of animals."[2.3]

Brilliant, isolated, ascetic, hyperintense, an almost pure example of late 19th-century romantic idealism, Thayer epitomized the popular image of a genius...

—RICHARD MERYMAN
"A Painter of Angels Became the Father of Camouflage," p. 121.

BY ALL ACCOUNTS, Thayer was mercurial, eccentric and excitable. Described by one biographer as "of slight build, of nervous temperament, penetrating in his glance, with a voice of fine timbre," he wore in all seasons "Jaeger underwear, a flannel shirt, a Norfolk jacket, golf trousers descending into high Norwegian boots and a battered felt hat."[2.4] It is said that he started the winter each year by putting on a new pair of long woolen underwear, then cutting it off an inch or two at a time as spring approached, until by summer it had become a pair of shorts.[2.5]

When asked about their buckskins, Hawk said, "The story is that it helped water drain off in a downpour instead of soaking into the cloth, but I don't go along with that...But I believe that one thing that it did do, whether they realize it or not: it helped to break up their silhouette when they were in the woods. I mean, if you were dripping with fringes and things, you would blend in with the woods easier than if you were just a hard silhouette."

—ELIOT WIGGINSON
Foxfire 5, p. 411.

Despite the severity of New Hampshire winters, his house (intended only as a summer home) was unheated except for fireplaces, and, when he built a fire, the doors and windows were left open in order to demonstrate that "a fire similarly heats an interior space whether the doors remain open or closed."[2.6] Only during blizzards and driving rain was the house closed, with the result, as one guest recalled, "In winter ice formed around the vegetables on the table, unless they were carefully drained."[2.7]

All members of the Thayer family—Abbott, his devoted wife Emma, son Gerald, and daughters Mary and Gladys—slept out of doors. It was Thayer's hypothesis (not an uncommon belief at the time) that constant exposure to fresh air was necessary for rigorous health. Winter and summer, everyone slept outdoors on hide-covered cots in separate makeshift sleeping huts, concealed in the woods in the bushes, but designed to make maximum use of the sun. Less hardy house guests were put up in what was referred to as the "guest room," which consisted of a "second-story sleeping porch, wide open on two sides to the breezes of heaven."[2.8] One visitor remembered that the shoes he placed beside the bed froze so solidly one night, at thirty degrees below zero, that he placed them under the covers the following night so as to be able to wear them the next day.

▲ **FIGURE 2.B**
Portrait photograph of ABBOTT H. THAYER by Peter and Paul Juley.

> We should note that the successful camouflage officers of the two world wars were artists rather than scientists, or sometimes scientists with artistic inclinations.
>
> —ALISTER HARDY
> *The Living Stream*, pp. 127-129.

Despite constant suffering from what Thayer himself called "the Abbott pendulum" (in which he swung back and forth between the emotional polar extremes of "all-wellity" and "sick disgust"), he had an active and mischievous sense of humor.[2.9] For example, one day he arrived at dinner carrying a covered basket which he said contained "the catch" from picking blueberries on Mount Monadnock. When the basket was dumped onto a platter, the family was surprised to find that it held a half-grown porcupine, which waded through everyone's chowder as it scampered across the table.

On another occasion, Gladys painted a face on the back of her father's bald head, the remaining fringe serving as a kind of beard. To the children's delight, Thayer then walked backwards toward them while flexing the muscles of his scalp to make the face appear to grin.

While he was visiting at the Thayer's, Louis Fuertes always came to call on the Brush family. He was full of high spirits and fun, and entertained us by hanging from the crossbeams of the living room, pretending to be an orangutan.

—Nancy Douglas Bowditch
George de Forest Brush, pp. 189-190.

When the family visited Europe, they used a madcap method of sightseeing, beginning at an arbitrary point of departure, then following a random rule like "three turns to the left and two turns to the right," with the intention that they would explore those aspects of the continent that the guidebooks omitted.[2.10]

In the same spirit, Thayer and Gerald sometimes collaborated with Louis Agassiz Fuertes, a friend and favorite student (who later became a well-known bird illustrator), on drawings of imaginary animals, constructed (far in advance of the Dadaists' use of the exquisite corpse) by mixing and matching the heads, bodies and tails of existing species and assigning them spurious Latin names.

The theory of concealment by countershading will always be associated with the name of Abbott H. Thayer, the American artist, who first fully grasped this important optical principle which operates so widely in the cryptic coloration of different animals.

—Hugh B. Cott
"Camouflage in Nature and War," p. 506.

Thayer and Fuertes had initially met in 1896 at a gathering of the American Ornithologists Union. The former had been invited to speak on the subject of natural camouflage because he had published an article on "The Law Which Underlies Protective Coloration" in the April issue of the *Auk*, the journal put out by the Union. In that article, Thayer had publicly announced his discovery of an effect called *countershading*, examples of which are abundantly found in the coloration of animals.

When an animal is out of doors, the upper surfaces of its body appear lighter than the undersides, which are shaded because of the light of the sun. Artists have long been aware of this, and they commonly simulate overhead lighting: Shading is used to create the appearance of roundness and solidity on a flat surface by coloring shapes darker on the undersides and progressively lighter toward the top.

Countershading, as the name indicates, is the exact opposite, because the upper surfaces of a countershaded body are progressively darker, the undersides lighter (Fig 2.C). Countless animals are countershaded—rabbits, squirrels, chipmunks, certain birds and so on—particularly those that are active during the day and respond to intrusion by "freezing" in place. Countershaded animals are darkest on those sections of their bodies that are most exposed to sunlight, and lightest on those that are mostly in shade (Fig 2.D). When a countershaded animal is observed out of doors, its coloration cancels out the shading effects of the sunlight, with the result that the animal is less visible, in the sense that it tends to look flat and insubstantial rather than solid and three-dimensional. This effect is what Thayer was talking about when he titled one of his articles "The Meaning of the White Undersides of Animals."[2.11]

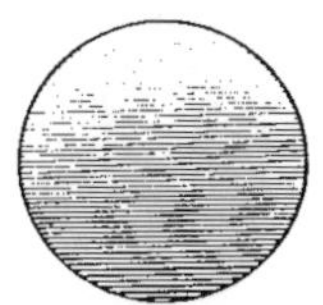

▲ FIGURE 2.C
In countershading or "Thayer's Law," the shading produced by the overhead sun (top) is cancelled out by the white undersides of animals (center), to create the appearance of flatness (bottom).

Thayer had discovered countershading as early as 1892, but the publication of his first article on the subject had resulted from a meeting in early 1896 when Thayer arrived unannounced at the office of Frank Chapman, editor of the *Auk*, at the American Museum of Natural History in New York, and demanded that they walk outside to look at something. Pointing to the ground near the building, Thayer asked, "How many decoys do you see?" Chapman replied that he saw two. As it turned out, Thayer has set out four wooden models of ducks, all of which "were the same size, all were colored earth brown, exactly alike, on the upper half, but the two nearly invisible ones were painted pure white on the lower half; whereas the conspicuous decoys were the same color throughout."[2.12] The two decoys that Chapman had overlooked were countershaded, while the remaining two were not.

▲ **FIGURE 2.D** Engraving of a countershaded mouse.

It will be noted that in countershading we have a system of coloration the exact opposite of that upon which an artist depends when painting a picture. The artist, by the skillful use of light and shade, creates upon a flat surface the illusionary appearance of solidity: Nature, on the other hand, by the precise use of countershading, creates upon a rounded surface the illusionary appearance of flatness. The one makes something unreal recognizable: the other makes something real unrecognizable.

—HUGH B. COTT "Camouflage in Nature and War," p. 506.

Thayer's younger cousin, Barry Faulker, an artist who later became a military camoufleur, recalled a similar incident, which may have occurred the same year, in which Thayer was seen "crouching in the dust of School Street [in Keene, New Hampshire], demonstrating to Mrs. Weeks, our teacher of drawing in the public schools, his newly evolved theory" by means of wooden ducks "mounted on wires, both painted the color of the dirt on which they stood," one of which was countershaded, the other not.[2.13]

Among ornithologists, as well as other scientists, the reaction to Thayer's theory of countershading was largely positive, even enthusiastic. Especially supportive was Edward B. Poulton, a prominent British entomologist who, as it turned out, had already discovered it in 1888. Through Poulton's influence, Thayer was invited to lecture on countershading in 1898 at the South Kensington Museum in London, at Oxford and Cambridge Universities, in Bergen, Norway, and Florence, Italy, installing in each of those places "permanent apparatus demonstrating the invisibility of a countershaded object."[2.14]

In addition, hoping to find practical applications of his discovery, he experimented with its theatrical use, for which purpose he invented and displayed in the Dublin, New Hampshire, town hall "a large wooden box wired for operating two sets of electric lights to demonstrate the disappearing act of a small countershaded Venus de Milo. It was the delight of the school children to press the buttons and make her come and go."[2.15]

Although concealing coloration, countershading and camouflage are now axiomatically understood, at the end of the 19th century it probably took an eccentric fanatic like Thayer—a freethinker antagonistic to all conventions, a man eminent in a separate field—to break with the rigid mindset of the naturalist establishment.

—Richard Meryman
"A Painter of Angels Became the Father of Camouflage,"
p. 120.

1898 was also the year of the Spanish-American War, a brief conflict precipitated by the sinking of the *Maine*, an American battleship, in a Cuban harbor. In another attempt to find practical applications for countershading, Thayer and his artist friend George de Forest Brush were invited by Theodore Roosevelt, then Assistant Secretary of the Navy, to come to Washington DC, to demonstrate countershaded models of battleships to the Department of the Navy.

They had experimented with these wooden ships on Dublin Pond while rowing around in Thayer's dory. On one model, Brush's daughter remembered, "All the visible undersurfaces of objects above deck were painted white, and all the upper surfaces blue-gray. They made another boat of uniform gray... They rowed about, getting different angles. Suddenly they lost sight of one of the boats; its silver sides reflecting the water, and the rigging merging in color with surroundings, caused the [countershaded] boat to disappear completely. Its recovery was finally made through the flashing of sunlight on the tinfoil. The plain gray vessel was never lost from sight."[2.16]

▲ **FIGURE 2.E** Portrait photograph of GEORGE DE FOREST BRUSH by Peter and Paul Juley.

An unthinking person must go on talking about the many creatures that he sees, and never reflect on the evidence that he misses many others.

—ABBOTT H. THAYER *Concealing Coloration in the Animal Kingdom*, pp. 461-462.

The Spanish-American War ended in December, while Thayer and Brush's presentation to the Department of the Navy was delayed until June of the following year. However persuasive their demonstration, the need to conceal American ships was no longer immediate and nothing came of the matter. But Thayer and Brush refused to give up: In 1902, Thayer and Brush's son Gerome were granted a patent for methods of concealing ships, and in 1908, they presented their proposals to the Bureau of Construction and Repair. However, according to government records, they "imposed such stringent conditions as to secrecy that the Bureau dropped the matter. When these conditions were later modified, the monetary consideration demanded was so high that in August 1911, the matter was definitely abandoned."[2.17]

Meanwhile, emboldened by his discovery of countershading, Thayer's interest in protective coloration intensified. While publishing more articles in scientific journals, he began working with his son Gerald, other family members, and a handful of student artists (among them Fuertes, Rockwell Kent and Richard Meryman) in putting together a large, lavishly illustrated volume on animal camouflage. After seven years of preparation, it was finally published in 1909, then reissued in 1918, with Gerald H. Thayer as the author of record.

Concealing Coloration in the Animal Kingdom quickly became controversial, not because of countershading, but largely because of the arrogant tone with which other less acceptable theories were presented. In Abbott Thayer's introduction, for example, he insisted that protective coloration had been "in the hands of the wrong custodians," and that "it properly belongs to the realm of pictorial art, and can be interpreted only by painters. For it deals wholly in optical illusion, and this is the very gist of a painter's life. He is born with a sense of it; and from his cradle to his grave, his eyes, wherever they turn, are unceasingly at work on it,—and his pictures live by it." In addition, he insisted that his

It was an artistic as well as a scientific principle that Thayer let loose in the war when his law gave the camoufleurs their art.

—Royal Cortissoz
American Artists, p. 42.

[About 1916, when he was more than sixty years old, George de Forest Brush acquired a small monoplane called "The Moran Sonnier"] in order to try out his camouflage and other experiments for war purposes. With the aid of a Mr. Harrison, he was experimenting with transparent wings and fuselage in order to make the plane less visible from the ground.

—Nancy Douglas Bowditch
George de Forest Brush, p. 152.

findings were irrefutable, that they were "not theories, but revelations, as palpable and indisputable as radium or X-rays."[2.18]

It was believed at the time, as it still is, that certain animal coloration is protective,

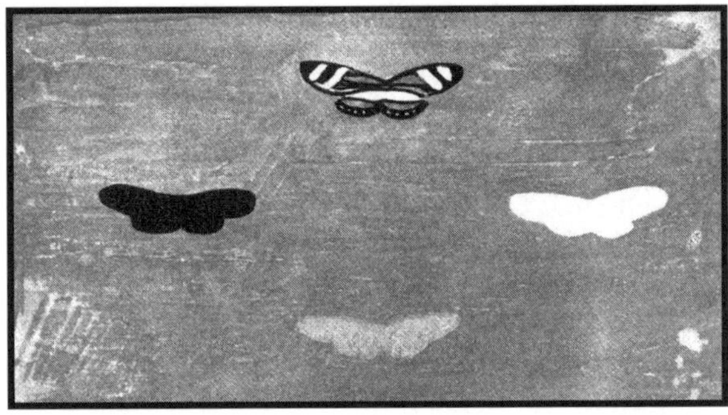

▶ **FIGURE 2.F**
A demonstration by Thayer of the comparative visibility of monochromatic and disruptive coloration.

that it contributes to low visibility, while other coloration is not for concealment but is designed to be quickly and easily seen, to assist in the process of attracting a mate, deceiving quarry or intimidating a predator. Thayer disagreed. All animal coloration, he protested, even the most brightly colored patterns, functions as concealing coloration, and whenever a creature is easily seen, it is simply because it is being observed outside of its optimal setting, or from the point of view of humans rather than that of its natural enemies. Even the conspicuous white tail and patches on the rear end of a pronghorn buck, Thayer argued, are protective markings, because, when observed from a crouching position (the viewpoint of its predators), the rump is a jumbled confusion of shapes that blend in with the sky in the background.

Hummingbirds are a beautiful demonstration of the fact that even almost constant conspicuousness is no evidence that the costume of a species is not obliterative.

—ABBOTT H. THAYER
Concealing Coloration in the Animals Kingdom, p. 462.

While Thayer acknowledged the importance of *figure-ground blending* (based on what Wertheimer later described as "similarity grouping"), he was one of the first to assert that monochromatic coloring was often less effective as camouflage, particularly if it lacked countershading, than was high difference *disruptive coloration*, which he called "razzle-dazzle" and which was later widely known as "dazzle camouflage" (Fig 2.F). In the latter, wrote Thayer, the figure is visually broken apart by "the employment of strong arbitrary patterns of color [which] tend to conceal the wearer by destroying his apparent continuity of surface."[2.19]

It is blending in combination with disruption (which Hugh B. Cott would later call "coincidental disruption") (Fig 2.G), Thayer said, that makes "the Mallard's dark green head tend to detach itself from his body, and to join the dark green of the shady sledge; or the ruby of the Hummingbird to desert him and to appear to belong to the glistening flower which he is searching."[2.20]

Mimicry is a special case of high similarity camouflage, in which a deceptive resemblance exists between two kinds of unrelated organisms (Fig 2.H). For example, some animals have an astonishing similarity to flowers, leaves, twigs and bark; while in other instances, harmless animals have evolved to look like harmful ones, or vice versa, as in the case of the Viceroy butterfly, which benefits from its

As all painters know, two or more patterns on one thing tend to pass for so many separate things. All art schools will tell you that it takes a far-advanced pupil to be able to represent the patterns on any decorated object so true in degree of light and darkness as not to "cut to pieces" the object itself, and destroy its reality.

—Abbott H. Thayer
"Camouflage," p. 488.

In Tanganyika a small moth resembling a bird-dropping was not uncommon. On one occasion I observed what I thought to be one on a leaf, but after a close examination from a distance of only a few inches I discovered (to my own satisfaction) that it was after all only a bird-dropping. Just as I turned away the said bird-dropping flew off!

—Hugh B. Cott
Adaptive Coloration in Animals, p. 184.

resemblance to the Monarch, which is noxious to birds. Thayer was doubtful of this latter kind of mimicry, so much so that he took a trip to the West Indies, where other mimics of the Monarch are common, with the expressed purpose of tasting the butterflies. "He actually tasted them," reported his daughter Gladys, who traveled with him, "and could find no difference in the flavor."[2.21]

The natural setting of an animal is forever changing, more or less, and one of Thayer's most extraordinary ideas was that of *background picturing*, his belief that the patterns on animals' coats, while not specific imitations, are epitomized emblems of their customary surroundings, "a generalization or distillation of the features of those physical settings in which the animal commonly was found, a surface that would be absorbed into a greater variety of specific backdrops."[2.22]

▼ **FIGURE 2.G**
Coincident disruption in the wings of a swallowtail butterfly.

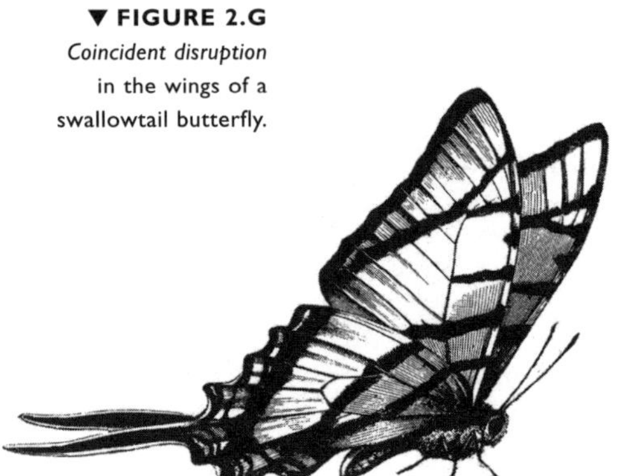

Nature weaves fantastic designs but she avoids round or angular patterns, or monotonously regular curves. Irregularity is what the camoufleur should seek at all times when designing disruptive camouflage.

—ERIC SLOANE
Camouflage Simplified, p. 44.

To demonstrate this, he cut out stencils of animal silhouettes, then looked through each stencil at the animal's background from the point of view of its predators (FIGS 2.I, 2.J). A few years later, he saw this as being a portable way for soldiers to design their own camouflage, since a person "has only to cut out a stencil of the soldier, ship, cannon or whatever figure he wishes to conceal, and look through this stencil from the viewpoint under consideration, to learn just what costume from that viewpoint would most tend to conceal this figure."[2.23]

Criticism of Thayer's writings intensified greatly in 1910 with the publication of *African Game Trails* by Theodore Roosevelt, the naturalist and former U.S. President, who had recently returned from a hunting expedition

▲ **FIGURE 2.H**
A conceivable (if bizarre) example of *mimicry* in the chrysalis of a North American butterfly, *Feniseca torquinius*, which bears a peculiar resemblance to a human or other primate.

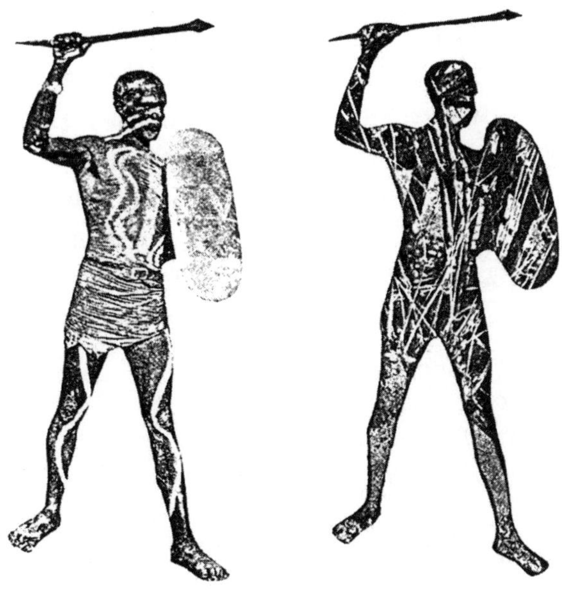

◀ **FIGURE 2.I**
As he demonstrated by these photographs, Thayer believed that the designs of "tattooed warriors," like the patterns of animals, were functional examples of *disruptive patterning* and *background picturing*.

in East Africa, where he had observed giraffes, zebras and other large animals in the wild. While at first praising Thayer's efforts, he thought that the basic ideas were "pushed to preposterous extremes."[2.24] In particular, he objected to the artificiality of the illustrations,

A fascinating addition to the theory was Thayer's perception that many birds and some animals carry on their plumage and hides a stylized picture of their most frequent habitats.

—Barry Faulkner
Sketches from An Artist's Life, pp. 18-19.

in one of which, for example, the brilliant blue head of a peacock is shown to have totally merged with the sky, conveniently painted the exact same blue.

To use an artistic contrivance like that to demonstrate a scientific fact, said Roosevelt, was comparable to "putting a raven into a coal shuttle in order to show that its coloration is concealing."[2.25] And as for the white tail and patches on the rump of a pronghorn buck, continued Roosevelt, "There is in Africa a blue rump baboon. It is also true that the Mediterrean Sea bounds one side of Africa. If you could make a series of experiments tending to show that if the blue rump baboon stood on its head by the Mediterranean you would mix up its rump and the Mediterranean, you might be illustrating something in optics, but you would not be illustrating anything that had any bearing whatsoever on the part played by coloration of the animal in actual life."[2.26]

▲ **FIGURE 2.J** Thayer's demonstration of *background picturing*, in which a stencil has been cut out in the shape of a duck, showing its typical background.

It is as though nature painted a picture upon the dress of bird or beast, a picture reproducing the general character of the science in which it lives...

—Royal Cortissoz *American Artists*, p. 36.

Thayer's exaggerations, Roosevelt suggested, may not have been intentional misdeeds, but were probably simply the consequence of "the enthusiasm of a certain type of artistic temperament."[2.27]

As the heated exchange between Roosevelt and Thayer went on, through letters and tempestuous articles in scientific journals, an unanticipated disaster occurred. On the night of August 14, 1912, more than 1,500 people died when the *Titanic*, a British ocean liner on its maiden voyage, sank in the North Atlantic, near Newfoundland, when it struck an iceberg. On the brink of nervous exhaustion from his argument with Roosevelt, Thayer was greatly disturbed by the news and proposed that the reason for the crash was the invisibility of icebergs. "How many more years of chancing it at sea," he wrote, "before the world realizes its deadly error in the universal notion that bergs at night are visible because they are white? It is precisely when they are purest white that they are at night invisible."[2.28]

A few years later, with the outbreak of World War I, the interests of Thayer and Brush in military camouflage were rekindled, although by then they had had a dispute and were no longer working together. By 1916, Brush had developed an "invisible" airplane, in which the fuselage and wings were covered with transparent silk treated with varnish. At the same time, Brush's son Gerome was asked to oversee the painting of merchant ships in various east coast harbors, including Boston, New York and Norfolk, Virginia. Using Thayer's system of countershading, the camouflage scheme for the ships was derived "from the general coloring of a seagull, worked in two shades of gray and pure white, the underpart of everything being painted white. The side surfaces were gray, the upper surfaces a slate color" (Fig 2.K).[2.29]

The application of Thayer's law to camouflage devices in the World War is a matter still controverted, but there is little doubt that England, France, and Germany studied *Concealing Coloration* in an effort to devise ways of concealing arms and movements, and that his theories had a general influence upon the designs used.

—Anon
The National Cyclopedia of American Biography.

[Thayer's book] was momentous as a contribution to the science of the naturalist. Its fame has since been greatly heightened by the fact that by application of "Thayer's law" the art of camouflage was brought into the Great War.

—Royal Cortissoz
American Artists, p. 35.

Six months into the war, Thayer traveled to New York to demonstrate military applications of protective coloration, then to Washington, DC, where he met with Franklin D. Roosevelt, Assistant Secretary of the Navy, to offer his services to the Allies. Put in touch with the British Admiralty, he cited the lesson that should have been learned from the *Titanic* tragedy, and urged that all vertical surfaces on warships be painted white, all horizontal surfaces the gray of the back of a seagull. Appealing to the British War Office, he advised that the khaki field service uniform (first adopted in in 1848 in India because of its general resemblance to dust) be replaced by a disruptively patterned uniform, so that soldiers, like pronghorn bucks, would seem to be jumbled confusions of shapes.

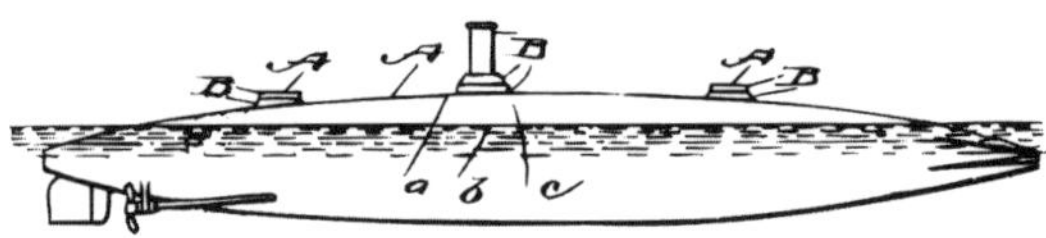

▲ **FIGURE 2.K**
GEROME BRUSH AND ABBOTT H. THAYER
Patent drawing dated December 2, 1902, for "Process of Treating the Outsides of Ships, etc., for Making Them Less Visible."

In World War I, devices and formulas taken from it [Thayer's book] were put to practical use in disguising war and merchant vessels, and Thayer was hailed in some circles as the "Father of Camouflage."

—PAUL RUSSELL CUTRIGHT
Theodore Roosevelt: The Naturalist, p. 233

THROUGHOUT THE WAR, despite episodes of emotional instability, Thayer had continued to paint and to teach a handful of loyal students, among them William James' sons, William Jr. and Alexander. Thayer admired their famous father, who had studied painting as a young man, and when the Harvard philosopher died in 1910, some of his clothing was passed down to "Uncle Abbott," including James' favorite duck hunting jacket, a brown Norfolk.[2.30]

In November 1915, Thayer sailed to England in order to meet with officials at the British War Office, to convince them that they should adopt his designs for a disruptively patterned field service uniform. A meeting with British staff officers had been set up by John Singer Sargent, the celebrated American expatriate painter who had known Thayer in Paris forty years earlier.

Hoping to contribute to both French and British camouflage, Thayer had written to Sargent earlier in the year, asking for introductions to the French painters Carolus-Duran (Sargent's former teacher) and Leon Joseph Florentin Bonnat, and the British author H.G. Wells, who had discussed camouflage in one of his books. Sargent had already met with the staff officers on Thayer's behalf, but the latter was impatient with the bureaucratic delays and had decided that he should appear beside Sargent at a second meeting.

As it happened, Thayer did not show up for the meeting. Anticipating rejection, he was overcome by anxiety. Displaced from the woods of New Hampshire and upset by the lack of support for his work, he "had partly lost his grip" when he had what he later described as a "fright-fit" or what we today call a "panic attack."[2.31] Tears streaming down his face, he boarded a ship to return to New York. At his London hotel, he left a note for Sargent and an old suitcase of drawings, sten-

The distinguished expounder of this principle [of countershading], Mr. Abbott H. Thayer, was in the strongest sympathy with the cause of the Allies, and I think it a great pity that it was not found possible to enlist his practical help, which I feel sure would have been gladly and freely given.

—JOHN GRAHAM KERR
"Camouflage of Ships in War," p. 205

As a boy of twelve I spent a good deal of time studying Thayer's great illustrated book on camouflage and was much influenced by it.

—PETER SCOTT
[WWII British naval camoufleur] quoted in White, *Abbott Thayer*, p. 137

Half of the ships that have been torpedoed would still be afloat had the naval experts perceived that there is a science of appearances, and that science does not form a part of a naval expert's training.

—ABBOTT H. THAYER
New York Tribune
(August 13, 1916)

cils and other materials to use in demonstrating his disruptively patterned uniform (FIG 2.L). Inside was a tattered Norfolk jacket, with irregular patches of fabric attached. It was William James' hunting jacket.

[Thayer's book] was used as a textbook by the United States in teaching the principles of camouflage, as adopted by the combatants on both sides in the World War.

—ANON
The National Cyclopedia of American Biography

▶ **FIGURE 2.L**
Photograph from an article by Thayer in which he advocates the use of a disruptively patterned field service uniform. [Could this be Thayer or his son, and is this William James' hunting jacket?]

The remaining years of Thayer's life were rewarding but greatly precarious too. In early 1917, he was delighted by a letter from the U.S. Naval Consulting Board, seeking his advice on ship camouflage. From Europe, he heard that the Germans, British and French had consulted his book in developing their military camouflage. And later in 1917, when America finally entered the war, surely he must have been pleased to be told that his cousin Barry Faulkner, Sherry Fry and other young artists (among them his apprentice Richard Meryman) had enlisted in the American Camouflage Corps.

[Gerald H. Thayer] states that it has recently come to light that, in Germany, the original edition [of his book] was "searched through with most diligent care for information which could be put to military or naval use."

—EDWARD B. POULTON
in "Naval Camouflage," p. 340.

But Thayer's breakdown in England had taken its toll. As his attacks of "nervous exhaustion" became more frequent, he consulted a doctor and was placed briefly in a sanatorium. Fearing suicide, his family no longer allowed him to go out alone on Dublin Pond in his dory.

According to William James Jr, Thayer once said that an artist is like "a man standing in a crowd above the heads of which there are thick clouds. But above the artist's head there is a tiny hole through which he can look all the way up to the blue zenith and to God. The people about him, who cannot see through the hole, of course deny his report and call him crazy."[2.32]

In the spring of 1921, at age 72, Thayer suffered a mild stroke, which paralyzed his painting hand. He was struck twice more in the following weeks and died quietly at his Dublin home on May 29. ✂

[Thayer's] theories were correct enough. In practice, however, neither his naturalist nor his military contributions proved important. In reality such well-meant enthusiasms distracted him from his place of sound value.

—Homer Saint-Gaudens
The American Artist and His Times, pp. 170-171.

Chapter Three

The Whole Theory of Art and Its Inevitability

Cubism and Camouflage

In October 1917, the painter John Singer Sargent was visiting Washington, DC, where he painted a portrait of U.S. President Woodrow Wilson. The United States had entered World War I on the side of the Allies only five months earlier. As the President sat, the subject of military camouflage came up in conversation, and Sargent could not keep from telling about his bizarre experiences two years earlier with Abbott H. Thayer in London.

▲ **FIGURE 3.B**
Portrait photograph of John Singer Sargent by Peter and Paul Juley.

◀ **FIGURE 3.A**
World War I French camouflage artists.

By coincidence, that same afternoon the President and Mrs. Wilson had been invited to drive out to a training camp on the outskirts of the capitol to inspect the amusing inventions of a new military unit, consisting mostly of artists, called the American Camouflage Corps. At Wilson's suggestion, Sargent joined the entourage, which included, among others, Secretary of War Newton Baker and several French military officers.[3.1]

There still exist photographs of that inspection. In one (FIG 3.C), President Wilson is standing with his wife and others in a flat, open field, speaking to an American military officer, apparently General John J. Pershing, while Sargent stands by in the background. Wilson has been told that a soldier is hidden somewhere within ten feet of him, and is astonished moments later when a middle-sized rock in in the foreground begins to move. That rock, as it turns out, was made of papier-mâché and served as the lid for a foxhole. Suddenly, a sniper pops out of the ground and salutes his Commander-in-Chief.

▲ **FIGURE 3.C**
U.S. President Woodrow Wilson (center foreground) speaks with General Pershing during a camouflage demonstration, as JOHN SINGER SARGENT (indicated by arrow) looks on.

He [T.S. Eliot's Prufrock] camouflages himself, at teas, on long foggy afternoons, where women come and go.

—WYLIE SYPHER
The Loss of Self in Modern Art and Literature, p. 85.

In contrast to Sargent's account of the strange behavior of Abbott Thayer, among the soldiers whose work was inspected that day was Thayer's cousin, Barry Faulkner, who was responsible, if indirectly, for starting the American Camouflage Corps. His collaborator, who was also present and who devised the papier-mâché foxhole lid, was Sherry Fry (FIG 3.D), an Iowa-born New York sculptor who had studied with Augustus Saint-Gaudens in Cornish, New Hampshire.[3.2]

In New York in the previous April, just as America entered the war, Faulkner had been approached by Fry, who showed him a photograph of "a French train and railway station painted in bold disrupted patterns, according to one of Abbott Thayer's theories of protective coloration."[3.3] No one can be sure which photograph it was, but the technique the French had presumably used was high contrast ruptive or disruptive coloring, the tactic that Thayer had proposed earlier for the British field service uniform.

Neither Faulkner nor Fry, as the former admitted later, "had clear ideas of how to apply Thayer's theories to warfare, but most other people had even less." Having learned that French artists had formed a camouflage unit, the two Americans organized the New York Camouflage Society, using Faulkner's connection to Thayer as "bogus prestige."[3.4] Quickly, the organization grew to two hundred members, with branches in San Francisco and Washington, DC.

Acting as civilians, Faulkner and Fry held meetings in New York with older artists, among them Daniel Chester French (Thayer's former studio partner), J. Alden Weir, Ernest Peixotto, and Herbert Adams. They collected the names of younger artists who had expressed an interest in serving as camoufleurs, and began training exercises in a Greenwich Village studio. Hoping to persuade the Army to use artists to set up a bona fide camouflage corps, they appealed to General Leonard Wood, the younger J.P. Morgan,

▲ **FIGURE 3.D**
A monument to Mahaska, Chief of the Ioway nation, as sculpted by Sherry Fry, in the town square of Oskaloosa, Iowa.

[Camouflage] is no vaudeville magic. It requires trouble, horse sense, and an ability to take advantage of the local conditions. It is Indian fighting.

—Homer Saint-Gaudens
"Camouflage Reminiscences," p. 248.

Colonel Edward House, and Franklin D. Roosevelt's influential mother.

In the meantime, within the Army, proposals to establish a camouflage corps were being initiated by others, including Major Evarts Tracy, a New York architect, and Wilfred Conrow, Laurence Hitt and Homer Saint-Gaudens at the Officer's Training Camp at Plattsburg, New York. Conrow had studied in Paris with Percyval Tudor-Hart, a Canadian-born painter who had invented a highly unusual plan for ship camouflage. Saint-Gaudens, a Broadway theatre director, had been Barry Faulkner's roommate at Harvard; while his father, with whom Fry had studied, was one of the best-known artists in America at the end of the 19th century.

▲ **FIGURE 3.E**
This may have been the news photograph of a camouflaged French railroad car that Sherry Fry showed to Barry Faulkner in 1917.

[The fascination of the Cubist painters] with continuities and discontinuities makes it very difficult for us to separate figures from their background.

—JOHN ADKINS RICHARDSON
Modern Art and Scientific Thought, p. 114.

Spurred by a cable from General Pershing asking that camouflage experts be deployed to France, the U.S. War Department issued a public appeal on August 29, 1917, calling for "ingenious young men who are looking for special entertainment in the way of fooling Germans."[3.5] Particularly needed, the article said, are "iron and sheet metal workers, sign and scene painters, carpenters, cabinet makers, stage carpenters, property men, plaster molders, and photographers." Despite the omission of artists, Faulkner and Fry were among the first to volunteer for this experimental section of the 40th Engineers, while Lieutenant Homer Saint-Gaudens, fresh from officer's training at Plattsburg, was appointed the unit's commanding officer.

This troop was initially located on the grounds of the American University on what was then the outer edge of the nation's capital. Preparations for battle consisted of marching drills, calisthenics and hiking, with virtually no combat training. In the afternoons, they experimented with camouflage techniques, often for public relations purposes, including the clever concealment of their own living quarters. It was reported in a magazine article, for example, that Saint-Gaudens had invented a mechanism that "converts old newspapers into blankets that can be tinted like the surrounding grass and used as a cover," while Wilfred Conrow had devised "an invisible helmet."[3.6]

Many American artists had read Thayer's book and when the United States entered World War I, a considerable number of them felt that camouflage was the branch of the service in which they could be most useful.

—BARRY FAULKNER
WKNE Radio Broadcast (1957).

◀ **FIGURE 3.F**
During a training session, an American sniper emerges from a concealed position, 1919.

Looking back on the American Camouflage Corps, Barry Faulkner said later that "The blind led the blind, and they did many useless and fantastic things. They knew that camouflage was mostly about aerial photography, but they could get no airplane and had never seen an aerial photograph."[3.7] Nevertheless, they replicated all of the various camouflage stunts, illustrated in the American newspapers, that the French and British had already invented: They "painted cars and trucks in disruptive patterns; constructed papier-mâché dummies of fallen tree trunks from whose interiors an unseen sniper could shoot; and dug trenches covered with sod and bushes from which soldiers could pop out."[3.8]

The French have named this art of concealment camouflage. The artists, with their forces of sign painters, scene painters, sculptors, mechanics and carpenters, are termed the camoufleurs.

—ANON
"Camouflage: Art's Aid in Modern Warfare," p. 50.

By October, the unit was ready to demonstrate its trickery to an audience of dignitaries, which is when President Wilson and John Singer Sargent arrived. Especially well-received was a battlefield observer concealed in a papier-mâché replica of a dead horse, created by the sculptor Harry Thrasher, another former student of the elder Saint-Gaudens.

...our friends in the French Army told us that "camouflage" was the only word in the French language which we Americans could pronounce correctly.

—BARRY FAULKNER
WKNE Radio (1957).

In addition to such field experiments, the Camouflage Corps had also produced a musical comedy with elaborate but inexpensive scenery and costumes, and had published several issues of *The Camoufleur*, a journal consisting of jocular poems about camouflage, skits and drawings, copies of which were peddled to patriotic civilians as a way to raise funds for the company's use.

Amateur civilian camouflage units had also been organized. There was, for example, a group in New York led by H. Ledyard Towle, sponsored by the New York Board of Education. Among its training sessions were lectures on military deception; hands-on instruction in which miniature land vehicles, artillery and other battlefield objects were visually embedded in small scale landscapes; and weekly field exercises using camouflage robes, which were hooded, loose-fitting costumes painted to blend in or disrupt with their surroundings, and which were described later in a govern-

◀ **FIGURE 3.G**
Members of the Women's Camouflage Corps, demonstrating the effectiveness of camouflage robes.

ment document as "resembling in appearance the teddy bear pajamas which little children wear."[3.9]

In New York, a women's camouflage corps had been formed, under the sponsorship of the National League for Women's Service. American women (although not allowed to vote), a journalist concluded, "excel the young men when it comes to the matter of camouflage robes, for they are naturally more skilled with the needle and can therefore make better robes."[3.10]

Camouflage, both as we practiced it in France and as we plan it for the future, has suffered from too much loose conversation, newspaper propaganda, and the inability on the part of the average soldier to use his eyes.

—HOMER SAINT-GAUDENS
"Camouflage Reminiscences," p. 242.

When the French Army first marched out to war, in the uniform of blue with the famous red breeches, little was thought of the part that concealment was to take in the conflict. It was not until the contending armies were deadlocked and had dug themselves into the long lines of trenches that stretched from Switzerland to the coast that the importance of being inconspicuous began to make itself felt.

—H. LEDYARD TOWLE "What the American 'Camouflage' Signifies," p. 14.

...though still not as well camouflaged as the British khaki or the German *Feldgrau*, after a few days in the mud of the trenches it [the French *horizon bleu*] blended with surroundings as well as any other.

—ALISSAIR HOME *The Price of Glory: Verdun 1916*, p. 68.

FOUR MONTHS AFTER its formation, the American Camouflage Corps was deployed to France, sailing from Hoboken, New Jersey, on January 4, 1918. Seventeen days later when they landed at the French harbor of Brest, remembered Faulkner, "we saw that camouflage had preceded us, for the harbor was full of boats, both French and American, painted in a riot of disruptive patterns."[3.11]

In fact, the camouflage experiments of the French had predated those of the Americans by about three years, since French ground camouflage had begun in late 1914, adjacent to the town of Metz in northeastern France, 25 miles south of the Luxembourg border. By most accounts, it had been the brain child of Lucien Victor Guirand de Scevola, a 43-year-old academic painter who was serving in the French infantry. As the telephone operator in the artillery division, he was an intermediary between headquarters and front line artillery teams.[3.12]

As de Scevola remembered, he was transmitting orders one day when it occurred to him that he could make a cannon less visible to aerial observers by painting it with abstract, irregular shapes, a technique that eventually came to be known as *zébrage* because of its similarity to zebra stripes. Initially, he proposed the idea to his military superiors at Pont-a-Mousson. Later, he made a similar presentation at Toul, a few miles west of Nancy, to an audience of the highest government officials, among them French President Raymond Poincaré and the French Commander in Chief, General Joseph Joffré.

In his demonstrations, de Scevola used a paint-streaked cannon manned by an artillery team whose loose-fitting hooded outfits (called *cargoules*) had also been streaked. When an aerial observer flew over the area at a height of 300 meters with instructions to look for the team, neither the men nor the cannon could be located from that altitude.[3.13]

As a consequence, on February 12, 1915, just seven months after the start of the war, the French government established the first *section de camouflage* in military history. Its primary workshop was located in Paris, with secondary workshops at Amiens, Chalons and Nancy, and smaller peripheral studios at Chantilly and Dijon. The person who was chosen to oversee the operation, which began with six men and grew to a total of 3000 men and women by 1917, was de Scevola, who no doubt deserves to be credited as "the father of French camouflage."

Nearly all the soldiers assigned to the French camouflage section were artists of one kind or another, from theatre set designers to portrait painters. While officially known as *les camoufleurs*, they were spoken of unofficially by unsympathetic fellow soldiers and the intrigued but skeptical French public (who saw

The French Government awakened to the fact that the artists of its country should not be thus wantonly sacrificed; that there were very useful things that they could do...It was the artists also—[Jean-Louis] Forain among them—who, at the beginning of the war, first thought of dissimulating war material by means of protective coloring.

—Ernest Peixotto
"Special Services for Artists in War Time,"
p. 2.

[At the age of sixty-two, Jean-Louis Forain] managed to enroll [in the French Army] as a camouflage artist and was put in charge of concealing the viaduct at Chantilly.

—Lillian Browse
Forain: The Painter,
p. 60.

camouflage as a soft or cushy job, *un bon filon*) as *les barbouilleurs*, the scribblers or the smearers.[3.14]

Of the French artists assigned to camouflage, the persons whose names are remembered today include Jacques Villon (the brother of Marcel Duchamp and Raymond Duchamp-Villon), Jean-Louis Forain, André

It's unbelievable, the marvelous things accomplished by the Cubists in the area of camouflage!

—ALEXANDRE BRACKE-DESROUSSEAUX in "Le Rire de la Semaine."

▶ **FIGURE 3.H** French Army personnel resting beneath a canopy of umbrella camouflage.

Dunoyer de Segonzac (who was the Chief of the Camouflage Corps for the Armies of the North), Othon Friesz, Abel Truchet, André Mare (the founder of Maison Cubiste), Pierre Laprade, Jean-Louis Boussingault, Luc-Albert Moreau, Jean Puy, Charles Camoin, and Charles Dufresné.

The complex, concealed identities of Cubist art found a surprising parallel in the military art of camouflage.

—ROBERT ROSENBLUM *Cubism and Twentieth-Century Art.*

Like most French camoufleurs, de Scevola was not an avant-garde artist; he had been an academic salon painter before the war, not a Cubist. But in his military capacity, he used the same methods as the Cubists to create deliberate distortions, methods which art historian Wylie Sypher has described as "a breaking of contours, the passage, so that a form merges with the space around it or with other forms; planes or tones that bleed into other planes and tones; outlines that coincide with other outlines, then suddenly reappear in new relations; surfaces that simultaneously recede and advance in relation to other surfaces; parts of objects shifted away, displaced, or changed in tone until forms disappear behind themselves."[3.15]

Looking back, de Scevola admitted that, as a military camoufleur, he had been consciously influenced by the Cubists: "In an effort to obliterate objects," he said, "I used the techniques the Cubists had used to simulate objects. Later, this enabled me, without having to justify my decisions, to assign certain painters to camouflage who—because of their visual adeptness—could prevent the recognition of virtually any object."[3.16]

The most famous account of Cubism's influence on camouflage appears in *The Autobiography of Alice B. Toklas*, which, notwithstanding its title, is the autobiography of Gertrude Stein, the American expatriate writer who lived most of her life in France. The book itself is camouflaged as a memoir by Toklas, who was Stein's friend and intimate companion.

In one of its passages, Stein remembers an evening in early 1915 in which she and Toklas, accompanied by Pablo Picasso and his mistress Eva Gouel, were strolling and talking in Paris

> ...Even in the trenches, where so many artists think, work and plan, Cubism is all the rage...
>
> —Jacques Émile Blanche
> Quoted in Kahn (1984), p. 98.

> That summer they went again to Spain and he [Pablo Picasso] came back with some Spanish landscapes and one may say that these landscapes... were the beginning of Cubism... In these pictures he first emphasized the way of building in Spanish villages, the line of the houses not following the landscape but cutting across and into the landscape, becoming indistinguishable in the landscape by cutting across the landscape. It was the principle of the camouflage of guns and the ships in the war.
>
> —Gertrude Stein
> *The Autobiography of Alice B. Toklas*, pp. 89-90.

on the Boulevard Raspail: "All of a sudden down the street came some big cannon, the first any of us had seen painted, that is camouflaged. Pablo stopped, he was spell-bound.

It is said that Cubism invented camouflage, and indeed the First World War used camouflage in a Cubist way.

—WYLIE SYPHER
The Loss of Self in Modern Literature and Art, p. 85.

▶ **FIGURE 3.1**
World War I photograph of camouflaged Italian artillery.

C'est nous qui avons fait ça, he said, it is we that have created that. And he was right, he had. From Cézanne through him they had come to that."[3.17]

While yet Verdun itself was out of sight, we came, quite unexpectedly, upon one of its mightiest defenders: a 400-millimeter gun mounted on a railway truck. So streaked and striped and splashed and mottled with many colors was it that, monster though it was, it escaped my notice until we were almost upon it.

—E. ALEXANDER POWELL
Italy at War, p. 150.

In Stein's other books, there are differing versions of the same incident. Nowhere does she describe the camouflaged cannon, but probably they were disrupted by abstract, broken zigzag shapes. It also seems likely that they were painted in shades of gray, because in a letter on February 7, 1915, Picasso wrote the following to his friend Guillaume Apollinaire, the French poet and critic, who was serving in the Army: "I'm going to give you a very good tip for the artillery. Even when painted gray, artillery and cannons are visible to airplanes because they retain their shape. Instead they should be painted very bright colors, bits of red, yellow, green, blue, white like a harlequin."[3.18]

A few months later, the poet Jean Cocteau appeared at Picasso's studio wearing a harlequin's costume beneath a raincoat. He asked Picasso to paint his portrait dressed as a harlequin, but the painter declined. Instead, Cocteau left the suit with Picasso, who was delighted by the gift and said jokingly that the French Army should issue harlequin outfits to the entire infantry, since the diamonds would make them confusing to see.[3.19]

Georges Braque, whom art historians regard as the co-founder with Picasso of Cubism, was not in Paris on the night that the camouflaged cannons were seen. He and Picasso were no longer close, and Braque was in the infantry. Long after the war, however, he recalled in an interview that he had been happy when "I realized that the Army had used the principles of my Cubist painting for camouflage. 'Cubism and camouflage,' I once said to someone. He answered that it was all a coincidence. 'No, no,' I said, 'it is you who are wrong. Before Cubism we had Impressionism, and the Army used pale blue uniforms, horizon blue, atmospheric camouflage."[3.20]

From 1915 onwards, harlequins appear frequently in Picasso's Cubist paintings, among the best-known examples of which are *The Three Musicians* and *The Three Masked Musicians*. That pair of paintings was completed in 1921, two years prior to the publication of Max Wertheimer's famous dot paper. "If

The batteries were all camouflaged, the guns themselves being painted in blotched colors, while over them all was grass matting in camouflage colorings. They were all very ingeniously hidden.

—William Mitchell
Memoirs of World War I, p. 74.

While at table, we saw a battery of long four-inch [diameter] naval guns, pulled by heavy tractors, going to the front. The guns and carriages were painted in blotchy designs to look like the ground they stood on.

—William Mitchell
Memoirs of World War I, p. 21.

Harlequin, Cubism and military camouflage had joined hands. The point they had in common was the disruption of their exterior form in a desire to change their too easily recognized identity.

—Roland Penrose
Picasso: His Life and Work, p. 205.

Camouflage [in World War I] meant whirls, blotches, stripes and curlycues with which "experts" made common objects look like a futurist's bad dream. Stripes and blotches were supposed to do for ships and tanks what strips and blotches are supposed to do for giraffes and tigers.

—ANON
"Camouflage" (1939),
p. 42.

Cubism broke up the object into fragmented patterns of changing appearance; eventually it deprived the object of identity entirely. Under the Cubist attack the object first disintegrated into uncertain planes, then disappeared into an illusion of the object.

—WYLIE SYPHER
The Loss of Self in Modern Literature and Art,
pp. 85-86.

one looks at these pictures [such as *The Three Musicians*] after having read Wertheimer's paper," writes Gestalt psychologist Fritz Heider, "one realizes immediately that Picasso's new technique [of Cubism] consisted partly in destroying the natural units of familiar objects by opposing one unit-forming factor to another. One specific part of the picture may make a good unit with a table according to one factor, but according to another factor it belongs to the wall."[3.21]

Wertheimer's dot paper pertains to camouflage as well, contends Heider, because the latter, like Cubism, destroys natural units by opposing one unit-forming factor to another, or simulates spurious units instead. The Berlin Gestalt psychologists, he writes, "were of course conscious of the fact that camouflage makes use of unit-forming factors, and there was a rumor that Wertheimer or Koffka helped in improving it."[3.22]

The relevance of Gestalt theory to camouflage (and, by implication, to Cubism) has been pointed out by other authors as well. For example, G.W. Hartmann recalls that Gestalt psychologist Kurt Lewin, who taught with Wertheimer at the Berlin Psychological Institute, was a captain in the German infantry in World War I, during which "he maintained sufficient composure to prepare a unique article on the figure-ground phenomena present in the camouflaged scenery of trench warfare!"[3.23]

In his book on *Gestalt Psychology*, Wolfgang Köhler refers to camouflage as a "difficult art," and alludes to coincidental disruption, the combined use of figure-ground blending (*unit forming*) and disruptive coloration (*unit breaking*) in a passage in which he refers to the concealment of military vehicles "by painting upon these things irregular designs, the parts of which are likely to form units with parts of their environment."[3.24]

Kurt Koffka, who co-founded Gestalt theory with Wertheimer and Köhler, offers a comparable example in his book, *Principles of Gestalt Psychology*: "If a gun is covered with paint in such a way that one part of it will 'fuse' with the bole of a tree, another with leaves, a third with the ground, then the beholder will no longer see a unit, the gun, but a multiplicity of much less important objects."[3.25]

Broken color or pattern is another fundamental of camouflage, which, of course, must be adapted to its environment. For our trucks, cannon, and many other implements of war, dark green, yellow, dark blue, light gray and other colors have been used in a jumble of large patterns. A final refinement is that of the blending of these colors at a distance, where the eye no longer resolves the individual patches, to a color which simulates the general hue.

—M. Luckiesh
"The Principles of Camouflage" (January 25, 1919), p. 86.

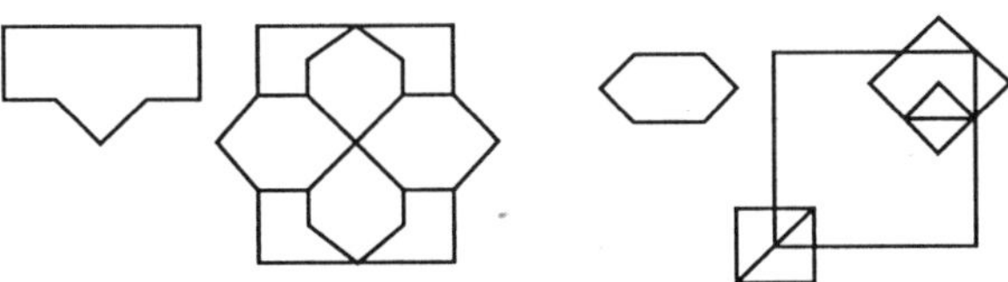

◀ **FIGURE 3.J**
Kurt Gottschaldt
Embedded figure diagrams used in his experiments in the 1920s.

Superb examples of coincidental disruption can be found in the *embedded figure* experiments of Gestaltist Kurt Gottschaldt, sometimes called "camouflaged figures," which are made up of complex arrangements of lines in which smaller, simpler shapes have been hidden.[3.26]

But none of the Gestalt psychologists wrote more extensively about camouflage than Wolfgang Metzger in *Gesetze des Sehens*. When visited in Germany after World War II by the American psychologist Heinz Ansbacher, Metzger described his wartime research specialty as "the psychology of perception as applied to camouflage problems."[3.27]

[Arriving unannounced to inspect the troops, U.S. Commanding General John J. Pershing] goes up and down our lines, shaking his head. I guess we weren't military enough for him. When he reached me [the company's camouflage expert], he really seemed appalled, particularly when he saw the sketchbook.
"What do you have there, Corporal?"
"Oh this is just my sketchbook."
"Sketchbook, sketchbook," he thundered, "what the hell do you think this is, an art school? You're in the United States Army, soldier. Give me that sketchbook."
Then he handed it to the lieutenant. I never saw it again.

—HENRY BERRY
Make the Kaiser Dance, p. 210-211.

IF WORLD WAR I French camouflage was directly influenced by Cubism, it was also inspired by 19th-century Impressionism, particularly Pointilism, in which precisely clustered colored dots appear to be single continuous hues when viewed from a distance. The bulk of World War I camouflage was designed to be seen from an airplane, from a considerable distance, directly by the human eye or through black-and-white aerial photography. At such distances, it was anticipated that a Pointillist pattern of blotches, or "the scientific use of broken color,"[3.28] as one journalist called it, would appear to be simply an indistinct gray.

In the mind of the French public, the employment of abstract, irregular shapes for camouflage reminded them of Cubism, while the quieter optical blending of dots was reminiscent of Impressionism. "There are two very distinct schools of camouflage," reported a World War I trench newspaper, "one clearly reminds us of the Pointillist Impressionists; the

Contrary to popular belief, it is the opinion of this writer that artists do not make good camouflage officers.

—PETER RODYENKO

other is infinitely closer to the Cubist school."[3.29]

Prior to World War I, Cubism was extremely unpopular with the French, who were still smarting from their humiliation by the Germans during the Franco-Prussian War. Cubist artists were often accused of being unpatriotic, of propagating an anarchistic, geometric style that was essentially German or *Boche*. A connection was even suggested between the art of the "Kubistes" (spelled with a K to make the term look more Germanic) and a suspect brand of boullion cube called "Kub," the sale of which was banned in France during World War I because it was manufactured in Germany.[3.30]

Like many others, I was not temperamentally suited to army life; but after the usual rookie training, I was fortunate in that I was transferred to the camouflage corps, where I was with kindred spirits doing interesting work.

—CHARLES BURCHFIELD
His Golden Year, p. 23.

▲ **FIGURE 3.K**
A WWII example of the use of overhanging nets (or umbrella camouflage), in which the shadows of canvas scraps are used to disrupt the shapes of personnel and artillery beneath them.

Ironically, German camouflage during World War I was more reminiscent of Impression than Cubism. German artillery was often covered with Pointillist blotches of color, and much of their airplane camouflage (some of which may have been painted by Paul Klee, who later taught at the Bauhaus) consisted of lozenge or polygon shapes that were also calculated to blend into gray at a distance.

In England, the British counterpart to Abbott Thayer and de Scevola was an academic portrait painter named Solomon J. Solomon. When the war began, the 54-year-old Solomon, who was a prominent member of the Royal Academy, suggested to the British Army that field positions be concealed by erecting overhanging nets, later called

In a week I shall return to my post on the Somme, where big guns camouflaged as if by Bakst or the Cubists are shaking all Picardy.

—JEAN COCTEAU
(letter to Igor Stravinsky)
quoted in Steegmuller (1986), p. 159.

"umbrella camouflage." Suspended on bamboo poles and interwoven with scraps of dyed muslin, burlap or canvas, these garnished nets impeded aerial observation by blocking out familiar forms, and, on a sunlit day, by casting

▶ **FIGURE 3.L**
An experiment in artillery camouflage in Hollywood by film producers, c. 1918.

disruptive irregular shapes on anything placed beneath them.[3.31]

Solomon's suggestions were largely ignored until late 1915, when British staff officers, impressed by the ingenuity of French camoufleurs, proposed that a similar unit be formed for their own army. Seeking a technical advisor, they approached Solomon, who sought the advice of the French and assembled a group of available men with artistic inclinations. As a result, a British camouflage section, which was itself camouflaged as the "Special Works Park," was formally established in March 1916. Appointed its commanding officer was a capable and experienced military officer with no artistic training, named Lieutenant Colonel Francis Wyatt.

To some the war [World War I] was like the materialization of a theory. "Nature," in a sinister meaning of the gay phrase of the 'nineties, crept up to art. The tremendous bombardments which left behind a stark tree-stump, a criss-cross of trenches on a barren shell-pocked plain from which all color had gone, created a cubist landscape. The science of camouflage, devised by the most correctly academic painters, arrived in some strange fashion at the abstract forms which had seemed too revolutionary a few years before.

—WILLIAM GAUNT
The March of the Moderns, pp. 173-174.

By mid-1917, the British organization had grown to sixty officers and 400 personnel, among them the painters Walter Russell, Ian Strang, Alan Beeton, and Colin Gill; sculptor Leon Underwood (who was Henry Moore's teacher); designers Oliver Bernard and Harry Paget; and theatre set designer L.D. Symington. Also in this unit was a young student of Solomon's named Alister Hardy, who was mistakenly chosen when he was confused with another Hardy, but was knighted many years later for his research in zoology, including protective coloration.[3.32]

Meanwhile, back in war-torn France, the American Camouflage Corps had constructed a "camouflage factory" on twenty acres of land near Dijon. By November 1918, it had grown to forty buildings, including specific facilities for blacksmithing, machine work, sewing, painting, a laboratory, and a toy production shop that also served as a painting and sculpture studio for artists. In addition to manufacturing daily 50,000 square yards of garnished nets, the factory produced observation posts, wooden silhouettes, dummy heads, sniper suits, armor-plated tree trunks, and airplane hangar covers.

Among its oddest products were armor-plated tree trunks, which the French, British

We saw a wonderful school for "camouflage," an institution that has come up in this war, meaning the painting or otherwise preparing ground or covering guns or trees, etc., so that in airplane photographs, they do not show.

—JAMES G. HARBARD
Leaves from a War Diary,
p. 114.

Around noon, we went to see the "camouflage" or disguising studio. Where this word comes from, I have not yet been able to discover. Any method or ruse that puts a different appearance on things so as to deceive the enemy, is camouflage.

—WILLIAM MITCHELL
Memoirs of World War I,
p. 56.

◀ **FIGURE 3.M**
WWI American soldier with a papier-mâché head on a stick, used to draw the enemy's fire.

and Germans used occasionally as camouflaged observation posts. When such a lookout was desired, a search would be conducted for an existing dead tree that stood at a useful

None of us, including the captain, knew a goddamn thing about camouflage, but it got us out of all the drilling and what have you.

—HENRY BERRY
Make the Kaiser Dance, p. 206.

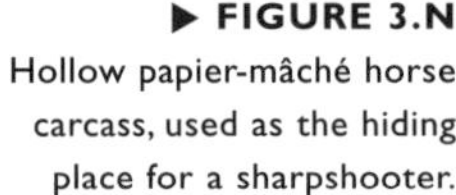

▶ FIGURE 3.N
Hollow papier-mâché horse carcass, used as the hiding place for a sharpshooter.

The sign of the camoufleur used to be a chameleon, but this has been lately removed. There could be no better insignia for camouflage than this—a disappearing chameleon.

—ERNEST PEIXOTTO
"Special Service for Artists in War Time," p. 3.

location, adjacent to one of the trenches. After making a detailed drawing of the existing tree, the camoufleurs returned to the factory, where a hollow duplicate was made in horizontal sections of manganese steel, covered with tin, and camouflaged on the surface with paint, plaster and actual tree bark. During the night, two trenches were dug to the existing tree, which was removed by way of one trench while the duplicate was brought in through the other. Inside the duplicate was a ladder which led to seat at the top, where there were peepholes and a telephone for relaying observations.

The heads and silhouettes produced were simulations of human figures, used to draw fire from snipers and, by that, reveal their positions. The silhouettes were life-sized figures, posed for by the camoufleurs, then cut out of wall board and painted. Several dozen of these might be placed in shell holes in front of the trenches at night, rigged with ropes and hinges. The British called it the "Chinese attack" when, on the following day, "the rope would all be pulled at once, and the appearance to the enemy would be that of a raiding party starting out at top speed."[3.33]

In addition, the Dijon factory made imitation tree branches containing periscopes, and covers for foxholes that became known as "beehives." In using these, the soldier looked out through a camouflaged lid that was covered "with paint and bits of grass to simulate the appearance of the surrounding terrain, often being studded with tin cans or old shoes to make it appear to be an accumulation of rubbish. The favorite way to make the peephole for a beehive was to cover with gauze a hole cut in the bottom of an old shoe, which was then fastened to the observation post."[3.34]

The ingenuity of the Dijon camoufleurs extended beyond their military responsibilities, when they applied it to ways of amusing

A town occupied by an army looks like a deserted shell of grey inhabitants watched over by khaki ghosts.

—Stephen Spender
in John Goldsmith (1986),
p. 62.

Along the line bloated, decomposing carcasses of horses and cattle, stinking and glittering and seething with flies and maggots under the burning sun, were varied by wrecks of trains, twisted rails, and war debris, and by fortified blockhouses festooned with barbed wire and still guarded by sweating, scarlet-faced tommies whose khaki uniforms, intended to blend with the biscuit-colored landscape vibrating round them in the heat, contrasted with the blue distances.

—William Plomer
The Autobiography of William Plomer,
p. 72.

Gertrude Stein's poetry, Schöenberg's music, the philosophical thought of Wittgenstein and the Vienna Circle, Cubism, and Formalist criticism all typify a general tendency in twentieth-century life towards the "construct" that is sufficient unto itself, ordered according to its own laws, dissociated from any moral cause, and associated exclusively with the hermetic experience of man confronted by man's creations.

—JOHN ADKINS RICHARDSON
Modern Art and Scientific Thought, p. 120.

By the war's end, more than three thousand French artists of all ages and artistic schools had served the nation in this capacity [of camouflaging].

—ALFRED E. CORNEBISE
Art from the Trenches, p. 6.

their friends, nurses and hundreds of French children whose mothers worked at the camouflage factory. These Americans "worked during their leisure moments and eventually produced the scenery and equipment for a genuine Yankee circus, animals and all, the menagerie, however, being principally made of papier-mâché with human operatives inside the beasts. The first performance of the circus was given on Thanksgiving Day 1918, and the audience was so delighted that it demanded a repetition. After three encores of this sort it was suggested that performances be given in Dijon, a city of upward of 50,000 population, with admittance charged. This advice was followed, and the circus made such a hit that the Engineers were able to turn over to the French orphan fund a considerable sum of money."[3.35]

The French, an American journalist wrote in 1917, "were quick to appreciate its [camouflage's] great usefulness and employ and continue to use it with rare skill; the Germans lost no time in their endeavor to outdo the French, and the English accepted it as a modern necessity, but practiced it as first with a heavy hand and with a lack of grace and imagination."[3.36]

As for the Americans, the writer continued, "If the French were ingenious enough to invent it and the Germans to copy it, it is safe to say that we Americans shall first of all systematize it; we shall make a business of it—not a cut-and-dried business, but one directed with level reasoning and touched by American humor and inventiveness."[3.37]

Two years later, when the fighting had finally ended, Gertrude Stein and Alice B. Toklas drove out to the front lines to survey the effects of the conflict. Fascinated by what they saw, they were particularly interested in "how different the camouflage of the French looked from the camouflage of the Germans, and then once we came across some very very neat camouflage and it was American. The idea was the same but as after all it was different nationalities who did it the difference was inevitable. The color schemes were different, the designs were different, the way of placing them was different, it made plain the whole theory of art and its inevitability."[3.38] ✂

Camouflage began with a bucket of paint. Now what it needs is a plumber's kit.

—Homer Saint-Gaudens quoted in Fox (1942), p. 156.

Chapter Four

A Flock of Sea-going Easter Eggs

World War I Ship Camouflage

DURING A TEN-MONTH PERIOD from March to December 1917, German submarines (called "U-boats" for *Unterseeboot* or "under-the-sea-boat") sank an average of more than 23 British ships each week for a total of 925 ships. The worst period was in mid-April, when 55 British ships were destroyed in one week, for an average of almost eight ships per day.

When a U-boat attacked an enemy ship, one of three methods was commonly used: First, the submarine might remain submerged and, aiming through a periscope from a safe distance, fire an expensive and often inaccurate torpedo. Second, the submarine might come to the surface (which left it vulnerable) and, allowing some time for preparation, attack with the cannon mounted on its deck. Third, if its target was an unarmed commercial vessel or "merchant ship," it might come to the surface, move alongside the captured ship, remove everyone on board, and then sink the empty ship by blowing it up.

▲ **FIGURE 4.B**
ANON
World War I-era British dazzle-painted ship.

◀ **FIGURE 4.A**
Camouflaged American soldier in Vietnam.

Prior to World War I, the Germany Navy preferred the third method. Its official stated policy was that "destruction may not take place before everyone on board has been brought to safety along with their goods and chattels..."[4.1] In late 1914, however, it adopted a new policy, one which proclaimed that "a U-boat cannot spare the crews of merchant ships, but must send them and their ships to the bottom of the sea. All shipping should be warned and all merchant shipping to England should be brought to a halt in a short period of time."[4.2]

▲ **FIGURE 4.C**
Anon
World War I-era dazzle-painted ship.

In the early years of the war, this new policy was not strictly carried out, because many of the merchant ships (often clandestinely carrying goods to aid England's war effort) were coming from the United States, which was a neutral power that Germany preferred not to offend. However, a more severe policy was introduced in January 1917 when Germany announced that its submarine warfare would be unrestricted. From then on, all ships traveling within a certain war zone, even ships from neutral countries, if suspected of transporting aid to England, would be attacked by U-boats. Four months later, the *Lusitania*, a British passenger ship, was struck by a German torpedo, and 1,195 passengers were killed, including 128 American citizens. The American public was outraged by the tragedy, and it was later a major contributor to the U.S. decision to enter the war on the side of the Allies.[4.3]

One reason for Germany's more severe policy toward ships of neutral countries was England's decision to use mimicry in its ship camouflage, resulting in what were referred to as "Q-Ships." These were armed British ships disguised as unarmed merchant ships. They often flew "false colors," erroneous flags of neutral countries, in the hope of enticing a U-boat to come to surface and to move in, at which time the guns of the British decoy would be unveiled and the submarine fired on at close range. While this strategy was moderately successful for a while, the element of surprise was soon lost, and the U-boats became increasingly cautious about approaching merchant ships, even those with neutral flags. For this and other reasons, it became least hazardous for U-boats to attack with torpedoes, remaining submerged and aiming through a periscope from a distance of at least 2,700 yards or about one and a half miles.[4.4]

Our ports are full of strange monsters such as the naval architects of the past never envisaged in their wildest dreams.

—Charles DeKay
"Ships That Fade Away,"
p. 105.

What would a deep water sailor of the old type have thought, if he had dropped into the midst of the particolored ships of 1918?

—Thomas G. Frothingham
The Naval History of the World War, p. 263.

That this kind of Cubist painting on a colossal scale should have proved useful in the world war is only one more example of the fact—that you can never tell!

—Charles DeKay
"Ships That Fade Away,"
p. 106.

As the war continued and the U-boat toll continued to rise, the chief concern of Allied ships was how to avoid a torpedo attack. This was the problem that came to be faced in the early months of 1917 by a 39-year-old British illustrator, marine painter and designer named Norman Wilkinson, who was a lieutenant in the Royal Navy. Years later, Wilkinson recalled the time and exact circumstances that led to his invention of *dazzle painting*: "On my way back to Devonport in the early morning, in an extremely cold carriage, I suddenly got the idea that since it was impossible to paint a ship so that she could not be seen by a submarine, the extreme opposite was the answer—in other words, to paint her, not for low visibility, but in such a way as to break up her form and thus confuse a submarine officer as to the course on which she was heading."[4.5]

The object of this [dazzle] camouflage is to get the enemy gunner groggy as to distance and direction, so that he will be unable to tell how far away the vessel is and what course it is holding, and so lead him to aim short or to overshoot his mark.

—CHARLES DEKAY
"Ships That Fade Away,"
p. 105.

Wilkinson concluded that prior attempts at ship camouflage had been ineffective because techniques used for ground camouflage had been used inappropriately for ships. In ground camouflage, the object to be camouflaged is often stationary, and one is more or less assured of a fixed and predictable background. In naval camouflage, however, the object to be camouflaged is nearly always moving, and its background is frequently shifting as well. Further, even if a ship were stationary, its two predominant backgrounds, the sea and the sky, are constantly changing in color and light.

Given these and other variables, thought Wilkinson, it was absurd to attempt to conceal a ship on the ocean. Since invisibility was impossible in naval camouflage, it would be more effective to paint erratic patterns on the ship's surface, making it even more visible, and thereby confuse or "dazzle" the submarine gunner so that he could not be sure about the target's course, size, speed or distance. The primary goal was to mislead the U-boat gunner about what position to fire from,

▶ **FIGURE 4.D**
NORMAN WILKINSON
Detailed dazzle-painting plan

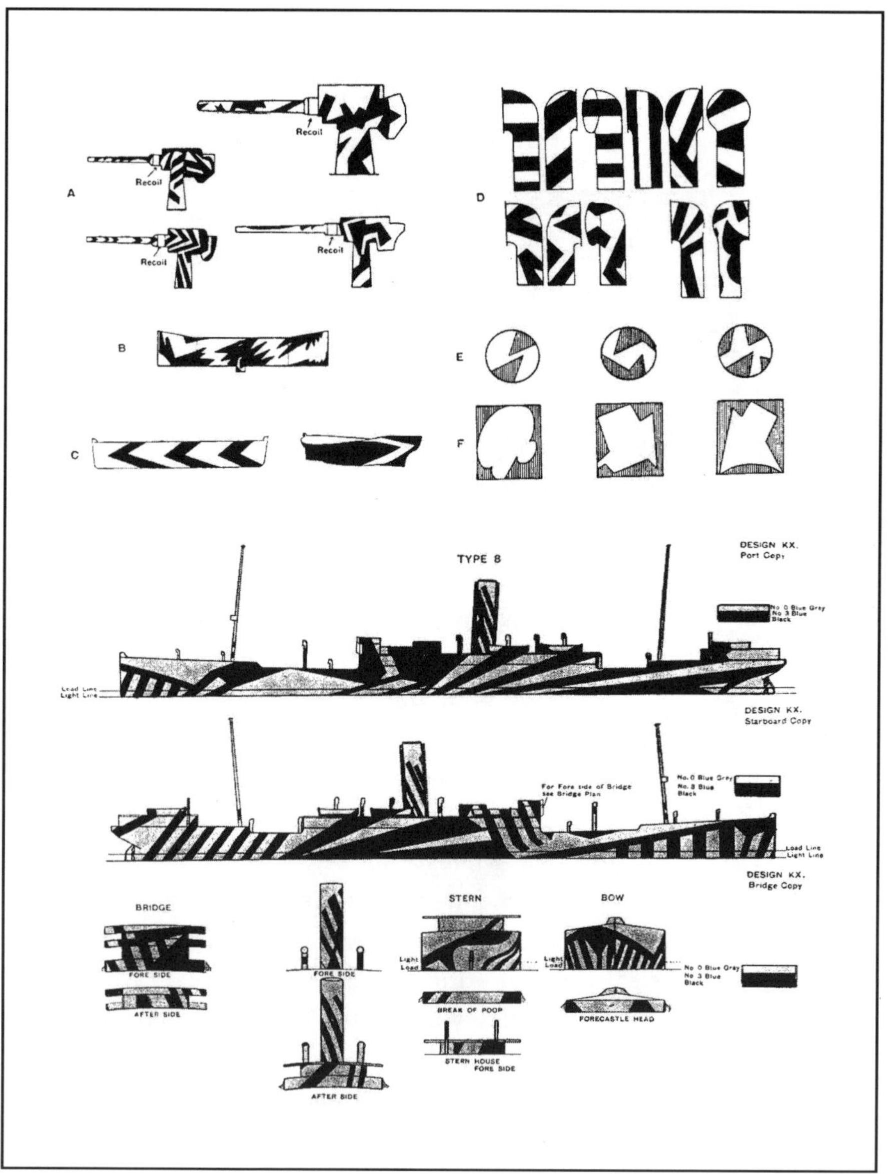

when the ship was first sighted. A submarine, explained Wilkinson, "having once failed to obtain a good position has little or no likelihood of regaining that position, owing to insufficient underwater speed."[4.6] And even if the submarine did get into firing position, the bewildering pattern might still cause the gunner to spoil his aim. This was possible because the torpedo was not aimed at the ship, but rather was fired ahead of the ship—it had to lead its target—so that to determine the course of the ship, quickly and accurately, was absolutely essential.

▲ **FIGURE 4.E** British news photograph of NORMAN WILKINSON in 1970, at age 92, the year before he died, holding a dazzle-painted ship model, against the background of one of his marine paintings.

When Wilkinson submitted his idea to the British Admiralty, it was initially ignored. Soon however, it was taken seriously, with the result that the *H.M.S. Industry*, a small store ship, was ordered to be painted in an experimental dazzle scheme under Wilkinson's supervision. Meanwhile, other British ships, the coast guard and shore stations were instructed to report their impressions whenever they sighted the curious boat.

A few days later, it was ordered that fifty troopships be dazzle-painted immediately, and Wilkinson was placed in charge of a newly-formed Dazzle Section. Located in a spare classroom at Burlington House, home of the Royal Academy of Arts, this unit was made up of seventeen workers: Wilkinson; five male artists chosen by him, either unfit or too old for military service, who designed the dazzle schemes; three ship model makers (two male, one female); and eleven young female art students, who prepared hand-colored mechanical drawings which were followed in painting the actual ships.[4.7]

Twenty or thirty ships elaborately camouflaged with streaks and blotches of violently contrasting colors, all zigzagging in formation, presented an uncertain and bewildering target.

—C.R.M.F. CRUTTWELL
A History of the Great War, p. 386.

In addition, ten other men were appointed dock officers at various harbors around Britain, including Bristol, Liverpool, Newcastle, Glasgow and so on. Initially, these men only supervised the painting of the ships, but later, when generic schemes were used on ships of varying sizes and shapes, they also contributed to modifying the dazzle schemes. One of these outport officers was Edward Wadsworth, a painter who played a significant role before World War I in the development of Vorticism, a British combination of Cubism and Futurism.[4.8]

In Wilkinson's words, the ships were prepared in the following way: "In the initial stages a small wooden model of each ship was made to scale. On this a design was painted in wash colors for the purposes of rapid alteration. This model was then carefully studied on a prepared theatre through a submarine periscope, various sky backgrounds being placed behind her alternately. A satisfactory design having been evolved giving the maximum distortion, the model was then handed to the trained plan

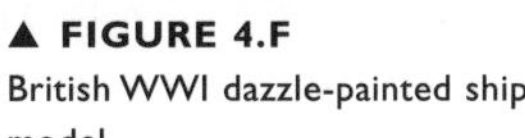

▲ **FIGURE 4.F**
British WWI dazzle-painted ship model.

maker and copied on to a 1/16th-inch scale profile plan of the ship on white paper showing port and starboard side. The plan was then sent to the outport officer at the port at which the particular ship was lying and transferred under his supervision to the ship."[4.9]

[A dazzle-painted ship] was like an enormous cubist painting with great sheets of ultramarine blue, black, and green, sometimes parallel but more often with sharp corners cleaving into one another, and although you don't quite make it out, you can divine a reason, a plan, a guiding principle, a scheme.

—RENE GIMPEL
Diary of an Art Dealer, p. 29.

Each of the first fifty dazzle painting

▶ **FIGURE 4.G**
Cartoon [detail] by C.H. SHEPARD from *Punch* (June 4, 1919) in which British street workers, filling up cracks with tar, are compared to dazzle camoufleurs.

schemes was unique, in the sense that a different design was applied to each ship. Further, on any one ship, the design on the port side was different from that on the starboard. As before, observers were asked to report what they saw when dazzle-painted ships were sighted. One was described as "almost impossible to say how she was steering," while it was said of another that it "sometimes appears to be going in the opposite direction."[4.10]

▲ **FIGURE 4.H**
British WWI dazzle-painted ship model.

As a consequence, in October 1917, the

Admiralty decided that dazzle camouflage should be applied to all armed and unarmed merchant ships, so that by the end of the following June, more than 2,300 British ships had been dazzle-painted. There were moments when as many as 100 ships were being dazzle-painted in a single harbor at one time.[4.11]

◀ **FIGURE 4.1** WWI-era news photograph of a ship being dazzle-painted.

IN THE MEANTIME, as a result of a visit to England by Admiral William S. Sims of the U.S. Navy, the American government requested that Norman Wilkinson be loaned to the United States. This request was submitted in spite of the fact that six camouflage methods had already been adopted by the U.S. Navy: One of these, called the "Brush System," was patented by Abbott Thayer and Gerome Brush, as mentioned earlier, and was based on the former's discovery of countershading in animals.[4.12] Another was the "Mackay System," a low visibility Pointillist plan invented by New York artist William Andrew Mackay. A third, known as the "Warner System," proposed by

It was necessary frequently for vessels to have their dazzle designs altered… Ships so treated would creep back to port with a particularly odd-looking coat of many colors, the wear and tear of a winter journey across the Atlantic having played havoc with the fresh paint of her new design, causing the old one to appear in patches.

—HUGH HURST
"Dazzle-Painting in War-time," p. 94.

Girls in tight jeans and dazzle socks.

—ANON
Economist
(January 11, 1958).

an Iowa-born artist and Naval Reserve officer named Everett L. Warner, was, like Wilkinson's method, designed to interfere with range finding.[4.13] Other systems were developed by

▶ **FIGURE 4.J**
An example of disruptive coloration or dazzle in the protective coloration of animals.

Maximilian Toch,[4.14] an authority on paint chemistry, Lewis Herzog, and a person named Watson. Encouraged by the Board of Marine Insurance Underwriters, which offered preferred insurance rates to

▲ **FIGURE 4.K**
British news photograph (c. 1919) of swimmers at Margate wearing dazzle-painted bathing suits.

camouflaged merchant ships, dozens of other suggestions were made by American artists, inventors and patriotic amateurs throughout the country. Thayer submitted two models, one in which the ship was draped by an enormous net, and another in which it was covered by "a huge spread of canvas painted to imitate a cloud."[4.15] In a proposal from Thomas Edison, an entire ship was apparently disguised as an island, complete with a lighthouse and pine trees. Thayer's proposals were rejected outright, but because of Edison's prestige, his scheme was actually applied to the *S.S. Ochenfels*, but his camouflage made the ship "so unseaworthy that it [the imitation island] got carried away before the vessel got out of New York Harbor."[4.15] A number of people suggested that ships be nickel-plated or completely covered in mirrors. Others proposed that they should be disguised to look like whales or icebergs.

Although the majority of women seem to prefer shoes with just two colors to match their frocks, "dazzle" footwear are a good second.

—Anon
Star
(May 8, 1931).

Norman Wilkinson sailed to America in March 1918 on the *Leviathan*, formerly the *Vaterland*, a large ocean liner captured from Germany by the U.S., then converted for use as a troopship. Arriving in New York, he was taken to Washington, DC to a meeting with Franklin D. Roosevelt, Assistant Secretary of the Navy, who expressed his admiration for dazzle painting. "We have no department of camouflage here," Roosevelt said. "Up to the present ship camouflage in the United States has been carried out by a number of private individuals, all of whose systems vary, but are mainly on the order of invisibility or low visibility treatment. They have been selling their plans at so many dollars a foot run to ship owners. We had no means of testing the results in a practical way…'"[4.16]

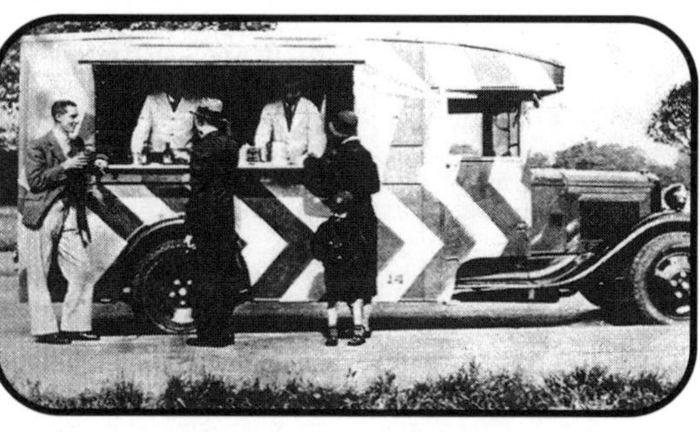

▲ **FIGURE 4.L**
Shortly after World War I, this dazzle-painted concession stand was staffed by British war veterans.

The boy…his yellow dazzle socks flashing like twin beacons.

—J. Townsend
Young Devils (1958).

During the next four weeks, Wilkinson assisted in organizing an American Camouflage Section, patterned after its British predecessor and established as part of the Bureau of Construction and Repair. Lieutenant Harold Van Buskirk was placed in charge of the unit, while two subdivisions were set up. The research subdivision at the Eastman Kodak Company in Rochester, New York, was comprised of scientists, while a design subdivision in Washington was made up of artists.[4.17]

Captain Schmidt at the
periscope.
You need not fall and faint.
For it's not the vision of
drug or dope,
But only the dazzle paint.

—G.F. NORTON
quoted in Wilkinson (1969), p. 78.

The person in charge of the research group at Rochester was Lieutenant Loyd A. Jones, who was head of the physics laboratory at Eastman Kodak. As a civilian, Jones had already contributed to the efforts of the Submarine Defense Association by inventing a "visibility meter," a device for obtaining a measurement of the visibility of an object in an ocean setting. Later, he set up a theatre for studying camouflaged ship models in which the periscope moved on a track and the lighting was much more elaborate than in other theatres.[4.18]

▲ **FIGURE 4.M**
WWI photograph of U.S. naval camoufleur EVERETT L. WARNER.

The artist in charge of the Washington subdivision was Lieutenant Warner, who escorted Wilkinson as he lectured at harbors at Boston, New York, Philadelphia, and Norfolk on the purpose, design and application of dazzle painting. Back in Washington, Warner assembled a small team of camouflage artists, including marine painter Frederic Waugh (who produced an especially wonderful plan for dazzle-painting the *Leviathan*), portrait painter Gordon Stevenson, sculptor John Gregory, Kenneth MacIntire, A. O'Connell, a person named Richardson, and several others.[4.19] Like their British counterparts, they applied dazzle patterns to miniature wooden models, tested the models in a periscope-equipped theatre, and prepared instructions for painting the ships.

◀ **FIGURE 4.N**
Like their British counterparts, U.S. naval camoufleurs tested their painted ship models by observing them through a periscope, under viewing conditions that simulated those of a submarine gunner.

In the meantime, official approval was withdrawn from all naval camouflage systems other than dazzle painting. It became the sole responsibility of the Dazzle Section to supply camouflage for all American ships, while the Shipping Board provided camoufleurs at ports (most of whom were professional artists and architects) who supervised the painting. In addition, the Office of Naval Intelligence used artists and photographers to make colored sketches and photographs for the Dazzle Section of camouflaged ships in American ports. One of the artists assigned to draw ships was Louis Bouché.[4.20] Another was Thomas Hart Benton, who wrote in a letter that "This is

To [Ernest] Peixotto's artist eye, the ships that he observed [during World War I], "brilliantly camouflaged like wasps, queerly striped with black and white, with spots between of yellow, grey-blue, and water-green," or painted with low-visibility colors and "toned like Monet's pictures with spots of pink and green" never failed to fascinate.

—Alfred E. Cornebise
Art from the Trenches,
p. 26.

done so that if the ship should be torpedoed or lost in any way all the facts concerning her appearance etc. can easily be found."[4.21]

But there were other reasons for making the drawings. It was, for example, of value to have drawings and photographs of camouflaged foreign ships, to compare and contrast with American schemes. In addition, by studying drawings, paintings and photographs (made by yet another team of artists) of dazzle-painted ships in American harbors, Warner and his team could tell if their camouflage designs had been applied correctly. As it turned out, often they had not, especially when the Shipping Board's dock supervisors had been asked to use a single scheme for several ships, each structurally different. It was evident in some cases that those artists had failed to understand the basic principles of course deception, so much so that it was decided that each week three of the Shipping Board camoufleurs would travel to Warner's Washington laboratory for a brief but informative seminar on dazzle painting.[4.22]

▲ **FIGURE 4.O**
U.S. marine painter and naval camoufleur FREDERIC WAUGH. Photograph by Peter A. and Paul Juley.

Dazzle camouflage aimed at deception rather than obscurity. Transports and cargo ships were decorated in huge zigzag designs, like so many floating Cubist paintings, until American ports resembled nightmare harbors beyond the gates of ivory and horn.

—PRESTON SLOSSON
The Great Crusade and After, p. 51.

It was during one of these seminars that Warner made a serendipitous discovery. In the process of explaining course deception, he sawed one of the dazzle-painted wooden ship models into about five sections. He then arranged these sections in a curve or oblique angle in front of a plain gray ship model. To his delight, he discovered that when the gray model "was placed at any angle behind one of those rows of blocks it invariably appeared to take the same direction as the blocks."[4.23] In other words, to create a new dazzle scheme, one had simply to position the blocks in a way that contradicted the orientation of the gray ship model, convert that arrangement to a flat pattern (through drawing or photography), and apply that design to the side of the ship.

Hulls and funnels alike were transformed into crazily festooned apparitions, intended to disorient any U-boat.

—Richard Cork
A Bitter Truth, p. 232.

From what is known about this simple yet effective method, it appears that Warner's arrangements of blocks were always thoughtful and deliberate; they were, in his own words, "very far from being haphazard." As a result, he objected when others began to refer to this method as "jazz painting"; while he conceded that it was an American-sounding name (and one which caused "a great deal of merriment"), he regarded it as inappropriate because jazz at the time was considered to be spontaneous, carefree improvisation. Nor did

▲ FIGURE 4.P
WWI camouflage scheme designed by Frederic Waugh, as applied to an American troop ship, the *Leviathan*.

The explosive diagonal and zig-zag bands [of dazzle camouflage] had a wild, ragtime impact.

—RICHARD CORK
A Bitter Truth, p. 232.

he agree that the method was based on the same principles as Cubism. On the contrary, he protested, "it was precisely when our work was most firmly grounded on the book of Euclid that the uninitiated were the most positive that the ships were being painted haphazard by a group of crazy Cubists."★[4.24]

▲ **FIGURE 4.Q**
U.S. Navy photographs of the use by EVERETT L. WARNER of irregularly-shaped wooden blocks in the invention of camouflage schemes.

Warner wrote about and provided illustrations of his innovative method on at least three occasions. In 1919, he published two articles on his World War I ship camouflage, one in *Everybody's Magazine*, the other in *Transactions of the Illuminating Engineering Society*; and then, in 1944, at age 67, while serving as a civilian advisor to the U.S. Navy during World War II, he prepared a 14-page document for the Bureau of Ships, titled *Ship Camouflage Manual for Pattern Design Application*, which was never published.[4.25]

Of particular interest is a passage in the *Transactions* article in which he compares his wooden block technique to the illusory effects of distorted wallpaper. He writes:

"If a room were papered with a pattern of recurrent design, and if it were possible to take a photograph with a filter which would eliminate everything but the pattern, it would be quite possible to reconstruct the room from such a photograph and a piece of wallpaper.

Every change in the direction of the walls—every corner and projection—would all be indicated by an alteration in the apparent size and shapes of our units of pattern. When

★ In 1917, L. Wolfe Gilbert and Anatol Friedland were authors of a "jazz rag" sound recording titled *Camouflage*. It was released for player piano as Imperial Songrecord No. 9471-85.

you have once thoroughly grasped this idea, marine camouflage holds no secrets for you.

You will realize that by changing the normal appearance of the pattern on one of the walls—by distorting it, as it were—we could alter your visual impression of the wall. A regular pattern will not have the same appearance upon a curved surface as upon a flat surface, and if, upon the latter, we paint the pattern as it normally appears upon the curved surface we can give the illusion of a curving wall. This is exactly what was done on some of the ships."[4.26]

▲ **FIGURE 4.R**
U.S. naval camoufleurs (including Frederic Waugh, second from right) applying camouflage schemes to wooden ship models, c. 1918.

DURING THE FINAL eight months of World War I, more than 1,200 American ships were painted with dazzle schemes produced by the Washington subdivision, about half of which were modifications of British designs. The results were astonishing. "Those who were not fortunate to see the docks at one of our great ports during the war," a writer recalled, "may imagine the arrival of a convoy—or, as frequently occurred, two at a time—of these painted ships, and the many miles of docks crowded with vessels of all sorts...each resplendent with a variety of bright-hued patterns, up-to-date designs of stripes in black and white or pale blue and deep ultramarine, and earlier designs of curves, patches, and semicircles. Take all these, huddle them together in what appears to be hopeless confusion, but which in reality is perfect order, bow and stern pointing in all directions, mix in a little sunshine, add the varied and sparkling reflections, stir the hotchpotch up with smoke, life, and incessant movement, and it can safely be said that the word 'dazzle' is not far from the mark."[4.27]

▲ **FIGURE 4.S** American painter THOMAS HART BENTON. Photograph by Peter A. and Paul Juley.

[Serving as a U.S. Navy camoufleur] was the most important thing, so far, I [Thomas Hart Benton] had ever done for myself as [an] artist. The mechanical contrivances of building, the new airplanes, the blimps, the dredges, the ships of the base, because they were so interesting in themselves, tore me away from all my grooved habits, from my play with colored cubes and classic attenuations, from my esthetic drivelings and morbid self-concerns.

THOMAS HART BENTON quoted in Adams (1989), p. 87.

Riding in a convoy of dazzle-painted ships, a journalist said, was "like being in the middle of a floating art museum," while others spoke of dazzled ships as "so many floating cubist paintings," "a futurist's bad dream," "cubist painting on a colossal scale" and "a cross between a boiler explosion and a railroad accident."[4.28] "You should see our Fleet!," exclaimed an American newspaper, "It's camouflaged so, it looks like a flock of sea-going Easter Eggs. If you shut your eyes good and tight, and stand behind a wall, you can't see a ship a cable's length away. It was an English guy [Wilkinson] thought of it first, and his name's the first toast now at all the paintmakers' social reunions."[4.29]

But was it Norman Wilkinson who first thought of dazzle painting? Not according to an American naval manual, prepared in 1961, which contended that Abbott Thayer had devised "a system of course- and type-decep-

[Norman] Wilkinson reported that dazzle saved many ships from destruction. Although a number of the decorated vessels were hit by torpedoes, "a far larger percentage of these made port than ships painted light grey, owing to the submarine making an erratic shot, and so injuring the vessel in a less vital spot."

Richard Cork
A Bitter Truth, p. 232.

◀ **FIGURES 4.T, 4.U and 4.V** Everett Warner WWII ship camouflage applied to [from top to bottom] *U.S. Destroyer O'Brien*, *U.S. Destroyer L.K. Swenson* (both May 1944), and *U.S. Carrier Yorkstown* (October 1944).

tion painting which used misleading painted-patterns to falsify real perspective and natural lines of construction" as early as 1915 (two years in advance of Wilkinson), a system which Thayer discovered while studying ship models

▲ **FIGURE 4.W**
EVERETT WARNER
WWII ship camouflage applied to *U.S. Cruiser Trenton* (August 1944).

on Dublin Pond, when "he noticed that a partly painted model appeared to be headed in the wrong direction."[4.30] "Such strong contrasting deception patterns," the manual explains, "when carefully designed by good artists, could make a ship appear to be headed on any course desired, regardless of [the] ship's actual course."[4.31] Regrettably, no source is listed for the claim that Thayer applied dazzle patterns to ships in addition to his counter-shading measures.

Nevertheless, as discussed earlier, there is no doubt that Thayer was fully aware of the camouflage function of disruptive coloring, and there are portions of his book that anticipate dazzle painting. There is for example a photograph of four butterflies, three with monochromatic coloring (black, white and gray) and one with high contrast disruptive coloring (Fig 2.E). In the caption, the reader is instructed to study the photograph from a distance of seven or eight yards, at which point the three monochromatic butterflies remain identifiable, while the fourth looks fragmented and incoherent.[4.32]

Looking at this image, one is reminded of a letter to the editor in *Nature* in May 1919 by John Graham Kerr, a Scottish professor of zoology and a Member of Parliament, who had spoken in favor of the ill-fated attempt by Thayer, with Sargent's assistance, to persuade the British to abandon the monochromatic khaki field service uniform in favor of a dazzle-like field service uniform. In this letter, Kerr claimed that Wilkinson's invention of dazzle painting was not unprecedented, and that, as early as 1914, he had invented a similar scheme, using disruptive coloring in combination with countershading. He had proposed this system to the British Admiralty at the start of World War I when he became convinced that uniform coloring, whether black, white or monochromatic gray, was ineffective camouflage, even dangerous, in the sense that—like Thayer's photograph of butterflies—it enabled the overall shape to remain clearly readable from a great distance. "I also directed attention," he writes, "to its [disruptive coloring's] use in confusing the details, especially vertical

[To see the formation of a convoy of dazzle camouflaged ships] was a kaleidoscopic effect as each vessel passed slowly down the river to take up her appointed station outside the bar; stripes crossing stripes, blue, black, green, and grey appearing and disappearing. At times a large patch of some strong color would detach itself from the side of a vessel, as if by a miracle, and eventually disclose the fact that it belonged to another vessel lying unsuspectedly alongside; and when, finally, all were in position and were viewed from a distance, there appeared again nothing but an interesting confusion.

—Hugh Hurst
"Dazzle-painting in War-time," p. 94.

lines, which are made use of by the enemy's range finders..."[4.33]

A month later, there was a reply from Wilkinson in the same journal, in which he

▶ **FIGURE 4.X**
U.S. naval camoufleur EVERETT L. WARNER (center) and four WWII co-workers, including (in foreground) Robert R. Hays and (in background, l to r) Bennet Buck, William Walters, and Arthur Conrad, preparing camouflaged ship models and transferring those patterns to the master plans of each class of ship.

argued that Kerr "has not thoroughly grasped the idea of the special form of camouflage on which I was engaged, and of which I still claim to be the originator."[4.34] Dazzle painting, said Wilkinson, was not derived from biological examples. It has little relation to disruptive coloring, in the sense that the latter attempts to decrease visibility, while his system merely confuses the aim of the submarine gunner and may even heighten visibility.

As for countershading, it is simply not practicable in ship camouflage, Wilkinson said, because any design requiring white patches or subtle coloration would soon be ruined by the heat, smoke, fuel, and rust that constantly leak from a functioning ship. All ships require

Everett Warner, one of the best artists employed by the U.S. Navy in World War I, was by far the most skillful in designing course-deception measures. In the second World War he returned to the Navy and trained and directed a staff of artists in the Camouflage Section of the Bureau of Ships—in addition to designing the best patterns used by the U.S. and British Navies.

—D.R.E. BROWN
Ships Concealment Camouflage Instructions: Vol. 2, p. 2.

repainting every six months, and dazzle-painted ships remain cleaner and more effective than others, Wilkinson explained later, "on the principle that a white table cloth will look

◀ FIGURE 4.Y
Robert R. Hays, working under Warner's direction, preparing camouflaged ship models during WWII.

dirty sooner than a patchwork quilt."[4.35]

Throughout World War I and long afterwards, frequent misgivings persisted about the usefulness of dazzle painting. To what extent could Wilkinson's assertions about its effectiveness be verified? American sources claimed that less than one per cent of dazzle-painted ships were sunk by torpedoes. But when the British Admiralty set up a Committee on Dazzle Painting, it reported in September 1918 that there was no clear evidence that dazzle painting had ever confused a submarine gunner. However, the report continued, it may be advisable to continue the practice because it is not disadvantageous and indeed it had caused an "undoubted increase" in the confidence

The pictorial qualities of dazzle were exploited by many painters...

—Paul Atterbury
"Dazzle Painting in the First World War,"
p. 27.

Considering that most of the artists involved [in World War I camouflage] were of academic outlook, some of the results they produced are astonishing. They often succeeded in out-cubing the Cubists, sometimes to the apparent detriment of the original objective.

—Barbara Jones and Bill Howell
Popular Arts of the First World War,
p. 77.

and morale of the crews aboard dazzled-painted ships.

World War I ended officially on June 28, 1919, with the signing of the Treaty of Versailles. Partly because ships require periodic repainting, dazzle painting soon disappeared. No longer menaced by German U-boats, the Allied navies chose to paint virtually all their ships in monochromatic gray, instead of expending additional time on the restoration of multi-colored dazzle schemes.

▲ **FIGURE 4.Z** Group photograph of EVERETT L. WARNER and his WWII American naval camouflage staff, including (l to r), Bennet Buck, Sheffield Kagy, William Walters, Warner (holding ship model), Arthur Conrad, and Robert R. Hays.

Shortly after the war, Warner was discharged from the Naval Reserve. He moved back to New York and resumed his career as a painter. A year later, he and his family moved to Pittsburgh, Pennsylvania, where, to ensure a steady income, he accepted a position as professor of art at the Carnegie Institute of Technology. Surely, it was not entirely a coincidence that his department head there was Homer Saint-Gaudens, who had commanded the American Camouflage Corps during World War I.

In December 1941, when the United States entered World War II, Warner was asked by the U.S. Navy to return to duty as the Chief Civilian Aid in charge of ship camouflage. He remained in that capacity until that war ended in 1945, at which time he retired from teaching. His plan was to go back to painting, and to rebuild his reputation.[4.36]

But it was too late; the attempt failed. Cubism, Futurism, Vorticism, Dada, Surrealism and Expressionism were now in predominance. Ironically, the man who had championed the use of abstract patterns in ship camouflage could not fathom Modern Art. He was, according to Helen Fusscas, "discouraged and bewildered by the lack of interest in realism."[4.37]

In 1963, at age 86, Warner was struck by a heart attack and died on October 20. Ten years earlier, he had written to a friend: "I have no public, but I continue to paint…I do not think that the critics now writing have even heard of my name…I am bewildered. After a long life spent in study and observation, I am assured that my time was just wasted."★[4.38] ✂

The art of our century has been characterized by shattered surfaces, broken color, segmented compositions, dissolving forms and shredded images. Curiously insistent is this consistent emphasis on break-up.

—Katharine Kuh
Break-Up: The Core of Modern Art, p. 11.

★ While researching this chapter, I was fortunate to locate Everett L. Warner's sons, James and Thomas, and one of his WWII co-workers, Robert R. Hays, all of whom were very helpful.

Chapter Five

The Language of Vision

Camouflage and the Bauhaus

In 1910, the Austrian composer Gustav Mahler underwent psychoanalysis with Sigmund Freud, who determined that he had been suffering from an Oedipus complex. As self-treatment, the 50-year-old musician decided to abstain from all sexual activity, a decision that greatly disheartened his wife, the enchanting Alma Mahler, who was 20 years younger and much sought after in Viennese society.

They were a tense and peculiar family, the Oedipuses, weren't they?

—Max Beerbohm

Soon after, she embarked on a steamy, clandestine romance with a young German architect, who sabotaged their secrecy when he mailed one of their love letters to her husband, then appeared at the Mahler home, demanding that Gustav and Alma divorce. The ailing composer refused, but a year later he died—on the architect's birthday.[5.1]

◀ **FIGURE 5.A**
Lionel Feininger
Cathedral
woodcut illustration for the *Manifesto and Programme of the Weimar Bauhaus* (1919).

That audacious young architect was none other than Walter Gropius, who is now widely remembered as the founder of the Bauhaus, the most influential art and design school of the 20th century. He and Alma Mahler later married. But when they first met, he had just been fired from the architectural office of German architect Peter Behrens, not for his curious inability to draw, but for miscalculating a ceiling height.[5.2]

Two women meet while shopping at the supermarket in the Bronx. One looks cheerful, the other depressed. The cheerful one inquires: "What's eating you?"... "Well, if you must know, it's my little Jimmy." "What's wrong with him, then?" "Nothing is wrong. His teacher said he must see a psychiatrist." Pause. "Well, well, what's wrong with seeing a psychiatrist?" "Nothing is wrong. The psychiatrist said he's got an Oedipus complex." Pause. "Well, well, Oedipus or Shmoedipus, I wouldn't worry so long as he's a good boy and loves his mamma."

—ARTHUR KOESTLER (a joke told to him by John von Neumann) *The Act of Creation*, pp. 32-33.

Gropius' career might have been ruined had he not been introduced by his brother-in-law to an enlightened industrialist named Fagus who was planning a shoe last factory. By its substitution of a glass and steel facade for load-bearing walls, that single innovative building, called the Fagus Factory, secured Gropius a place in architectural history.

Meanwhile, he had also become acquainted with Henry van de Velde, a prominent Belgian-born architect who was living in Germany. Shortly after the outbreak of World War I, van de Velde was declared an enemy alien and forced to resign his position as head of the Weimar Kunstgewerbeschule (School of Arts and Crafts). Gropius was among those he recommended to replace him.

Four years later, when the war ended, Gropius was appointed director of a reorganized version of the school, for which he proposed the ambiguous name *Bauhaus* (literally "building house"), a deliberate allusion to the *Bauhütten* of the Middle Ages, the union of artists and craftsmen who designed and built the great Gothic cathedrals.

"Let us create a new guild of craftsmen," Gropius proclaimed in a manifesto announcing the school's opening (Fig 5.A), "without the class distinctions which raise an arrogant barrier between craftsman and artist. Together let us conceive and create the new building of the future, which will embrace architecture and sculpture and painting in one unity and which will rise one day toward heaven from the hands of a million workers like the crystal symbol of a new faith."[5.3]

Unfortunately, the people of Weimar were opposed to both the name of the school and its progressive philosophy, and it was controversial even before it opened. As a convenient scapegoat in a setting of severe economic and political turmoil (in 1923, for example, a cup of coffee cost 17 million marks and workers were paid twice daily in order to spend their money before it lost its value), the tax-supported Bauhaus lived only as long as the reign of the legendary Weimar Republic, from 1919 to 1933.

[The German public] remained angry that their taxes were being spent on such a hare-brained institution. Mothers continued to warn unruly children that if their behavior failed to improve they would be packed off to the Bauhaus.

—Frank Whitford
Bauhaus

Forced out of Weimar in 1925, the Bauhaus moved to the city of Dessau, where it was housed in a Modernist structure designed by Gropius. Increasingly controversial, it moved again in 1932 to an abandoned telephone factory in Berlin, where a year later (when Adolf Hitler had become the Chancellor of the Third Reich) it was closed down by the Nazis, who condemned it as a breeding ground of Bolshevist radicalism—which indeed it was to some extent.[5.4]

If artists see fields blue they are deranged and should go to an asylum. If they only pretend to see them blue, they are criminals and should go to prison.

—Adolf Hitler

The Bauhaus type of art education is infinitely closer [than academic art school training] to what is needed [to train camoufleurs].

—MILTON FOX
"Camouflage" (1942), p. 137.

You have to think of this [the 1920s and early 30s] as a period when we went to see the first performances of the plays of Bert Brecht, and we bought the first editions of Sigmund Freud for fifty cents (I still have those), and we went to see the first exhibitions of the German Expressionists—of Kokoschka, and Feininger, and Kirchner, and all those sorts of people.

—RUDOLF ARNHEIM
"My Life in the Art World"

WHILE THE WORD "Bauhaus" was coined in 1919, "Gestalt" was an older respectable term that had been popularized by the German writer Johann Wolfgang von Goethe. That there are implicit connections between the Bauhaus and the concept of "form" or *Gestalten* is seen by the school's German subtitle: *Hochschule für Gestaltung* (College of Design). Further, in light of their interest in vision research, including Gestalt theory, it is not surprising that some of the Bauhaus artists and designers were also explicitly interested in military camouflage.

In 1927, Gestalt psychologist and art theorist Rudolf Arnheim, who was close to completing his doctorate at the Psychological Institute in Berlin, visited the newly opened Dessau Bauhaus, and soon after published an article in the magazine *Die Weltbühne* in which he praised the honesty and clarity of its design.

As "a building of pure utility," wrote Arnheim, this structure by Gropius "shows more clearly than ever that the practically useful is at the same time beautiful. Even from the viewpoint of esthetic composition it feels good to see how railings, chair legs, door handles, or tea pots can be made of the same metal tubes. The old 'unity in complexity,' which up to now could be applied only to architecture, statues, or pictures, acquires here a new meaning. One can now comprehend a building, which contains a thousand different objects, as an organized whole."[5.5]

At nearly the same time, Kurt Lewin, who was teaching at the Psychological Institute and later applied Gestalt theory to social psychology, commissioned Peter Behrens (Gropius' former teacher) to design a new home for him in Berlin, but because of some confusion, Marcel Breuer, the Bauhaus architect and furniture designer, was brought in instead to complete the interior.[5.6]

In 1929, the Gestalt psychologist Wolfgang Köhler had to cancel an appearance at the Bauhaus because of a scheduling conflict, so Karl Duncker, one of his graduate students, spoke instead on his behalf. In the audience that day was the Swiss-born painter Paul Klee, who was already making deliberate use of unit-forming factors in his artwork as well as his teaching, apparently having been influenced by Wertheimer's dot paper and, possibly, an earlier paper on grouping by the latter's teacher, Franz Schumann. It seems certain that Klee was acquainted with Wertheimer's writings as early as 1925, and that, in the 1930s, he used portions of diagrams from the Gestaltists' publications in several of his paintings.[5.7]

But other Bauhaus teachers were also influenced by Gestalt theory, among them the painters Wassily Kandinsky and Josef Albers, both of whom attended a series of talks on the subject (sponsored not by the faculty but the students) presented in the winter of 1930-

Some years ago, I [took] a trip to China with a group of women in psychology and related fields. Near the end of the trip, we were, for the first time, introduced to a Chinese social psychologist. Four of us received permission to visit her at her university. The young woman explained that she had recently received her MA in social psychology… She told us that the topic of her thesis had been the work of Kurt Lewin, although she had only been able to obtain a copy of one of his books. As I sat speechless, my colleagues shouted excitedly, "This is his daughter." The young woman stared at us for a minute and then burst into happy tears. It seemed amazing to all of us that ideas that began to develop in the mind of a man born in Mogilno, Germany/Poland in 1890 had caught the attention of a young, isolated graduate in China a century later.

—MIRIAM A. LEWIN
"Kurt Lewin: His Psychology and a Daughter's Recollections," p. 118.

31 by Count Karlfried von Durckheim, a visiting psychologist from the University of Leipzig. "Up until that time," writes Bauhaus student Hannes Beckmann, "design problems were more or less solved on the feeling level. It looked as if the artists asked the scientists for reassurance that they were on the right track. The Gestalt psychologists had after all for years investigated how we perceive and interpret form and color in the mind."[5.8] Kurt Kranz, also a Bauhaus student, recalls that he too was influenced by von Durckheim's lectures, so much so that, for many years afterward, Gestalt theory "continued to preoccupy me."[5.9]

▶ **FIGURE 5.B**
The small squares within the larger squares are all of the same lightness. Yet, they appear to dramatically change as the lightness of their backgrounds change.

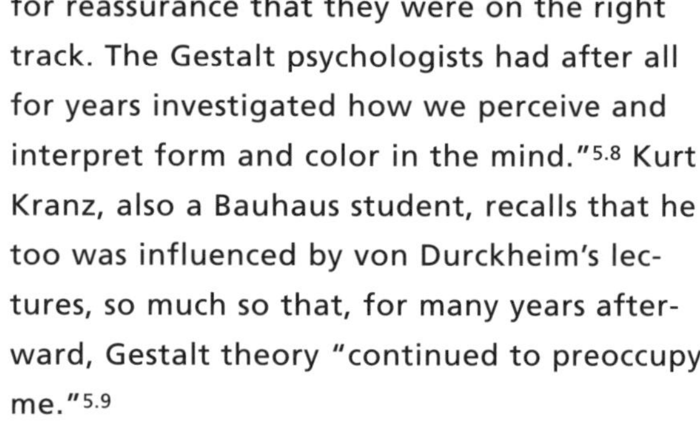

▼ **FIGURE 5.C**
The number 5 is the same size in both examples here, yet one appears larger.

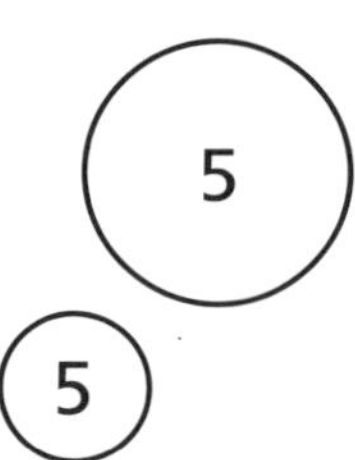

Of particular interest is Josef Albers' interest in Gestalt theory because he is now commonly credited with the resurgence of artistic interest in "simultaneous contrast" and "selective attention," which von Durckheim discussed in his lectures.

Recognized and used by artists for centuries, *simultaneous contrast* was described scientifically in 1839 by the French chemist,

Michel-Eugene Chevreul, who had found that a swatch of color may change appearance, often dramatically, when moved from one surrounding to another. A certain red, for example, may appear to be of one intensity on a green background, another on orange.[5.10]

This phenomenon is not limited to color: It can also be demonstrated using black, white and gray (Fig 5.B), or any size (Figs 5.C and 5.D), shape or angle; and, in fact, the effect can be made to occur using *any* attributes, visual or not. As a result, there are no simple answers when asked "What color is this?," "Of what lightness is this gray?" or "How large is this shape?" Such questions can be answered reliably, but only by noting the context (or the standard of comparison) within which they are observed, so that the preponderant question becomes, for example, "What color is this swatch when viewed under these conditions in this surrounding?"

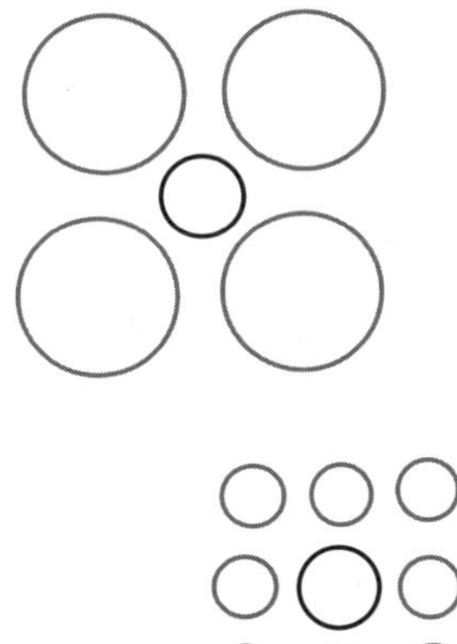

▲ FIGURE 5.D
The central circles in these two clusters are measurably identical, and yet one appears to be larger than the other.

Chevreul's color research was an important influence for the French Impressionist painters, whose intention was not to paint objects as fixed invariant entities, but as things whose

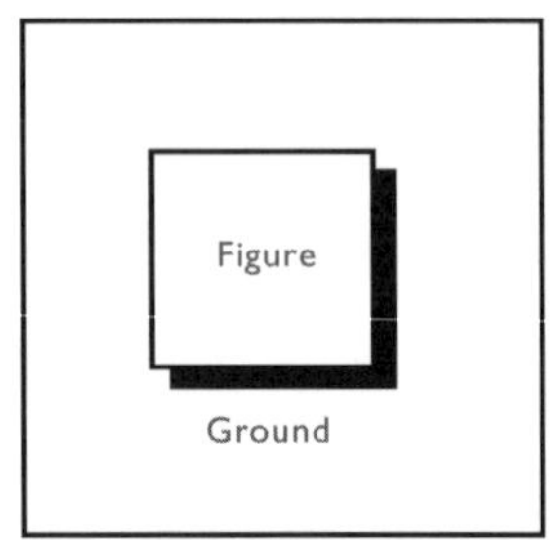

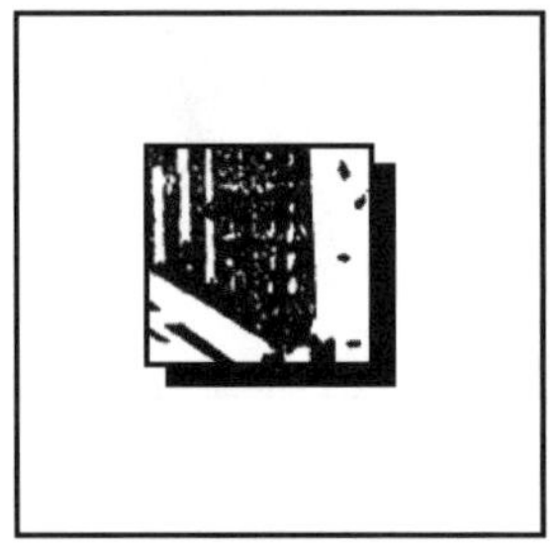

▲ **FIGURE 5.E**
Author's diagram of three figure-ground relationships: *blending camouflage* (top), *disruptive* or *dazzle camouflage* (middle), and the two combined as *coincidental disruption* (bottom).

appearance may vary as the conditions in which we observe them are changed. The subject of Claude Monet's famous paintings of haystacks, for example, is not so much a haystack as the altered, exotic "impressions" that come from viewing that mundane subject under a wide range of conditions.

It also anticipated the findings of Max Wertheimer, as confirmed by the maxim so commonly linked with Gestalt theory: "The whole is greater than the sum of its parts." Like the Impressionists, the Gestaltists believed that the variant appearances of a color (or a size, shape, angle and so on) may all have some legitimacy because we only experience perceptual wholes, never isolated parts. As Alan Watts has written, what we perceive at any moment "is never a figure alone but a figure-ground relationship. The primary 'unit' of perception is therefore neither the thing (figure) nor the space (ground) in which it appears: it is the field or relationship of the two."[5.11]

The relevance of figure-ground to camouflage is self-evident. When figure and ground are highly similar, no "thing" may be perceivable. Perceptual information is essentially "news of difference," writes the anthropologist Gregory Bateson, and "it takes at least two somethings to create a difference."[5.12] Or, as British psychiatrist R.D. Laing put it, "The condition of the possibility of anything being at all is that it is in relation to that which it is not."[5.13] In Gestalt theory, figure-without-ground or ground-without-figure (the goal of blending camouflage) is technically known as a *Ganzfeld*, while in Zen Buddhism it is "the sound of one hand clapping."[5.14]

The salience of a figure is largely dependent on two conditions: (1) the degree of contrast between figure and ground, and (2) the extent to which the figure is structurally cohesive within its own borders. Both conditions are essential. Not surprisingly, as earlier examples have demonstrated, camouflage is typically the subversion of one or both of these conditions: by high similarity between figure and ground (*blending camouflage*), or high difference within the confines of the figure alone (*dazzle camouflage*). Often, the most effective camouflage is a combined use of blending and dazzle (called *coincident disruption*), as demonstrated by puzzle pictures or what Gestalt psychologist Kurt Gottschaldt called "embedded figures."[5.15]

Edgar Rubin, a Danish psychologist who was in contact with the Berlin Gestaltists, and who wrote about figure-ground perception as early as 1915, is especially known for his interest in *reversible figure-ground* patterns. It was he who popularized the ubiquitous vase-and-faces diagram in which two black human profiles can also be interpreted as a white vase. Equally familiar are the prints of the Dutch artist M.C. Escher, among them an image that easily reads as black ducks or, by selectively

[The sculptor Alexander] Archipenko remembers his parents bringing home two identical vases. He said that as he looked at them, he was seized by the urge to place them close to each other. No sooner had he done this, he discovered a third, immaterial vase formed by the space between the first two.

—Katherine Michaelsen and Nehama Guralnik, *Alexander Archipenko*

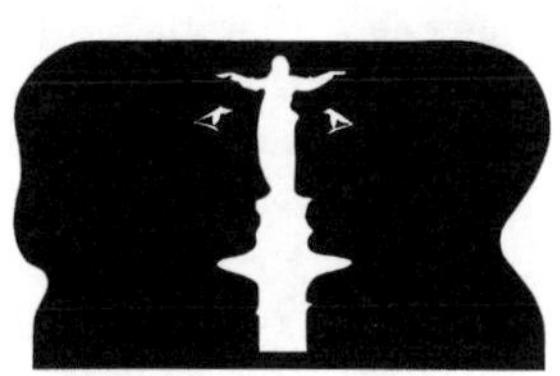

▲ **FIGURE 5.F**
Aliyah Marr
A logo comprised of two facing profiles, c.1989. The space between them takes the form of a statue in Fountain Square in downtown Cincinnati, Ohio.

switching attention to the space between the ducks, as white fish.[5.16]

▲ **FIGURE 5.G**
AARON CUMMINS
A logo in which the letter s appears in the space between two butterflies, c.1997.

IN EXPLANATIONS of *selective attention*, it is commonly said that the input capabilities of our sense organs are greater than the processing capabilities of the central nervous system. Simply, we have the physical ability to take in far more information than the brain can possibly handle. To avoid an overload, or a bottleneck at best, the system "tunes in" to significant parts of our surroundings, and delays or neglects the remainder.

In a sense, to perceive we must also be partially blind; or to attend we must also ignore, because, as Alan Watts wrote, "we think by ignoring—by attending to one term of a relationship (the figure) and neglecting the other (the ground)."[5.17] In a famous experiment, for example, subjects were instructed to watch a video of a basketball game. Those who were assigned the task of observing all the fouls were rarely aware of a woman who walked past the court, carrying a conspicuous, multicolored umbrella.

As he glanced around, [the graphic designer Alvin] Lustig [awaiting the arrival of Frank Lloyd Wright at an interview at Taliesin East] noticed that there was a blue vase against a blue wall and a white vase against a white wall. He exchanged the blue vase and the white vase. Wright entered the room, and as he spoke his first words to the young Lustig, replaced the blue vase against the blue wall and the white vase against the white wall.

—R. ROGER REMINGTON AND BARBARA J. HODIK
Nine Pioneers in American Graphic Design.

The extent to which we are blinded by selective attention is confirmed by the misdirection tactics of pickpockets and sleight of hand magicians, who camouflage their "groundwork" by diverting our attention to an otherwise insignificant event. The inverse of that process occurs typically in inventions, discoveries, humor, and other forms of creative activity, when we cast off the blinders of habit and suddenly turn our attention to aspects that had gone unnoticed before. In the writings of Arthur Conan Doyle, this is the decisive strategy of Sherlock Holmes, who confesses in one of his stories: "You know my method. It is founded on the observation of trifles."[5.18]

Few examples of this are more delightful than a famous essay by the Danish theologian Sören Kierkegaard, titled "The Rotation Method," which describes how he rotates his vision, as farmers rotate crops, by changing the "crop and mode of cultivation," instead of moving on to a new plot of land. He discovered this method by accident, when he was forced to listen to a tedious speaker: "At every opportunity," writes Kierkegaard, "he [this lecturer] was ready with a little philosophical harangue. Almost in despair, I suddenly discovered that he perspired copiously when talking. I saw the pearls of sweat gather on his brow, unite to form a stream, glide down his nose, and hang at the extreme point of his nose in a drop-shaped body. From the moment of making this discovery, all was changed. I even took pleasure in inciting him to begin his philosophical instruction, merely to observe the perspiration on his brow and at

Both read the Bible day and night,
But thou read'st black where I read white.

—William Blake
The Everlasting Gospel (1818)

▲ **FIGURE 5.H**
Thomas J. Lechtenberg (top) and Chris Thilges (bottom): Examples of reversible figure-ground in the design of corporate logos, c.1996.

◀ **FIGURE 5.I**
Two profiles of Richard Nixon butt heads in the space at the top of the Canadian maple leaf.

the end of his nose."[5.19]

When Josef Albers enrolled at the Bauhaus in Weimar in 1920, he was a World War I veteran and, at 32 years old, one of the school's oldest students. Three years later, while still a student, he was asked to assist the Hungarian photographer and designer Lazslo Moholy-Nagy in teaching the *Vorkurs*, the basic or "foundations" course. After graduating in 1925, he continued to teach in that program, then served as its director until he left the Bauhaus in 1933. After emigrating to the United States, he taught at Black Mountain College from 1933 to 1949, and then became the head of the Department of Architecture and Design at Yale University until his retirement in 1960.[5.20]

Emil Willimetz [a student at Black Mountain College] described [Josef] Albers' method of typesetting and designing as the "tausands technique... You do a *tausand* and then you can see which one is right."

—MARY EMMA HARRIS
The Arts at Black Mountain College, p. 28.

As an artist, all of Albers' later work is geometric abstraction. "Art should not represent," he once said, "but present."[5.21] And nearly all of it falls within two categories: the simultaneous contrast of color, and shifts in selective attention. Beginning in 1950, he produced an extended series of paintings in which colored squares are positioned within increasingly larger squares but displaced toward the bottom. Erroneously titled *Homage to the Square*, these paintings pay homage to color. Squares within squares are redundant, so our attention is drawn instead toward the color changes (where there is "news of difference"), in which modifications are produced by simultaneous contrast as the widths of the borders

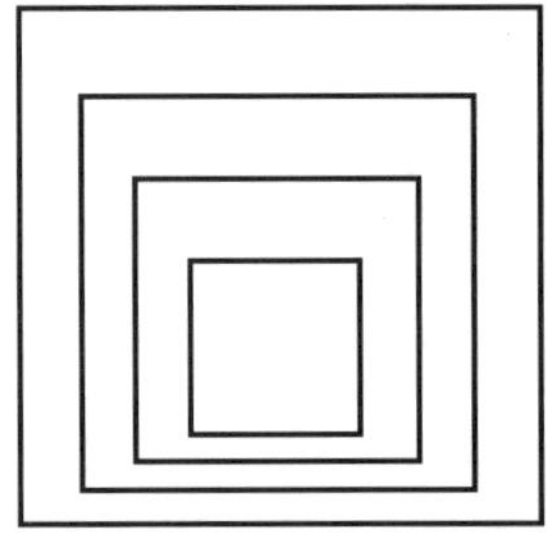

▲ **FIGURE 5.J**
Author's diagram derived from a series of paintings by JOSEF ALBERS titled *Homage to the Square*.

are varied. In another series, he produced black and white compositions—some of which he called "structural constellations"—in which geometric elements appear to change in significance and spatial position as the viewer's attention is shifted.

As a teacher, Albers is best known for his writings on simultaneous contrast and related color phenomena, which he described and demonstrated in his well-known, classic volume on the *Interaction of Color* (1963).[5.22]

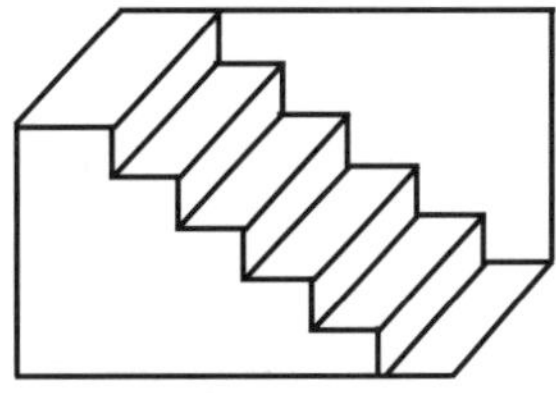

▲ **FIGURE 5.K**
A reversible staircase illusion from William James' classic textbook on the *Principles of Psychology* (1890). A half century later, Josef Albers used similar examples of shifts in selective attention in works that he referred to as "structural constellations."

It would be interesting to know if Albers was in the audience in 1929 when the Gestaltists' graduate student Karl Duncker lectured at the Bauhaus, and if Duncker and he were aware of their mutual interest in"problem-solving." Six years after that talk, having emigrated to the U.S. (where he would later commit suicide), Duncker published a paper in which he described his experiments with "functional fixedness" (which he had researched earlier at the Berlin Psychological Institute) in which subjects were asked to improvise solutions to various problems, using inappropriate materials.[5.23]

In one, for example, the subjects were shown a table with a variety of common items on it—with a cord, nail and weight scattered among them—and asked to construct a pendulum. Most solved the problem by using the weight as a hammer to pound the nail into the wall, tying the cord to the weight and suspending the improvised pendulum from the nail.

But that solution occurred less readily to other subjects if, during the instructions, the weight was described as a "pendulum weight" and already tied to the cord. In those instances, Duncker concluded, the weight and the cord were assumed to be linked (as a constellation or Gestalt), making it more difficult to perceive the weight separately as a hammer.

▲ **FIGURE 5.L**
MICHAEL NEUMANN
An example of the inventive use of prosaic materials in which a "type face" has been improvised entirely from letterforms, 1997.

At nearly the same time, Albers and Moholy-Nagy were using comparable problems at the Bauhaus. As recalled by Howard Dearstyne, an American who enrolled at Dessau in 1928, students in Albers' foundation course, seated at long tables, were confronted with such unlikely art materials as "wire, wire mesh, paper, corrugated cardboard, sheet metal, match boxes, newspapers or whatnot. We were supposed to do something with these—just *basteln*, or play around with them, to see if we could make something out of them or discover something about them."[5.24]

The purpose of these exercises, in Albers' words, was "unprejudiced experimentation"—the opposite of functional fixedness—with the goal that the student would "search by oneself and learn how to discover for oneself."[5.25] At the beginning of each problem, said Albers, the most common ways of using these materials are identified and discussed "and, since they can no longer be discovered, they are banned." Paper, for example, is nearly always used by manufacturers not as an edge but as a flat sheet that is glued. "That is a reason for us to use paper standing up," he continued, "uneven, plastically mobile, two-sided and with the edges emphasized. Instead of gluing it, we tie it, pin it, sew it, rivet it, that is, fas-

▲ **FIGURE 5.M**
MICHAEL NEUMANN, a type face made of letterforms, 1997.

◀ **FIGURE 5.N**
Cover of the package for a modern edition of FRIEDRICH FROEBEL's geometric wooden blocks, called "gifts," which were an essential ingredient in his concept of *kindergarten*, or "child garden." Courtesy of Uncle Goose Toys. For more information, see <www.froebelgifts.com> or call 888 774-2046.

ten it in other ways and we also investigate its capacity to withstand tension and pressure..."[5.26]

Duncker need not have influenced Albers, nor vice versa, since improvisational problem-solving was more or less going around at the time. That trend may in part have been influenced by Friedrich Froebel, the founder of kindergarten, and his pedagogy of "education through play," which was manifested by providing children with sets of abstract wooden blocks and other materials (called "gifts"), then prompting inventive arrangements of these.[5.27] Frank Lloyd Wright, Walter Gropius, Georges Braque, Paul Klee, Wassily Kandinsky, Piet Mondrian, Le Corbusier, and R. Buckminster Fuller were all educated in the Froebel system. In addition, Johannes Itten, the first director of the foundations course at the Bauhaus, was also Froebel-trained and had been previously employed as a kindergarten teacher.

He [the British art critic Roger Fry] was taking Lady Violet Bonham-Carter round the Post-Impressionist Exhibition, in which Cézanne, Van Gogh, Gauguin, etc., first blazed upon London, and finally led her up to *La Ronde*..."What do you think of that?" Lady Violet, whose soul was already a little fatigued by its adventures among so many novel masterpieces, gazed upon it in stupefaction, and at last brought out apologetically, "I don't think I quite like the shape of their legs." "Ah!" said Roger in a tone of triumph, "but don't you like the shape of the spaces between their legs?"

—EDWARD MARSH
A Number of People, p. 55.

BY 1933, WHEN Hitler became Chancellor, most of the Bauhaus masters had fled the country. But Oskar Schlemmer, who was in charge of the theatre workshop, chose to stay, as did Klee and the sculptor Gerhard Marcks.

Within several years, Schlemmer was forbidden to teach, and in 1937, his work was denounced as "degenerate art." Under unbearable personal strain, he subsisted by taking on menial jobs, including, by a twist of fate, the camouflage of buildings for the German army. Some of his grief-stricken letters survive. From Giebelstadt, he wrote his wife: "I shall see if I can make little models in Stuttgart which the painters could follow, so that I would only need to come now and then. The camouflage itself is turning out well. Gigantic paintings."[5.28] But his health broke shortly after that, and he died five years later, at the early age of fifty-five.

Laszlo Moholy-Nagy, the gifted Hungarian painter, photographer, film-maker, graphic designer, kinetic sculptor, theorist, and teacher, was considerably more fortunate. Sometimes unpopular, he was ridiculed by some of his Bauhaus colleagues as "Gropius' drummer boy," while his student devotees were known as the "Last of the Moholigans." When Gropius resigned as director of the Bauhaus in 1928, Moholy also left the school. He eventually moved to Chicago, where in 1937 he founded a small private design school, which he called the "New Bauhaus." The Ukrainian sculptor Alexander Archipenko was on the faculty, as was the Hungarian painter György Kepes, who later wrote *Language of Vision*.[5.29]

The New Bauhaus was forced to close within a year, due to financial problems, but Moholy revived it the following year under the new title of the "School of Design." Soon after, World War II began, and the school was again in jeopardy because "Students and teachers were called up, personnel left for factory jobs, and the raw materials needed for instruction vanished from the civilian market."[5.30]

Facing the likelihood of a second closing, Moholy proposed an emergency plan in which (as his wife recalled later) his little design institute would seem to be "as essential to an American victory as, say, Mrs. Roosevelt's smile."[5.31] His three-point plan was centered

▲ **FIGURE 5.0**
Marcel Breuer
Wassily Chair. Produced at the Bauhaus in 1925, this icon of Modernism resulted from Breuer's surprising application of bicycle manufacturing techniques to furniture.

About the time I first met Picasso, he had made a sculpture of a bull's head out of the seat and handlebars of a bicycle. He used to say that this sculpture was reversible. "I find a bicycle and handlebars in the street, and I say 'Well, there's a bull,' until a cyclist comes along and says, 'Well, there's a bicycle seat' and he makes a seat and a pair of handlebars out of it again..."

—Françoise Gilot
Life With Picasso, p. 321.

on (1) therapeutic rehabilitation for disabled American veterans; (2) research of industrial uses of wood and other prosaic materials in the manufacture of chairs, for example, or bed springs, because of the wartime requirement for metal for military purposes; and (3) research and instruction in art and visual perception, for the purpose of teaching the public about civilian camouflage.

As a design student [at Moholy-Nagy's Institute of Design] with creative flair and a love for art, Jo Mead did such a good job camouflaging Navy destroyers that the enemy couldn't even tell in which direction the ships were going.

—BRENDA WARNER ROTZOLL "Obituaries: Jo Mead"

In 1941, Moholy was appointed to the Chicago mayor's Civil Defense Commission and given the responsibility of disguising the shoreline of Lake Michigan, making it harder to recognize from the air, in the event of an enemy bombing attack. Unfortunately, the project required "stormy trips on patrol boats that made him seasick, and precarious flights in small reconnaissance planes that made him airsick."[5.32]

Nevertheless, through Moholy's efforts, his school was officially certified by the U.S. Government as a camouflage training center in January 1942. Kepes was placed in charge of the Camouflage Workshop, as shown by the following entry among a list of the 1942-43 evening classes: "The Principles of Camouflage Research in natural camouflage; surface covering; mimicry; visual illusions; basic photography; investigation of camouflage techniques. Conducted by George [sic] Kepes."[5.33]

A number of the art students [at Ohio State University] are receiving special training in camouflage.

—CAROLYN BRADLEY "A Department of Fine Arts Integrates with War," p. 220.

At least three of the students who worked with Kepes during this period went on to contribute to camouflage during World War II:

Architect and designer Myron Kozman, who graduated from the School of Design in 1941, was a U.S. Army camoufleur in Europe for three years; Robert O. Preusser, who later taught with Kepes at MIT, served for the same length of time, perhaps with the same unit; and Jo Mead, who remained a civilian but contributed to ship camouflage.

In 1944, Kepes published *Language of Vision*, on page 45 of which are two black and white illustrations of a camouflaged snake, one clearly visible on a plain white background, the other effectively camouflaged on a background of leaves. "A snake camouflaged by nature is no longer a snake," writes Kepes. "It is an aggregation of small units of color-shape."[5.34]

In the book's acknowledgments, Kepes' opening sentence is an admission of his indebtedness to the Gestalt psychologists (Wertheimer, Köhler and Koffka), whose ideas and visual examples, he notes, are used "in the first part of the book to explain the laws of visual organization."[5.35] ✂

The study of camouflage provides a vast store of interesting and timely material that may be used in art and other school courses.

—Harry Rubin
"The Art of Camouflage,"
p. 9.

Chapter Six

How Easy Is A Bush A Bear

Ambiguity, Madness and Camouflage

GESTALT THEORY IS a variety of "holism," and as such, it is often contrasted with its opposite, called "atomism" or "reductionism." As Harvard philosopher Paul Weiss has written, atomism is like looking through the customary end of a telescope and thereby enlarging the details, while a holist looks into the opposite end and focuses on "the big picture," the overall plan or the structure.[6.1]

Not only do Gestaltists claim that "the whole is greater than the sum of its parts," they also insist that a part is defined by the context in which it functions, not vice versa. In other words, we see from the top down, not from the bottom up. Or, as E.H. Gombrich writes, "we do not respond to individual stimuli of isolated sounds but to configurations as a whole. Only after the medley of sounds has fallen into a distinct pattern do we allocate each individual sound its distinct place within the whole."[6.2]

The lunatic, the lover, and
the poet,
Are of imagination all
compact.

—WILLIAM SHAKESPEARE
A Midsummer Night's Dream

◀ **FIGURE 6.A**
HARLAN TARBELL
Chalk talk drawings in which numbers are embedded in the facial features of New Years babies (1924).

This, says Gombrich, is the "crucial fact" in Gestalt psychology, and one that might best be explained by a humorous example: "I would boldly assert," he continues, "that when a famous young Frenchman rushed into the English girl's room and exclaimed 'je t'adore' only to receive the answer 'shut it yourself, you idiot' the persons present heard different sounds according to the interpretation they accepted."[6.3]

A man who would go to a psychiatrist ought to have his head examined.

—SAMUEL GOLDWYN

Je t'adore is French for "I adore you" while also a reasonable homophone for the English phrase "shut the door." So, when the amorous intruder utters his French solicitation, it is misunderstood as an English command. The sounds are genuinely ambiguous (from the Latin root *ambi*, meaning "on both sides"), with the result that, far from being meaningless, both statements are credible interpretations of the same sequence of sounds.

Je t'adore is one Gestalt—one constellation, one configuration—while "shut the door" is another. Depending on the interpretation we favor, the component *Je t'a* will be heard as either a French fragment or a slurred version of the English words "shut the."

Hearing that story, one might be reminded of countless examples of nonverbal or visual ambiguity. Among these are humorous drawings employed in the late 19th and early 20th centuries in a kind of public speaking called "chalk talks." The term refers to entertaining lectures given with the aid of a chalkboard, but it also implies a sequential, simply-drawn cartoon in which (to the surprise of the audience) one picture is concealed within another

and, as the talk progresses, the first drawing is magically transformed into the second.

In FIG 6.B, for example, what begins as a pig has become, by the second drawing, a portion of its exact opposite, its predator, the wolf. Of particular fascination is the second drawing, which is a visual ambiguity because it contains all the aspects of both interpretations: the pig as a pig and as part of the wolf. (It is interesting that the artist cheated a bit by giving the pig a turned-up nose in the first drawing, then straightening the wolf's forehead in the second.)

The "rabbiduck" (FIG 6.D), a 19th-century illusion later made famous by being discussed in an essay by the Viennese philosopher Ludwig Wittgenstein, can be seen as either a rabbit or a duck. In it, as in the pig-and-wolf (and in the pun on *Je t'adore*), the function of parts of the drawing may change as the viewer sides with one interpretation or the other.

▲ **FIGURE 6.C**
HARLAN TARBELL
Chalk talk metamorphosis in which a young man evolves into his bearded grandfather (1924).

◀ **FIGURE 6.B**
HARLAN TARBELL
Chalk talk drawing in which a pig becomes a wolf (1924).

Ambiguous figures like those in chalk talks have long been used in visual art. There is a rider in the clouds in Andrea Mantenga's painting of St. Sebastian (c.1460), a face in a rock in a landscape by Albrecht Dürer (c.1495),

▶ **FIGURE 6.D** Popular 19th-century puzzle picture, the rabbiduck, which may have appeared for the first time in *Fliegende Blätter* in 1892.

and a toy car and tea cup handles in the face and ears respectively of a bronze sculpture by Pablo Picasso of a mother baboon and her infant (1951).[6.4] In *Art and Illusion*, Gombrich reproduces a photograph of a prehistoric sculpture on a cave wall in France that appears to have come from the shape of a rock in which the artist saw the accidental image of a horse. Similarly, says Gombrich, constellations could be thought of as suggested ambiguous forms in the sky.[6.5]

This guy goes to a psychiatrist and says, "Doc, my brother's crazy. He thinks he's a chicken." And the doctor says, "Why don't you turn him in?" And the guy says, "I would, but I need the eggs."

—Woody Allen

Accidental natural shapes (or "chance images") are mentioned in a celebrated passage by Leonardo da Vinci. If one needs ideas while painting, he advises, you can find landscapes, miniature battlefields and strange figures in violent action in the stains on rain-soaked mildewed walls. "In such walls," he continues, "the same thing happens as in the sound of bells, in whose stroke you may find every named word which you can imagine."[6.6]

Among those who used similar techniques were British artists Alexander Cozens, who wrote a book about accidental ink blots as points of departure, and Aubrey Beardsley, who said of his own method, "I make a blot upon the paper and begin to shove the ink about and something comes."[6.7] Even more astonishing are the experiments of the French novelist Victor Hugo, who made drawings and paintings not only from ink blots, but from soot, black coffee, mulberry juice, burned onion, cigar ash, fingerprints, matchsticks, stencils, sprays of water, lace and cloth impressions. He even signed and dated stones.[6.8]

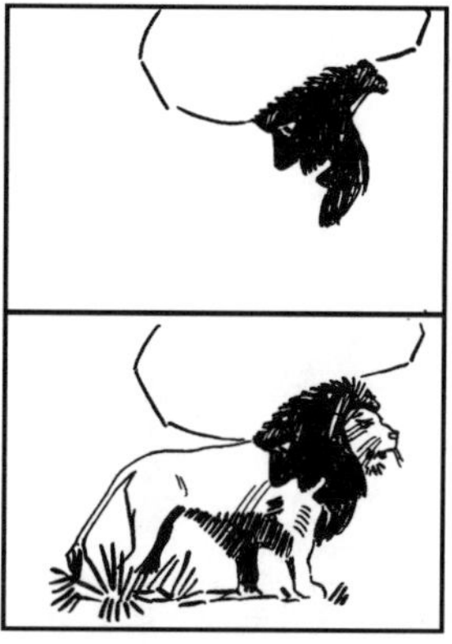

▲ FIGURE 6.E
Harlan Tarbell
Chalk talk drawing in which a hunter is concealed within a drawing of the creature he hunts (1924).

Chance images are not always desirable. There is a wonderful story about Picasso and Braque in their Cubist days, when they were painting in ways that were largely abstract. One day, as Picasso was looking at Braque's latest painting, "he became aware that there was a squirrel in the picture, and pointed it out to Braque, who was rather abashed at this discovery. The next day Braque showed him the picture again, after reworking it to get rid of the squirrel, but Picasso insisted that he still saw it, and it took another reworking to banish the animal for good."[6.9]

An Arab came to the river side
With a donkey bearing an obelisk:
But he would not try to ford the tide
For he had too good an *

—Anon

In perceptual psychology, the term "embedded figure" is applied to visual puzzles in which smaller, simpler shapes are concealed within larger, more complex designs. As mentioned earlier, some of the best-known examples are associated with the Gestalt psychologist Kurt Gottschaldt, who received his Ph.D. from the Berlin Psychological Institute in 1926. In his dissertation on past experience in relation to visual perception, Gottschaldt used a number of embedded figures, all of which were abstract geometric shapes (Fig. 6.G).[6.10]

What garlic is to salad, insanity is to art.

—AUGUSTUS SAINT-GAUDENS

Embedded figures such as those used by Gottschaldt reminded his teacher, Wolfgang Köhler, of "the puzzle-pictures which years ago amused the readers of magazines..." They rely on the same principles as military camouflage, said Köhler, which has been used in modern wars "to make objects such as guns, cars, boats, etc., disappear by painting upon these things irregular designs, the parts of which are likely to form units with parts of their environment."[6.11]

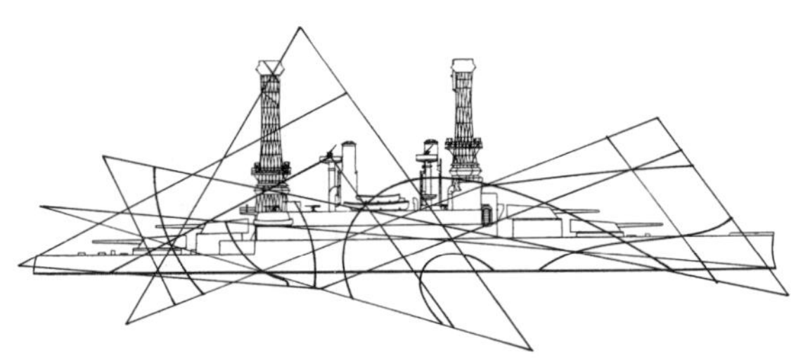

▲ **FIGURE 6.F** Author's drawing, showing how dazzle ship camouflage schemes might have been developed from embedded figure diagrams.

Which craft was persecuted by the Puritans of New England?

—ANON

A step-by-step procedure for camouflaging an object in its surroundings was discussed and demonstrated in 1942 by American artist Eric Sloane in *Camouflage Simplified* in a section on "The Disruptive Pattern."[6.12] By dividing up the object (a building, airplane or whatever) with lines and shapes that contradict (are "not in harmony with") its own attributes, a camouflage artist can prevent its being detected as a single, self-contained entity, and at the same time can blur the distinctions between the object and its surroundings.

The combination of figure disruption with figure-ground blending, which is what Sloane was suggesting, has been given the appropriate technical name of "coincident disruption" by Hugh B. Cott, a British zoologist and scientific illustrator who served as a camouflage officer in both world wars. On the one hand,

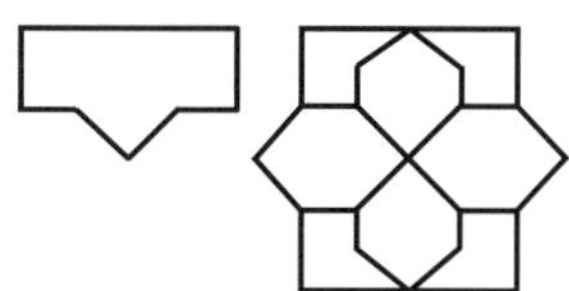

▲ FIGURE 6.G
KURT GOTTSCHALDT
Geometric puzzle (right) in which a simple shape (left) has been hidden, c.1926.

◀ FIGURE 6.H
Artists, illustrators and designers commonly embed recurrences of shape and other grouping attributes in their compositions. As shown by this diagram, for example, there is a trail of elliptical shapes (indicated by arrows) in this *Self-Portrait* by Francis Bacon (1970).

such forms are *disruptive*, he writes, because "they appear to break up what is really a continuous surface" (the figure), while, at the same time, they are also *coincident* because they "unite [visually] what are actually discontinuous surfaces" (the figure and ground).[6.13] As Cott illustrates, coincident disruption in nature occurs not only between a figure and its surroundings; it also takes place in relations among distinct regions of the same figure, as shown by the misleading bands that result when a frog's legs are folded up or a butterfly's wings are unfurled and aligned (FIG 2.F).

Coincident disruption is observable not just in camouflage but in a wide range of phenomena, both natural and man-made. In poetry and song lyrics, for example, it is common for writers to end a line (for the sake of rhyme or rhythm) in the middle of a sentence, then continue that sentence in the next line. There is no shortage of examples, but one that quickly comes to mind is a comic verse by Hilaire Belloc, a portion of which reads:

> A trick that everyone abhors
> In little girls is slamming doors.

In graphic design, comparable effects are accomplished through *edge alignment*. An implicit network of horizontal and vertical lines (called *broken continuity lines* or a *grid lines*) provides an embedded structural plan for a magazine, newspaper or printed book, including this one. Through edge alignment (recalling Wertheimer's unit-forming factors), the resulting implied axes make distinct aspects of a page layout appear to be connected (to belong together), while, at the same time, their incompleteness allows for closure.[6.14]

▲ **FIGURE 6.1**
LISA CROSLEY
Collage portrait of Sigmund Freud with an analysis of its implied grid lines (bottom), 1996.

JOSEPH JASTROW, the Polish-born American psychologist who first discussed the rabbiduck in a textbook, said of the dream that it "smug-

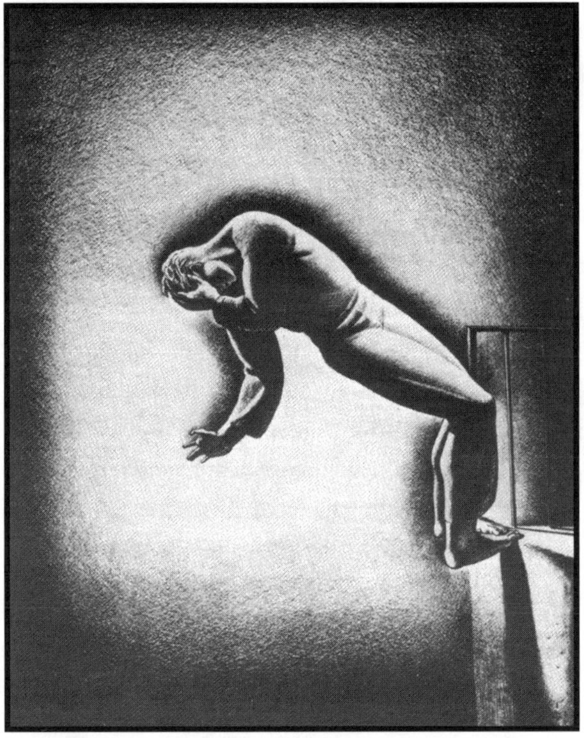

◀ **FIGURE 6.J**
ROCKWELL KENT
Nightmare, lithograph, from Carol Zigrosser, ed., *Medicine and the Artist* (Mineola NY: Dover Publications, 1970), from the Dover Pictorial Archives.

gles its wares by wrapping them in camouflaged packages and employing ingenious dramatic disguises..."[6.15] In light of his comment, one wonders if the rabbiduck (or other ambiguous figures that allow for multiple interpretation) is indicative of the kinds of disguises that are typically experienced in dreams.

When we see the rabbiduck as a rabbit, we are seeing its "manifest content" while the

I dreamed I was out coursing with two greyhounds each of which had only one eye. They started a hare apiece at the same moment, but each greyhound could only see the hare that the other was coursing. The consequence was that both hares escaped and both greyhounds knocked their heads against a stone wall.

—FRANCIS KILVERT
in Plomer (1960),
p. 103.

I didn't know the full facts of life until I was 17. My father [Sigmund Freud] never talked about his work.

—MARTIN FREUD

Sometimes a cigar is just a cigar.

—SIGMUND FREUD

▲ **FIGURE 6.K**
ALBRECHT DÜRER
The Men's Bath (detail), woodcut, c.1497. From Willi Kurth, ed., *The Complete Woodcuts of Albrecht Dürer* (Mineola NY: Dover Publications, 1963), from the Dover Pictorial Archives.

duck is its "latent content." Those are the terms that are commonly used in psychoanalysis when dreams are interpreted. According to Sigmund Freud, dreams are hallucinatory forms of subconscious urges, sexual or otherwise. They are examples of camouflage in the sense that the tactics employed by the mind are identical to those used in nature and by the military, techniques that (at least in psychoanalysis) are frequently said to consist of *condensation*, *substitution* and *displacement*.

In condensation, the latent content of the dream is concealed by making two or more things appear to be one. The usual result is a hybrid, like a unicorn (a combination of a horse, goat and lion), centaur or cameleopard, whether a person, place or time period, which combines portions of this and that into a new single form that feels vaguely familiar, and yet is disturbingly alien too. Equivalent art forms, many of which are fanciful spin-offs of Freudian dream interpretation, include collage, montage, assemblage, frottage, fumage, decalomania, coulage, froissage, double exposure, automatic drawing, and the exquisite corpse.[6.16]

In substitution (also known as symbolization), one thing stands for something else, either by taking the place of it (proximity grouping) or because the two entities are auditory or visual rhymes (similarity grouping). In one experiment, for example, when the name "Robert" was spoken repeatedly to a sleeping subject, he dreamed about a "distorted rabbit." Among the artistic examples of this is a woodcut by Albrecht Dürer (Fig. 6.K), in which a faucet is positioned in such a way as to resemble a penis. More than four centuries later, the Surrealist photographer Man Ray used nearly the same "Freudian symbol" in a nude photographic portrait of Surrealist artist Meret Oppenheim, by posing her behind a mechanical wheel with its shaft-like handle jutting out in imitation of a penis.

In displacement, a component may be moved from its customary, suitable setting to one that is unsuitable; or the dreamer's focus is displaced, diverted, or, as magicians and pickpockets say, "misdirected" toward aspects that reinforce the manifest interpretation of the dream but (recalling Sherlock Holmes' advice about the observation of trifles) are nonessential, irrelevant or misleading in relation to its latent content.

I've always
used dreams the way you'd use mirrors to look at something you couldn't see head on—the way that you use a mirror to look at your hair in the back.

—Stephen King
Writers Dreaming

"Find out all about dreams," said the British neurologist John Hughlings Jackson, "and you will find out all about insanity."[6.17]; while the philosopher Arthur B. Fallico writes that "if we seek for an object which resembles the art object, we will find none better than the dream."[6.18] These are but two of the dozens of scholars who have suggested throughout history that there is somehow an affinity between art and insanity, with dreams as a bridge that connects them.

In the 20th century, the movement most closely identified with dreams and mental instability has been Surrealism, which was founded in 1922 by the French poet André Breton. As described earlier, it was born of an unlikely marriage of art with psychoanalysis; its artistic parent was Dada, which began as a protest of World War I and deliberately tried to provoke its audience through chance, nonsense, errors, and contradiction.

What is a double petunia? A petunia is a flower like a begonia. A begonia is a meat like a sausage. A sausage-and-battery is a crime. Monkeys crime trees. Tree's a crowd. A crow crowd in the morning and made a noise. A noise is on your face between your eyes. Eyes is the opposite of nays. A colt nays. You go to bed with a colt, and wake up in the morning with a case of double petunia.

—ALEX OSBORN
Applied Imagination

During that war, Freud's innovative method of "free association" (to say aloud while lying on a couch whatever comes to ones mind) had been used with some success to treat the victims of trench warfare. Working with shell-shocked soldiers in a hospital, it was Breton who saw the connection between Freud's famous "talking cure" and the Dadaists' nonsense-producing techniques. But the link between Freud and Breton was direct, and they actually met in Vienna in 1921.

I was in analysis. I was suicidal. I would have killed myself but my analyst was a strict Freudian and if you kill yourself they make you pay for the sessions you miss.

—WOODY ALLEN

In 1938, Salvador Dali, the Spanish Surrealist painter, also met Freud, in London, in an encounter that, according to the former, was an utter failure. Freud was old and ill by then. Only a month earlier, he had withstood a Nazi raid of his home in Vienna, had fled to England, and would soon die of cancer of the jaw. Under the circumstances, he could not have been greatly amused by a crank with billiard ball eyes and a moustache as sharp as a scorpion's tail. "Contrary to my hopes," Dali recalled of their meeting, "we spoke little, but we devoured each other with our eyes."[6.19]

Dali, then in his mid-30s, was already widely known for his technically painstaking paintings of dreams. During his visit, he tried to convince Freud to look at an article he had just published on paranoia. Opening the magazine, he begged Freud to read it not as a "Surrealist diversion" but as an "ambitiously scientific article." Still, Dali reported later, "Freud continued to stare at me without paying the slightest attention to my magazine."

Faced with what Dali described as such "imperturbable indifference," his voice grew "sharper and more insistent." As the meeting ended, Dali said, Freud continued to stare at him "with a fixity in which his whole being seemed to converge," then turned and said, in Dali's presence, to Stefan Zweig, the Austrian writer who had arranged the meeting, "I have never seen a more complete example of a Spaniard. What a fanatic!"[6.20]

How wonderfully appropriate—how dreamlike!—that the painter of dreams should be incompatible with the father of dream analysis. No less appropriate, however, is the discovery that Dali's interpretation of Freud's reaction was apparently mistaken, and that Freud actually found their encounter that afternoon both pleasant and instructive. In other words, Dali really was paranoid! "I really owe you thanks for bringing yesterday's visi-

After falling into a sound sleep, [Elias] Howe dreamed that he was kidnapped by a band of savages who threatened to kill him if he did not invent a sewing machine in twenty-four hours. Unable to meet the deadline, the machinist was led to his execution. As the spears of the savages descended on him, Howe noticed that they had eye-shaped holes close to the tips. At that moment he shook off the nightmare, woke up, and knew exactly where to place the eye in his sewing machine needle.

—Carol Orsag Madigan and Ann Elwood *Brainstorms and Thunderbolts*, pp. 81-83.

The name of the inventor of the sewing machine is pronounced how?

—Anon

tor," Freud wrote to Zweig on the day after the meeting. "For until now I have been inclined to regard the Surrealists, who apparently have adopted me as their patron saint, as complete fools (let us say 95 percent, as with alcohol). That young Spaniard [Dali], with his candid fantastical eyes and his undeniable technical mastery, has changed my estimate."[6.21]

> Dreams are often most profound when they seem most crazy.
>
> —SIGMUND FREUD

A DECADE EARLIER, Dali had made a shocking classic film in collaboration with another Spaniard, Luis Buñuel. Titled *Un Chien Andalou* (An Andalusian Dog), it is a film, as Buñuel said, "in which there are neither dogs nor Andalusians."[6.22] It is a celluloid nightmare, made up of 17 minutes of ludicrous and horrific sight gags, one after another, with little if any discernible plot.

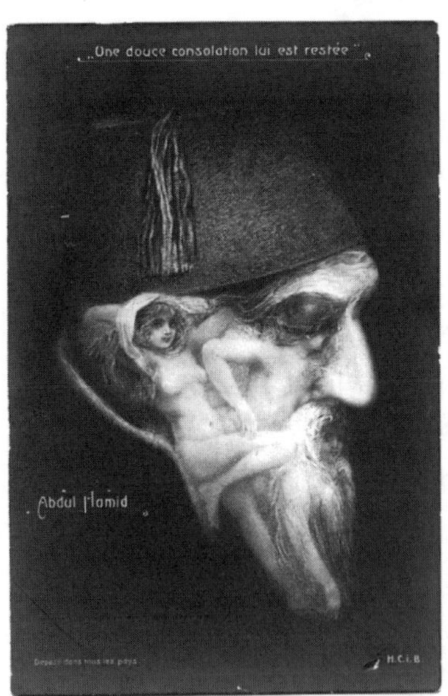

In the opening sequence that many viewers find unforgettable, a man (played by Buñuel) with a cigarette dangling from his lips sharpens a straight razor as he stands by a window in the moonlight. A cloud in the night sky cuts across the full moon, faintly suggesting the slicing of an eyeball. As the camera moves in for a close-up on the face of a young woman, the man (who is standing behind her) holds her eyelid open as he draws the insidious razor across her eyeball.

Throughout the film, there are other visual metaphors in addition to that of the eye and the moon. In one scene, for example, a young woman is being fondled by a hallucinating madman when, in his mind, her breasts are transformed into buttocks. But most of the scenes are inexplicable instances of radical juxtaposition: for example, the ants that crawl out of a hole in the palm of someone's hand; a woman's armpit hair that becomes a goatee on the chin of a man; or the curious moment in which two identical grand pianos, each bearing a donkey carcass, are dragged by ropes across a room by two priests, while a woman stands back in a corner, preparing to defend herself with a tennis racket.

There is only one difference between a madman and me. I am not mad.

—Salvador Dali

Soon after the completion of that film, Dali embarked on a series he called "critical paranoid" paintings, which came from what he once described as "a spontaneous method of irrational knowledge based upon the critical and systematic objectification of delirious associations and interpretations."[6.23] It was during this period that he completed some of his best-known paintings, among them *The Persistence of Memory* (1931), in which a limp watch is suspended from a tree branch, and *The Metamorphosis of Narcissus* (1937), in

◀ **FIGURE 6.L**
Anon
19th-century naughty French postcard featuring a visual sight gag in which a portrait is composed of three smaller human figures. Author's collection.

which a human figure rhymes with the shape of a very large hand that is holding an egg with a lily inside.

Most, perhaps all of us experience mild paranoia, in the sense that we all are mistrustful at times and may suspect others of undermining our efforts. Such suspicions are not always unfounded, as is stressed by the comic but truthful remark that "just because you're paranoid, it doesn't mean they're not after you." In *A Midsummer Night's Dream*, William Shakespeare credits the chimerical mind with the readiness to see a threat where there really is none. "Or in the night," writes Shakespeare, "imagining some fear, / How easy is a bush suppos'd a bear?"

Dali was a Renaissance man who converted to psychoanalysis.

—SARANE ALEXANDRIAN

▶ **FIGURE 6.M**
Drawing of a detail from *Slave Market with Disappearing Bust of Voltaire* by Salvador Dali (1940).

In Dali's critical paranoid paintings, he often portrays one thing as if it were another, more ominous thing, by which he appears to be saying that the delusional system of the paranoid is as distinct and logical as any other. It is simply an alternate constellation, in much the same way that the rabbit is one interpretation of the rabbiduck, the duck another. In a painting by Dali, for example (Fig. 6.M), one can interpret a cluster of marks in the center of the painting as the figures of two nuns, or, by a switch of attention, a portrait of the French philosopher Voltaire.

THERE IS A DELIGHTFUL little-known essay titled "Neurotic Camouflage" by Theodor Reik, the Viennese-born psychoanalyst who was one of Freud's earliest and most gifted students, in which he does not talk so much about the skewed interpretation of reality in the minds of psychoneurotics as about the clever ways by which they disguise their symptoms, to prevent others from knowing about them.

Reik cites the example of a middle-aged American man who suffered from an obsessive-compulsive neurosis which required that he stamp his right foot on the ground repeatedly whenever he crossed a line, such as whenever he entered a room, crossed a geographic boundary, and so on. He devised ways of justifying this foot stamping: for example, by claiming that his foot had gone to sleep from riding in the car, or by singing a portion of a song and stamping his foot to the rhythm.

One of Reik's women patients was unusually self-conscious about blushing. To disguise her apparent redness, whenever she passed other people in the hallway of her apartment building, she pretended to be looking in her purse for rouge or other make-up. Because of a tendency to blush when alone in her apartment and having to answer the door bell, she quickly put her hands in a basin of water, then opened the door while drying herself with a towel, as a way to account for the redness.

"I venture to assert," says Reik, "that social camouflage constitutes a typical feature

A neurotic is a person who builds a castle in the air. A psychotic is the person who lives in it. And a psychiatrist is the person who collects the rent.

—JEROME LAWRENCE

▲ **FIGURE 6.N**
BRAD FLANAGAN
Logo for Moon Dog Coffee Shop (1996).

Freud was the father of psychoanalysis. It had no mother.

—GERMAINE GREER

in the behavior of all psychoneurotics at a certain stage in the development of their neurosis."[6.24]

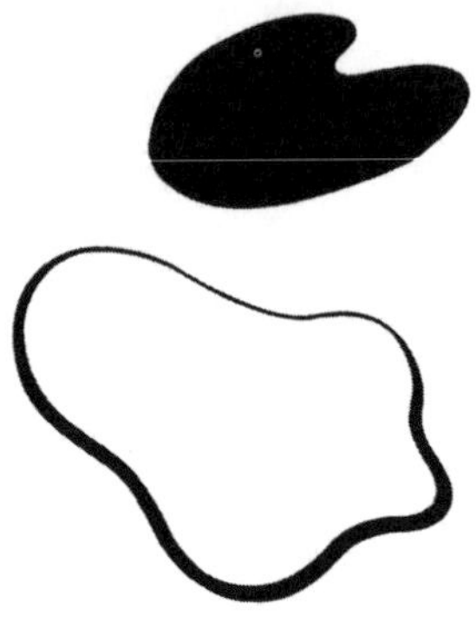

One of Reik's sources for the idea of social camouflage was an incident in the life of Austrian composer Anton Bruckner, who was visited one day in Linz by Franz Herbeck, the director of the Vienna Conservatory. As the two conversed while walking, the bells of a nearby Catholic church began to toll. Being deeply religious, but suspecting that Herbeck was cynically not, Bruckner was reluctant to doff his hat in response to the bells, for fear of being ridiculed. So, to disguise the activity, he suddenly took off his hat and exclaimed, "Gosh, but it's hot!"—although it was winter and bitterly cold.[6.25]

IT IS COMMON to think of Surrealist paintings as meticulously detailed, even if the subject matter is unrecognizable. As a result, it may be surprising that Surrealism was a major influence on Abstract Expressionism, in which the primary subject is the gestural act of painting and rarely are objects depicted at all. As it turns out, the link between the two movements was provided by free association or automatism: the belief that subconscious desires emerge during spontaneous self-expression.

Poetry is an imaginary garden with a real toad in it.

—MARIANNE MOORE

Among the transitional figures that link Surrealism with Abstract Expressionism was the Armenian-born painter Arshile Gorky.

While indebted to Joan Miro for the use of biomorphic shapes (which may also have been inspired by the amoeba-like shapes in certain camouflage fabrics), Gorky's work is gestural as well as abstract: He is, as Harold Osborne said, the last of the great Surrealists and the first Abstract Expressionist.[6.26] As proof, he was blessed by André Breton, "the Pope of Surrealism," who lived in the U.S. in the early 1940s, and wrote the catalog essay for Gorky's pivotal one-man show at the Julian Levy Gallery in 1945.

Six years earlier, when war broke out in Europe in 1939, Gorky had approached the Grand Central School of Art in New York about the possibility of teaching a course in camouflage. But the U.S. was not yet involved in the war, and the idea was dismissed as premature.

In 1941, Gorky revived the idea of becoming a camoufleur, in part because he was convinced that he would soon be drafted. He appealed to Homer Saint-Gaudens (who had commanded the Camouflage Corps during World War I) at the Joint Chiefs of Staff in Washington, D.C.; and in a letter to his sister, he wrote: "It seems I too shall be called to do camouflage painting. We artists are getting organized so that if called we shall serve as painters and not as soldiers."[6.27] He returned to the Grand Central School of Art and proposed once again that he teach a camouflage course.

◀ **FIGURE 6.O**
During and after World War II, a popular motif in design was a biomorphic or amoeba-like form, referred to then as a "wiggly," two examples of which are shown here. Julian Trevelyan believed that it had come from WWII camouflage patterns. Others suggest that it may have derived from the abstract logo-like reliefs of Jean Arp (as seen here on the cover of Rudolf Arnheim's famous book), or from the cross-section of Alvar Aalto's Savoy glassware (1937).

His idea was approved this time, and the course on camouflage began in late 1941. In the formal description, it states that the course will encompass "the data on protective coloring in zoology, optical illusion in the physics of light, and visual reactions to movement in Gestalt psychology. To complete the instruction and give it proper perspective is the history of camouflage and its application in the past."[6.28]

Distributed at the same time was a printed statement by Gorky about the purpose of the course, and the intrinsic connection between art and camouflage. "In the study of the object, as a thing seen," writes Gorky, the artist "has acquired a profound understanding and sensibility concerning its visual aspects. The philosophy as well as the physical and psychological laws governing their relationships constitute the primary source material for the study of camouflage."[6.29] According to his son-in-law and biographer, the books on camouflage he read in preparation for that course (which undoubtedly would have included the work of Abbott Thayer) "stayed with Gorky for the rest of his life, and he studied them with the same concentration he gave to his art books."[6.30]

It is funny why do the Germans wear camouflaged raincoats but not camouflaged uniforms now why do they. The first I saw was the other day, they went by on bicycles, and they reminded me of the chorus of the Tivoli Opera House in San Francisco, it used to cost twenty-five cents and the men in mediaeval costume looked so like these camouflaged coats, with sort of keys and crosses on them in contrasted colors. Oh dear. It would all be so funny if it were not so terrifying and so sad, this in January forty-four.

—GERTRUDE STEIN [while living in France, during the German occupation] *Wars I Have Seen*, pp. 147-148.

Unfortunately, on the very day the class began, FBI agents showed up to question Gorky about his new-found expertise. A year or so earlier, they had harassed his American wife about the liberal leanings of some of their friends. Now they wanted to know: How could he, a foreign-born artist with supposedly no military training, have sufficient knowledge of camouflage to teach a course on it?

Understandably, Gorky was so enraged by this intimidating intrusion that he could barely go on with his lecture. It also provided justification for his mounting paranoia, a psychoneurotic condition that grew until 1948, when, profoundly depressed by a cancer operation, a car accident, and the departure of his wife, he committed suicide.

I think Picasso is often guilty of camouflage.

—Hiram Williams
Notes for a Young Painter
(Englewood Cliffs NJ: Prentice-Hall, 1984), p. 119.

A quarter of a century after Gorky's suicide, his New York gallery dealer, Julien Levy, wrote the foreword to the catalog for an exhibition of his work at the Museum of Modern Art. "The unconscious," wrote Levy, "is, so to speak, the domain of camouflaged objects, and Gorky was to discover that if the realistic object can be camouflaged, so can the unreal, or 'surreal' object be decoded and decamouflaged."[6.31] ✂

Chapter Seven

Now You See It, Now You Don't

Camoufleurs, Conjurers and Pickpockets

IN 1842, THE BRITISH novelist Charles Dickens visited the United States, a trip he described in *American Notes*. That same year, having returned to England, he purchased the tricks, equipment and props of a retiring stage magician, and began a tradition of putting on shows for his family and friends on birthdays and other occasions.

Dickens as a magician, writes Phyllis Rose, "turned watches into tea caddies, made pieces of money fly through the air, burned up pocket watches without burning them. He caused a tiny doll to disappear and then to reappear with little messages and pieces of news for different children in the audience. But his greatest trick, the climax of it all, was his manufacture from an ordinary gentleman's hat of a plum pudding."[7.1]

The "first fundamental principle" of magic, claims the Great Merlini, a fictional magician in a mystery novel by Clayton Rawson, is

[Magic] takes us for a time into an unreal world.

—WARREN E. STEINKRAUS "The Art of Conjuring" in the *Journal of Aesthetic Education* (1979).

◀ **FIGURE 7.A**
JOHN TENNIEL
Illustration [detail] for Lewis Carroll's *Alice's Adventures in Wonderland*, 1865.

misdirection. "The other two—and they are used by magicians, criminals, and detective story authors alike—are *imitation* and *concealment*. Understand how these principles operate, and you should be able to solve any trick, crime, or detective story."[7.2]

Of course, Merlini might also have listed camouflage artists, since camouflage is governed by the exact same principles as magic—regardless of whether we call them "unit-forming factors" or "laws of disguise"—one proof of which is offered by the contributions of a British stage magician named Jasper Maskelyne to Allied combat efforts in World War II.[7.3]

At that point, early in '42, anyone in the arts was invited to apply for camouflage work—and we all rushed out there very green; not even knowing how to salute.

—WILLIAM PAHLMANN quoted in Reit, p. 79.

Personally I dreaded going into the army. I mean, who wants to go into the army? That's how I got involved in the Camouflage Society, I figured if I had to go into the army, I might as well do something behind the lines.

—SAM LEVE quoted in Naverson, p. 43.

MASKELYNE WAS a grandson of one of the most famous stage magicians of the 19th century, John Nevil Maskelyne, whose career as a magic performer began by duplicating on stage the "inexplicable manifestations" of spiritualists. He went on to develop one of the most enduring magic acts in history, an endeavor which finally ended in 1917, when, at age seventy-seven, he became ill during a performance and died a few weeks later. His son Nevil took over the act, but, seven years later, when Nevil died, the firm was inherited by his three sons, the youngest and most notable of whom was Jasper.

So this family of performers was widely known in England when Jasper Maskelyne interrupted his stage career in 1939 in order to offer his services to the Royal Engineers as a camouflage expert. Soon after, he was directed to the Camouflage Training Center at Farnham Castle for six weeks of instruction in how to conceal, deceive and distract. As it turns out, he was not the first Maskelyne to participate in a British war effort: As explained in his autobiography, his famous grandfather had contributed to military balloon research during the Boer War, while his father had shared information on artillery and gunpowder during World War I.

> As you know, a conjurer gets no credit when once he has explained his trick and if I show you my method of working, you will come to the conclusion that I am a very ordinary individual after all.
>
> —A. CONAN DOYLE
> *A Study in Scarlet*

The camouflage training at Farnham, recalls Maskelyne, "almost drove me out of my mind." For six weeks, he listened to lectures in which "I learned how Artic rabbits suffer a change of color when snow falls, and why tigers hang about in tall grass," whereas his experience as a stage magician "had taught me more about the subject than rabbits and tigers will ever know. I could, in fact, have hidden myself and most of the rest of the class so efficiently that the lecturers would never have found them in the duration of the war, but that would only have caused trouble."[7.4]

> Crouched in a corner of that imaginary railway compartment, he [E.M. Forster] would have worn a kind of protective coloring, like an oak-egger or a stick insect—or, rather, like a retired booking-office clerk from a station on a branch line.
>
> —WILLIAM PLOMER,
> *The Autobiography of William Plomer*, p. 304.

Among Maskelyne's lecturers and classmates were people who would later be recognized for a variety of achievements, if rarely in the area of camouflage. One of the chief instructors, for example, was Hugh B. Cott, the British zoologist, who had been a student of John Graham Kerr, and who had just written a classic book on biological camouflage, with notes on its military applications, titled *Adaptive Coloration in Animals*.

Julian Trevelyan, an artist with the unit, recalls that he and others laughed at Cott's "passionate addiction to countershading" although they acknowledged its value. Cott was himself an artist, a scientific illustrator, who made exquisite pen-and-ink drawings for his own book.[7.5] When he and others from Farnham were sent to the war zone in North Africa, he continued his scientific research with a menagerie of snakes, lizards and beetles that he kept in empty gas cans and studied in breaks between duties.

Trevelyan was a printmaker and the brother-in-law of Robin Darwin (a descendant of Charles Darwin), an artist who also contributed to military camouflage. Before enlisting, Trevelyan had founded a company called the Industrial Camouflage and Research Unit with three other artists: Stanley William Hayter, John Buckland-Wright and Roland Penrose. As independent consultants, they claimed to have knowledge of how to create camouflage designs that would protect factories from bombardment by enemy aircraft. In truth, as Trevelyan admitted later, "we in our camouflage unit knew very little more about it than the man in the corner garage. We had none of us done much flying, and when we had flown we had not addressed ourselves particularly to the problem of what makes things conspicuous from the air. Had we done

[Shortly before World War II, Sybil Moholy-Nagy received a book in London from Bauhaus designer Marcel Breuer in Germany] which, when opened, was found to be [Hitler's autobiography] *Mein Kampf*. It was worse than a poor joke, she and Carola [Giedion] were furious and threw it away with the rubbish. Breuer arrived soon after, apparently happy at being away from Nazi Germany, only to find two furious dames attacking him with no mercy. When he could get a word in he explained that, in order to get some of his money through German Customs, he thought it would be a bright idea to interleave their leader's great book with bank notes. They would surely not examine it with any great care. There was immediate pandemonium, all rushed down, hoping the rubbish had not yet been taken away. When they found the book, all was forgiven.

—JACK PRITCHARD
View From a Long Chair
p. 111.

so we would soon have realized that a lot of our assumptions were false, and that the pattern of the world from above is read very differently from the way in which we had supposed."[7.6]

Nevertheless, he continues, "it was easy to sell any kind of camouflage" in the early months of the war, especially greenish squiggly shapes, applied indiscriminately, in part because citizens seemed to believe "that the green stripes were a charm that somehow bought them immunity from the unknown hazards of war."[7.7]

After Trevelyan had become a camouflage officer, he would occasionally "be asked to give a demonstration of how to paint some piece of equipment so as to merge it with the broken country around. I would arrive on the barrack square with pots of paint and brushes, and set to work daubing the shield of some anti-tank gun with spots of different greens and browns, touching in the underside of the barrel itself with pure white on the principle of Cott's gazelles. Against the dreary barrack walls it looked an unholy mess, but when it was wheeled out into the country and placed against a hedge, there were cries of astonishment at my magic. This role, half-clown, half-magician, was one that I found camouflage officers were more or less expected to fill."[7.8]

A needle is much simpler to find in a haystack than in a bin of other needles.

—Colin Watson

For some time I have been trying to find the right word for the shimmering glancing twinkling movement of the poplar leaves in the sun and wind. This afternoon I saw the word written on the poplar leaves. It was "dazzle." The dazzle of the poplars.

—Francis Kilvert in Plomer (1960), p. 91.

At Farnham at the same time was Trevelyan's former partner, Roland Penrose, a Surrealist painter who later produced a pioneering biography of Picasso. In fact, he was one of the first to point out the significance of Picasso's recognition of the resemblance between Cubism and World War I camouflage. Penrose was not in the military, but sat in on the training as a civilian camouflage instructor. In 1941, he wrote and illustrated a guidebook for civilians called the *Home Guard Manual of Camouflage*.[7.9]

Even the face of the soldier is streaked with bars of color like that of an Indian and he thus becomes quite invisible and is as effectively concealed as any wild animal lying under cover in the woods.

—ERNEST PEIXOTTO
"Special Service for Artists in War Time," p. 6.

▲ **FIGURE 7.B**
In his civilian guidebook, ROLAND PENROSE included drawings of disruptively camouflaged clothing, much like this example from World War I.

▶ **FIGURE 7.C**
World War II instruction sheet for a camouflage face painting kit for soldiers, using techniques like those LEE MILLER used.

It is hard to believe that a Surrealist as puckish as Penrose could lecture about trickery without introducing pranks as part of the lecture. Thus, Penrose found a clever way of demonstrating the conspicuousness of even the slightest movement: He would, Trevelyan remembers, "stand his audience round a piece of grass in which a small button was lying, which was of course invisible. He would then pull it rapidly along with a thread, and immediately all eyes were fixed on it."[7.10]

Penrose's wife was Lee Miller, the American model and photographer who had earlier been the wife of the Surrealist photographer Man Ray. In his notebook, Penrose provides a written account and a photograph of an afternoon tea in an outdoor garden with friends during which, as a "camouflage experiment," Miller removed her clothing and smeared herself with a matt dull greenish camouflage cream developed by a cosmetics company. It was Penrose's theory, he writes, "that if you could hide such eye-catching attractions as hers from the invading Hun, smaller and less seductive areas of skin would stand an even better chance of becoming invisible."[7.11]

Among those trained as World War II British army camoufleurs were the painters Robert Medley, Edward Seago, Patrick Phillips, Blair Hughes-Stanton and Frederick Gore;

designers Victor Stiebel, Steven Sykes, James Gardner, Jack Keefer, and Ashley Havindon; sculptor John Codner; film producer Peter Proud; theater set designer Oliver Messel; and a host of others, among them stained glass artisans, a *Punch* cartoonist, a circus manager, an art restorer, and art connoisseurs.

Like Penrose, Seago found it hard to be totally serious when designing camouflage. He was, for example, once asked to provide hundreds of life-sized human dummies, each of which was mounted on a remote controlled turntable and placed beside a dummy anti-aircraft gun on the south coast of England. As a joke, Seago made all of the dummies appear to be imitations of the discredited British prime minister Neville Chamberlain, but dressed in a helmet and battle fatigues.[7.12]

Monday, 7th April [1941] This afternoon reported to Victory House, along with forty other miserable recruits, all clutching their suitcases. We were conveyed to Paddington in camouflaged cattle-trucks, hurling from one wall to another as we went round corners, and arrived in Gloucester at six p.m.

—JOAN WYNDHAM
Love Lessons: A Wartime Journal, p. 187.

READING BETWEEN the lines of Trevelyan's autobiography, one senses that he was not fully convinced of Jasper Maskelyne's extraordinary command of camouflage, or, at any rate, not as convinced as the magician himself. Maskelyne, recalls Trevelyan, "entertained us with his tricks in the evenings [at Farnham], and tried, rather unsuccessfully, to apply his techniques to the disguise of the concrete pill-boxes [in which anti-aircraft guns were hidden] that were then appearing everywhere overnight. He was at once innocent and urbane, and he ended up as an Entertainments officer in the Middle East."[7.13]

By Maskelyne's account, which he recorded later in a book titled *Magic—Top Secret*, nearly all the entertainments devised by himself and the team that he fondly referred to as the "Magic Gang" were directed toward Adolf Hitler. "I and others made the mailed fist [of the Third Reich] strike wildly against empty air, with considerable loss to its sense of balance," recalls Maskelyne. "We made it draw timidly back when nothing but cardboard and canvas opposed it; and, at other times, crash home upon knobby obstacles from which it recoiled hurt, surprised and bleeding."[7.14] As proof of his effectiveness, he continues, there were no more satirical drawings of him in German newspapers after 1941: "Instead, Hitler did me the honor of placing my name on his dreaded 'Personal Black List,' and a reward was offered for my capture, perhaps because it was hoped that the Gestapo 'magic' might make me talk."[7.15]

A town occupied by an army looks like a deserted shell of grey inhabitants watched over by khaki ghosts.

—Stephen Spender
in Goldsmith (1986),
p. 62.

Papa was an airplane watcher in south Georgia; he even had this little hat to wear. He'd count every plane that came over and check to see if it was an enemy plane. They made camouflage nets in the gym at the high school.

—Bunny Johnson
in Sutton and Waite (1992),
p. 22.

Many of the Magic Gang's projects were tricks that might best be described as mimetic distractions and decoys, objects and events that not only called attention to themselves but also appeared to be some other thing than what they actually were. In one case, for example, he and his soldiers used scrap metal to build dozens of tanks and artillery guns, then filled the gun barrels with a stage magician's recipe for a harmless but conspicuous flash that looked and sounded like real artillery fire. Then, to create the effect of a column of tanks moving across the desert, he hired North Africans to drive their camels across the dunes, each animal dragging behind it a dust-producing wooden frame. In another incident, he and his crew constructed "a fleet of dummy submarines, full size, able to float

▲ **FIGURE 7.D**
DAN SCHRAD
Hand-drawn metamorphosis in which Beethoven becomes a clarinet.

like real submarines, but also able to be folded up by a few men so as to travel in a five-ton truck."[7.16]

Black, slack, stack, stark, stare, stale, shale, whale, while, white.

—E.J. KAHN, JR

IN DISCUSSIONS OF magic, the inevitable explanation is that "the hand is quicker than the eye." But that itself is a diversion, since the success of most magic depends not on extraordinary swiftness and manual dexterity but rather, as advised earlier by the Great Merlini, on the misdirection of attention, or distraction. It is to the performer's advantage that we, as vigilant and sophisticated audience members, should follow very closely the actions pointed out to us (figure), while ignoring the seemingly marginal acts—the trifles, Sherlock Holmes would say—that really enable the trick to occur (ground). The magician, writes Warren Steinkraus, "requires that his viewers watch every overt move diligently, thereby missing secretive moves."[7.17]

While the viewer attends—as directed—mainly to the figure, the magician must follow both figure and ground. This requires a sort of double consciousness, explains Steinkraus, with the result that "there are always two performances going on, the one we obviously see and the one carefully screened from our view. A conjurer must be double-minded as no other performer dares to be. He can never lose himself totally in the effect he is presenting, but at the same time he must appear so intently involved in doing what we observe that he gives us not the slightest hint that he is doing quite otherwise."[7.18]

▲ **FIGURE 7.E**
TOM GROTHUS
Adjusting the Antenna (1984).

[So-and-so] would not have thought of concealing his whereabouts, being a person who considers himself a "tough" soldier.

—JOHN GAITHA BROWNING
quoted in Toliver, p. 34.

Those two performances, one manifest, the other latent, are essentially two constellations or two Gestalts. They are comparable to the alternating interpretations of the rabbiduck, although in magic, as in dreams, one of them is deliberately made visible while the other remains inconspicuous. The primary tactic of magic, writes Max Dessoir, "lies in the power to direct the thoughts of the audience into such a groove [the explicit Gestalt] that a solution of the trick seems for a moment the natural result of the artificially underlying causes."[7.19]

In his biography of William James, the scholar Jacques Barzun describes an amusing moment in the life of that philosopher and psychologist when he and a student were taking a stroll near Harvard University. As they walked, they encountered on the street an elderly gentleman who was talking to himself and who appeared to be oblivious to the world, so much that they might collide if they had not stepped aside. When the stranger had

All the arts seem to have gravitated to the camouflage unit—even musicians.

—CHARLES BURCHFIELD
His Golden Year, p. 24.

passed, the student turned to James and said, "Whoever he is, he's the epitome of the absentminded professor," in reply to which her teacher said, "What you really mean is that he is present-minded somewhere else."[7.20]

Likewise, it is not that magicians persuade an audience to be absentminded, but rather that they cleverly prompt them to be present-minded toward other events that are of little or no consequence. Misdirection means simply directing the mind toward diversionary aspects; and magicians insure that this happens by methods that everyone uses daily. However, unless we are employed in sales, we probably use them more often to be clearer, not misleading, in the process of communicating. "My dentist informs me," writes Nathaniel Schiffman, "that dentists and doctors use the same [misdirection] trick when administering shots to patients. They first use the fingers to pinch the skin, rendering the patient a bit less sensitive to the needle to come."[7.21]

When I was in the Air Corps during World War II, I tried to get into camouflage, but they needed radio operators at that time. Because I was a drummer I passed the Morse Code aptitude test 100% and as it turned out my entire platoon consisted of jazz musicians...A less military group I never saw.

—BYRON BURFORD
in a letter to the author
(August 26, 1998), p. 62.

Perhaps the most familiar means of misdirection is the simple act of pointing. Magicians direct the attention of an audience by giving them verbal instructions about where to look, by pointing with the hands, fingers, thumbs, elbows, and feet, by motioning with ones head, by facing something, or simply by staring at it.

▲ **FIGURE 7.F**
John Dopita
A hand-drawn metamorphosis in which Beethoven becomes a piano, c.1995.

Another common way of calling attention to an object is through contrast (color, size, sound, movement, position, and so on), by creating what Gregory Bateson would call "news of difference," a technique that is often effectively used by pickpockets.

Cock-cook-cool-fool-foul-soul-sour-slur-slum-glum-glim-frim-gram-cram-craw-crow.

—E.J. Kahn, Jr

The pickpocket's use of misdirection is mentioned in Hugh B. Cott's lecture to the Royal Engineers: "When a pickpocket intends to rob you of your watch or wallet," he writes, "he, or his confederate, takes care to distract your attention from what he intends to do by creating a diversion. He draws your eyes from what is really happening to what seems to be happening."[7.22]

He compares pocket-picking to the confusing effects of disruptive coloration in animals. "Distributed over the body are irregular patches of contrasted colors and tones," continues Cott, which "tend to catch the eye of the observer and to draw his attention away from

the underlying form of the animal which exhibits them. The patterns themselves may be conspicuous enough, but since they contradict the form of the animal on which they are superimposed, they pass for part of the background, in the same way that the pickpocket's tactics of bluff pass for a commonplace incident."[7.23]

IN BOOKS ABOUT magic, dreams, camouflage, and other forms of misinformation, it is customary to include an inventory of methods, a list of the kinds and varieties of deceptive tactics. Rarely are two of these lists the same, but they typically include such strategies as condensation, substitution and displacement (described earlier as Freudian dream techniques), or, in the lingo of stage magicians, such categories as *production*, *restoration*, *modification*, *transposition*, *relocation*, and so on. In general, one might simply say that all of these are variations on one overriding strategy, the tactic of doing the opposite from what is really going on, or what would normally be expected.

That exact same principle was recommended in 500 BC by Sun Tzu, a Chinese army tactician, who said: "All warfare is based on deception. When able to attack, we must seem unable; when using our forces, we must seem inactive; when we are near, we must make the enemy believe that we are far away; when far away, we must make him believe we are near.

Hold out the bait; entice the enemy. Feign disorder and crush him."[7.24]

In magic performances, a thing appears where nothing was. Or, where something was only a moment ago, there is suddenly nothing. The parts of a thing are restored to a whole. One thing becomes some other thing, or exchanges places with another. That which is solid and heavy becomes insubstantial and weightless. The impenetrable becomes penetrable; the inanimate animate. That which is vulnerable becomes invulnerable. The mental becomes physical; the physical mental. Large becomes small; front becomes back; top becomes bottom; in becomes out, and so on. The list could continue indefinitely, in the sense that so long as an attribute can be defined and identified, the opportunity exists for a magic trick (or dream technique or camouflage strategy) to counteract that attribute.

Art historian Wylie Sypher said that "the great Cubist achievement was camouflage." With that in mind, it is of value to compare the above roster of magic categories with Sypher's surprisingly parallel list (cited in an earlier chapter) of techniques used by the Cubists. Among these, he writes, are "a breaking of contours, the passage, so that a form merges with the space about it or with other forms; planes or tones that bleed into other planes and tones; outlines that coincide with other outlines, then suddenly reappear in new relations; surfaces that simultaneously recede

Plagiarists are always suspicious of being stolen from—as pickpockets are observed commonly to walk with their hands in their pockets.

—Samuel Taylor Coleridge
Table Talk (1836)

◀ **FIGURE 7.G**
Victorian-era metamorphosis of a musician and his cello.

When it was dark we stood on the balcony and leant back looking at the sky and the barrage balloons, and G said, "I've never known it so warm in the evenings, not in three years. All the blimps are up tonight, they should paint them blue like the sky for camouflage."

—Joan Wyndham
Love Lessons, p. 68.

and advance in relation to other surfaces; parts of objects shifted away, displaced, or changed in tone until forms disappear behind themselves."[7.25]

Suzi Gablik has compiled a similar list for her book about the life and work of the Surrealist artist René Magritte, an account of the primary methods by which Magritte's paintings "disrupt any dogmatic view of the physical world."[7.26] She also reveals that his interest in art began during his childhood, when, as he was playing in an abandoned cemetery, he happened upon a painter who (in Magritte's words) "seemed to me to be performing magic."[7.27]

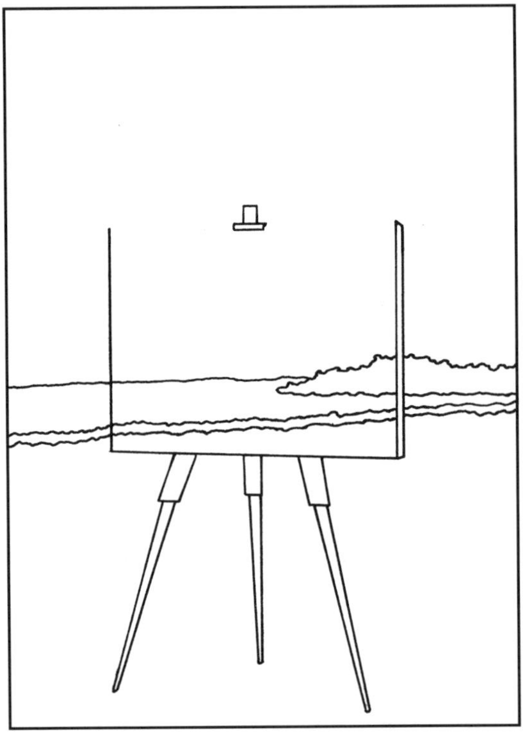

▲ FIGURE 7.H
Author's diagram, loosely based on paintings by the Belgian Surrealist René Magritte, in which the boundary is blurred between a painting and the thing painted.

In various of Magritte's paintings, a carrot turns into a bottle. A bird becomes a leaf. A man's head is a light bulb. Leather shoes are also feet. A rock floats. A figure is a hole through which it is also the background. An image of a landscape is itself the thing it represents. A painting of a pipe is labeled *Ceci n'est pas une pipe* ("This is not a pipe"). A flying bird is made of stone. A single apple fills a room. The smoke from a man's pipe becomes his nose. Hundreds of businessmen float in air, while precisely aligned in perspective. And a steam locomotive juts out of a fireplace wall, its smoke rising into the chimney.

By day I wore a dashing uniform, and Flossie dressed in an immaculate waitress outfit that could not camouflage her glorious body.

—ART BUCHWALD
Leaving Home

THERE WAS A sensation in London in 1875 when Jasper Maskelyne's famous grandfather, the magician John Nevil Maskelyne, announced a new addition to his stage performance. It was a robot, a cross-legged seated mechanical man called "Psycho" who was good at playing whist, a forerunner of bridge. This Oriental manikin, which was only twenty-two inches high, was seated on a small platform which was in turn supported by a transparent glass cylinder. Having withstood an inspection by members of the audience, it moved its head to look at cards (both playing cards and alphabets), and used its arm to pick them out as a means of responding to questions about mathematics, or to spell out words. It also took an occasional puff from a cigarette.[7.28]

▲ **FIGURE 7.1**
LES COLEMAN
Dislocation (c. 1996)

At a performance by Psycho on June 24, 1876 (which was, incidentally, the day before the Battle of Little Bighorn), one of the audience members was the Rev. Charles Lutwidge Dodgson, who was an Oxford College don and a teacher of mathematics. A prolific writer, within the previous decade he had published two children's classics, *Alice's Adventures in Wonderland* and *Through the Looking-glass*

Show business is dog eat dog. It's worse than dog eat dog. It's dog doesn't return dog's phone calls.

—WOODY ALLEN

and What Alice Found There, which he signed with the now famous pseudonym of Lewis Carroll (in which he hid his given names, Charles Lutwidge, by translating them into Latin as Carolus Ludovicus, then reversing the order and changing them back into English again). He had specifically come to observe Maskelyne's amazing mechanical man, after which he concluded (incorrectly) that "I have no doubt [that it] has a dwarf in it."[7.29]

But Carroll was also presumably there for another, more general reason, which was to satisfy his lifelong fascination with magic. A generation younger than Charles Dickens, he had practiced magic all his life. As a child, Martin Gardner writes, Carroll "dabbled in puppetry and sleight of hand, and throughout his life enjoyed doing magic tricks, especially for children. He liked to form a mouse with his handkerchief then make it jump mysteriously out of his hand. He taught children how to fold paper boats and paper pistols that popped when swung through the air."[7.30]

Lewis Carroll's *Alice* books are exemplars of the adroit use of ambiguity—they are, as one critic befittingly said, "an infinite onion, with many layers"—in the sense that they lend themselves willingly to a wide variety of complex interpretations, from psychoanalytic to literary to religious and political, on a level for children as well as adults. Since at least the 1930s, there have been frequent, repeated attempts to dissect both the writer's psyche

[Camouflage violated] the military obsession with neatness, spit-and-polish, drill-field regularity… [It] was considered careless and "undisciplined." It made a virtue of dispersion, irregularity, and improvisation; and like modern ecologists, camoufleurs tried to blend with the natural landscape instead of exploiting and dominating it.

—SEYMOUR REIT
Masquerade, pp. 65-66.

We [military camoufleurs] actually helped the soldiers' morale. They said they slept better at night knowing we had camouflaged the barracks…Many of the officers I worked for thought of us as dreamers with magic paint buckets and expected far more from us than we could possibly deliver.

—HARPER GOFF
quoted in Naverson, p. 98.

and his writings (which he claimed to have been "nothing but nonsense") through filters as heavily tinted as Freud's, or that of his disaffected student, Carl Jung. It was in reply to such "psycho-analyses" of Carroll's writings, as if they were transcripts from his therapy sessions, that James Joyce wrote in *Finnegans Wake* that "We grisly old Sykos have done our unsmiling bit on 'alices, when they were jung and easily freudened."

▲ **FIGURE 7.J**
JOHN TENNIEL
Illustration of the bread-and-butterfly from Lewis Carroll's *Through the Looking-glass and What Alice Found There*, 1871. This paradoxical creature has wings of bread-and-butter, a body of crust, and a lump of sugar for a head. It lives on weak tea with cream. If it doesn't eat, it will of course die; but if it eats it will also die, since its head will dissolve while drinking the tea.

Ignoring for a moment their enormous differences, the *Alice* books might have been written by Magritte, while Lewis Carroll might have made Magritte's paintings. Or maybe the Magic Gang could have produced the dream-like magic works of both.

In various episodes of Carroll's books, a little girl fills up a room. A poem is printed backwards. There is a grin without a cat, and an insect with bread for wings and a sugar cube for a head. Memory is discredited since it "only works backwards." The text of a tale about a mouse has been typeset to resemble the shape of a tail. A wooded landscape is a giant chessboard. The sea is hot, and pigs have wings.

The *Alice* books are the literary equivalent of a Victorian magic show, like those that Charles Dickens gave for his family and friends. "Like all great magicians," writes John Fisher, Carroll "needed only simple, everyday objects such as a ball of wool, a kitten and some chessmen, together with the almost obligatory mirror and the assistance of a little girl to produce a spectacle unrivalled in later years by Houdini or Disney."[7.31]

> "The time has come," the Walrus said,
> "To talk of many things:
> Of shoes—and ships—and sealing wax—
> Of cabbages and kings—
> And why the sea in boiling hot—
> And whether pigs have wings."
>
> —LEWIS CARROLL
> *Through the Looking-glass and What Alice Found There.*

The *Alice* books are said to rely on the language of dreams, which explains why they often gets targeted for literary psychoanalysis, and why Carroll's writings were praised and promoted by the Surrealists as the antecedents of their tradition. But it is also camouflage, in the sense that its enigmatic author—for whatever reason—made clever and often astonishing use of "the guise of nonsense" to demonstrate "the ephemerality and unimportance of our most cherished categories."[7.32] ✂

> He [Pablo Picasso] was thought to be dead at birth in Málaga on October 15, 1881. Then his uncle Salvador Ruiz, a celebrated Spanish physician who had delivered the boy, calmly puffed cigar smoke up the baby's nose, provoking howls of protest. Thus did Picasso embark on 91 years of rugged life.
>
> —ROBERT HUGHES
> *Time* magazine (May 26, 1980), p. 79.

THE ETYMOLOGY OF "CAMOUFLAGE"

THE WORD "CAMOUFLAGE" can be traced back to the 16th century to the French term for a practical joke (a variation on a hotfoot) by which a person who fell asleep in a chair could be abruptly and rudely aroused. It was called a *camouflet*, a term that may have been derived from *chault mouflet*, an archaic expression for "hot face." The joke was accomplished by lighting the tip of a hollow paper cone, then holding the opposite smoldering end under the victim's nose. The stupefied sleeper would spring to his feet as soon as a noseful of smoke was inhaled.

Three centuries later, *camouflet* had come to mean a small but lethal powder charge by which a tunneling enemy troop could be entrapped beneath the ground, buried and suffocated. From that came *camoufler*, a verb that means "to get made up," to put on cosmetics and costumes in order to play a theatrical role—or, in a somewhat more sinister sense (it was an underworld slang term), to be deceptive, to blow smoke, or, more specifically, to disguise oneself for illicit purposes.

It was from this lineage of root words that "camouflage" became the term for the purposeful use of a visual disguise as a military stratagem. During World War I, the term was exported to English from French. According to the *Oxford English Dictionary*, it first appeared in British print on May 25, 1917, in the *London Daily News*, where it was used in a sentence that said "The act of hiding anything from your enemy is termed 'camouflage.'"

A few months later the same newspaper announced that the King of England had "paid a visit to what is called a camouflage factory" where he was introduced to "all the latest Protean tricks for concealing or, as we all say now, 'camouflaging' guns, snipers, observers."

By the end of World War I, "camouflage" had amassed so many figurative, nonmilitary connotations that *The Anthenaeum* observed that the word "has met with more wear and tear in a few months than many receive in a century." During the same period, one finds reference to a "camouflage autocracy," to eggs "camouflaged" in a scramble, and even to a telephone as having been "camouflaged" by its design. "Instead of saying 'He is a bluff,'" wrote one journalist in 1917, "we say 'He is nothing but camouflage.'"

Chapter Eight

The Forms of Things Unknown

A Potpourri of Camouflage Artists

ONE: THE AMERICAN PAINTER Ellsworth Kelly was a nineteen-year-old art student in Brooklyn, New York, when he was inducted into the U.S. Army on New Year's Day in 1943. Soon after, as he had requested, he was assigned to the 603rd Engineers Camouflage Battalion at Fort Meade, Maryland, a unit described by its historian as "composed mainly of artists from New York and Philadelphia with an average IQ of 119."[8.1]

Kelly did not design camouflage, but was instead assigned to print a series of silkscreen training posters, each of which featured a single aspect of camouflage, with such headings as Blending, Texture, Shadows, Color, and Shape. A year later, his unit was transferred to the 23rd Headquarters Special Troops in Camp Forrest, Tennessee, where its mission was redirected toward deception instead of concealment.

The poet's eye, in a fine
frenzy rolling,
Doth glance from heaven to
earth, from earth to
heaven;
And, as imagination bodies
forth
The forms of things
unknown, the poet's
pen
Turns them to shapes, and
gives to airy nothing
A local habitation and a
name.

—WILLIAM SHAKESPEARE
A Midsummer Night's Dream

◀ **FIGURE 8.A**
MARILYN LYSOHIR
[see p. 182] standing beside a portion of her ceramic installation called *The Dark Side of Dazzle* (1986).

Rather than making personnel and equipment less visible, there was a new emphasis on distraction, misinformation and the use of false targets as decoys. At Camp Forrest, Kelly was taught how to construct fake military vehicles and other equipment. Initially made of chicken wire and plywood, these were eventually replaced by inflatable rubber dummies.

[Just as Picasso had expressed an interest in World War I camouflage, so] the camouflage units of the French army took a reciprocal interest in modern art, to the extent that they named their regimental mascots "Picasso" and "Matisse."

—JOHN RICHARDSON
A Life of Picasso (1996), p. 414.

Once erected, these were deceptively made to appear to be ineptly camouflaged, using overhanging garnished nets or "umbrella camouflage."[8.2] As described earlier, this technique, which had commonly been used during World War I, consisted of large fish nets interwoven with strips of muslin or canvas, suspended on poles above an artillery position, a truck or other vehicle. On a sunlit day, the interwoven strips cast high-contrast zebra-like shadows on everything beneath the nets (like the shadows of venetian blinds). Even when overcast, these nets diffused the contours of the covered objects to such a degree that they could not readily be seen from the air.

When the United States entered the first World War, [Kimon] Nicolaides [whose famous book, *The Natural Way to Draw*, would later be a handbook for generations of art students] volunteered in the Camouflage Corps and served in France for over a year...

—ANON

Kelly's unit was sent to Europe in May 1944, where it functioned in various regions of France during the final months of the war. Three years later, he returned to that country as a civilian, enrolled at the École des Beaux Arts, then continued to live and teach in Paris until 1954. In the summer of 1950, while staying at the Villa La Combe outside Paris, Kelly became interested in an effect that must surely have made him recall his wartime experiences with camouflage nets.

He was renting a balcony room, which he entered by an outside staircase that consisted of nine metal steps, supported by hand rails arranged in an X. On sunlit days, the shadows of the hand rails cast complex geometric shapes as they fell on the upright and vertical planes of the steps, patterns that changed as the position of the sun changed. Kelly made drawings and photographs of this, which he then used as the basis for at least two pivotal works, an oil painting titled *La Combe I* (1950), and a curious wooden folding screen, titled *La Combe II* (1950), consisting of nine elongated panels, arranged in a shallow accordion fold, as if they were upturned irregular steps (compare Fig 5.K). According to critics, these were pivotal early works for Kelly, who would eventually become a leading American artist.[8.3]

TWO: With the advent of Modernism in art, architecture and design, the use of shadows as disruptive elements became almost commonplace, as artists felt compelled to conform to the avant-garde and to emphasize aspects of nature ignored in academic, Beaux-Arts traditions.

There are, for example, two photographs by Lazslo Moholy-Nagy, created at the Bauhaus, in which shadow disruption is central: In one, the bodies of a pair of dolls are broken up by the shadows of an iron fence

The work [of camouflaging field artillery during World War I] was pleasant and I would set my drawing board under a young oak tree, more or less by myself. To make my designs more interesting [to me] I would invent themes, which I kept secret, which embodied some previous experience in Nature (such as March wind, sunlight and rocks). To see these later, on say, a field gun, gave me quite a thrill.

—Charles Burchfield
His Golden Year (1965), p. 24.

(1926); while in the other, the reclining figure of Oskar Schlemmer is bisected by the shadows of what may be the same fence (1927).

Also from that time period is a photograph of Jean Cocteau by Man Ray (1926), in which the poet's face is partly obscured by the shadows of a wire sculpture on which he appears to be working. Four years later, Man Ray again used disruptive shadows in two well-known portraits of Lee Miller (cited earlier for her outdoor camouflage demonstration): one in which the shadows of a screen-like grid are projected across her torso (1930), and another, titled *Leebra* (1930) as in zebra, in which a diagonal system of lines is superimposed on her face.

Mobilized in August 1914, he [Othon Friez] served at first with a territorial regiment; then, after having been wounded, he did topographical work at the front; and finally he worked on airplane camouflage.

—THEDA SHAPIRO
Painters and Politics, p. 244.

Other familiar uses of shadow disruption can be seen in the photographs of the Russian Constructivists, notably Alexander Rodchenko and El Lissitzky, and in the "light workshop" experiments of other Bauhaus and New Bauhaus artists, as shown by the wealth of examples in Kepes' *Language of Vision* and Moholy-Nagy's *Vision in Motion*.

[The work of Robert Lawson, illustrator of the famous children's book, *The Story of Ferdinand*] was interrupted by a year and a half in the Army, of which a year was spent in France with the 40th Engineers, Camouflage Section, A.E.F.

—ANON

Today, accidental occurrences of this same phenomenon can be witnessed almost daily in any darkened lecture hall, whenever a teacher steps into the path of a slide projector. Depending on the person's clothes and the complexity of the slide, the puzzling and often delightful result is that of coincidental disruption, in which the figure is broken apart while at the same time it blends with the slide on the screen.

This ubiquitous pedagogical blooper may have played some minor part in the work of Andy Warhol, the American pop artist, who embarked on a series of paintings about camouflage in 1986, shortly before his death. Some of these are photographic self-portraits, in which he appears to have stood in the path of a projected slide of camouflage fabric. Through this and other methods (name change, wigs and evasive remarks), this person born Andrew Warhola "camouflaged who he was, where he came from, what he thought, and how he felt, as well as his baldness, his blotches and blemishes, his scars."[8.4]

Warhol had been born in Pittsburgh in 1928. The son of a Czech immigrant who worked in the West Virginia coal mines, he was first introduced to art in 1939, when, as a student in the Pittsburgh public schools, he was offered the chance to participate in an art education program at the Carnegie Museum of Art. A few years later, after completing high school, he went on to study art at the Carnegie Institute of Technology, where he was surely influenced, if not actually taught, by two of the country's most experienced camouflage experts: Homer Saint-Gaudens, who was head of the school's art department at the time, and Everett L. Warner, who was a senior professor of art.

Aside from Warhol's self-portraits, the majority of his camouflage paintings are close-

[The camouflage task that he was assigned to] has a totally practical purpose to hide artillery emplacements from airborne spotters and photography by covering them with tarpaulins painted in roughly pointillistic designs in the manner of bright natural camouflage... I am curious what effect the "Kandinskys" will have [when viewed from the air] at 2,000 meters. The nine tarpaulins chart a development "from Manet to Kandinsky"!

—Franz Marc
quoted in Cork (1994), p. 111.

up, abstract patterns from military camouflage fabric, sometimes in colors so gaudy and sweet that stalemates of pattern and color result. Some of those color schemes and their teardrop biomorphic shapes are reminiscent of the wallpaper cut-outs of Henri Matisse, a connection that Warhol deliberately planned. According to an assistant, at one time he wanted to cover a wall (as background) with camouflage patterns ("so large that the camouflage paintings *become* the wall"), on which to hang other, smaller camouflage paintings (as figure).[8.5]

By 1916 he [French artist Jacques Villon, the brother of Marcel Duchamp] was transferred from an infantry regiment serving at the front to a camouflage unit at Amiens. There is reason to believe that the two years during which he worked at camouflage caused him to study color theory...

—DANIEL ROBBINS
in Villon entry
in Turner (1996).

Looking at Warhol's camouflage wallpaper (the largest of which is 9 and a half feet high by 35 feet wide), and recalling the fact that he learned about art at the Carnegie Institute, it is tempting to wonder if he may have read (or at least was told about) Everett L. Warner's essay on ship camouflage that appeared in the *Transactions of the Illuminating Engineering Society* in 1919. In that article, as noted earlier, Warner compared his use of abstract colored blocks in producing camouflage schemes to the illusory effects of distorted wallpaper. It was, thought Warner, a critical point: "When you have once thoroughly grasped this idea," he said, "marine camouflage holds no secrets for you."[8.6]

From an early age, [Swedish painter Bruno (Andreas)] Liljefors had been fascinated by the relationship between animals and their habitat; animal and bird camouflage was a theme to which he often returned.

—BRITA LINDE
in Liljefors entry
in Turner (1996).

THREE: ONE OF the most compelling uses of coincidental disruption is found in the work of an artist, model and film actress named Vera

Lehndorff, whose professional name is "Veruschka." As a European art student, she studied painting and design in Germany and Italy, but was put off by the prospect of having to live by producing textile patterns and wallpaper. After working with Lee Strasberg in New York, she turned instead to fashion modeling and acting, appearing most notably, as herself, in 1966 in Michelangelo Antonioni's *Blow-Up*.

In that same year, she also began to experiment with painting her own body. While working as a fashion model, it had occurred to her that fashion photographs would be more interesting "if I changed the color of my skin, giving the image a strangeness that would distract attention from the often very boring dresses. As a model I could transform myself into many characters. Soon I began to paint myself as different animals and plants, knowing that they are often more beautiful than we are. The nakedness of human skin always disturbed me. By painting myself I could create the illusion of having feathers, fur, scales or leaves. When I saw a photograph of myself painted like this, it pleased me. Camouflaging myself also made me feel that the public could not trap me so easily."[8.7] Later, she painted her body to merge with specific backgrounds, as when, for example, she painted her head to blend in with the stones of a terrace on which she was sitting.

In 1970, Lehndorff became associated with Holger Trulzsch, a musician, painter and pho-

His [Arthur B. Carles'] greatest contribution to the [World War I] war effort, however, was as a camoufleur in the Philadelphia Navy Yard where he worked in 1918 with many of his friends and students, including Franklin Watkins, Adolphe Borie, Jean Knox, Waldo Pierce, and Carroll Tyson. Watkins devised some of the camouflage designs, but it was Carles who actually oversaw the application of the paint on the vessels, supervising the work from various angles and distances.

—Barbara A. Wolanin
Arthur B. Carles, p.64.

tographer. In subsequent years, they worked together to produce scores of astonishing photographs of the unclothed but painted Lehndorff blending in with a wide variety of indoor and outdoor surroundings. Collected and published in book form in 1986 as

> The main qualifications which artists feel they can bring to camouflage work are a visual sensitivity, keen and quick in its discriminatory powers, a knowledge of color, texture, and modeling, imagination, and enthusiasm.
>
> —MILTON FOX "Camouflage" (1942), p. 137.

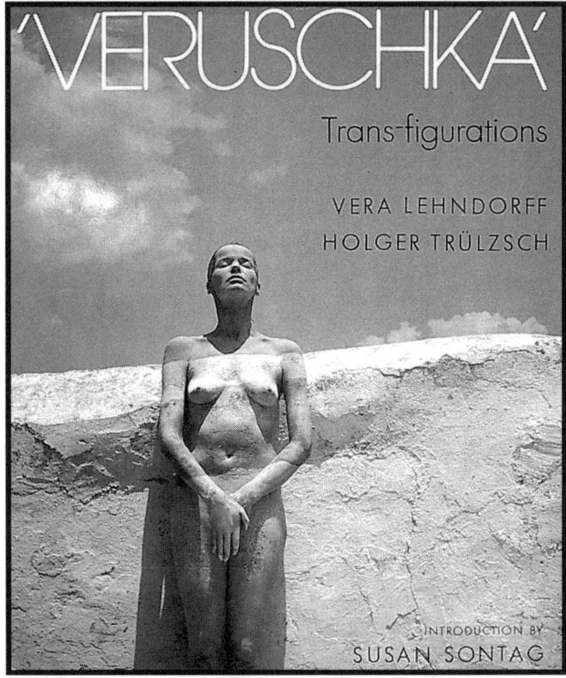

▶ FIGURE 8.B
Dust jacket for *Veruschka: Trans-figurations* by Vera Lehndorff and Holger Trulzsch (1986).

Veruschka: Trans-figurations, these amazing photographs include examples of mimicry (in which she is painted to seem to be dressed in various articles of clothing), and of blending and disruption in the context of both natural and man-made settings (in which she is barely distinguishable from a background of rocks, fungus, bark, brick walls, iron girders, decaying doors, and window frames).

"Sometimes people wonder," concludes Lehndorff, "why I should want to identify myself with doors, windows or walls... For me, things around us have symbolic meanings: a door is not only a door, it could also be an entrance or exit into something different and new; windows are also eyes through which we perceive and therefore communicate with the outside world; walls can be seen as separations, disconnections or forms of protection. I feel that it is important to deal with the surface of things because the surface may reveal to us a secret world, a new aspect. I believe strongly in the multiplicity of aspects in an image or a situation, in things seen from many different viewpoints, in resisting habit—the passive acceptance of how through convention we see ourselves or others. An artist's vision has to do, after all, with new ways of seeing, ways that make the artist and the work one and the same thing."[8.8]

Poetry is the opening and closing of a door, leaving those who look through to guess about what is seen during a moment.

—Carl Sandburg
Complete Poems

This specimen page is from "Color in Camouflage," a portfolio of instruction reference material for teachers diverting their Art Classes to useful studies in this direction.

—From an advertisement for Eberhard Faber Pencil Company in School Arts (March 1942).

FOUR: Not unrelated to the body paintings of Lehndorff and Trulzsch is the bark-covered sculpture of Tom Czarnopys, a Chicago-based artist who has often explored the relation between human figures and their physical surroundings, in forms that are uneasy statements about border skirmishes between wildness and domesticity, between nature and culture.

Born in 1957 in Grand Rapids, Michigan, Czarnopys is the grandson of a furniture craftsman. As early as six or seven, he began to accompany his father on trips into the National Forest in northern Michigan, a tradition the two have continued, although Czarnopys now lives in the city. "My father and I go up during the rut and bow hunt for deer," he explained in an interview. "He's up in the trees, all that stuff. We've always taken it very, very seriously. And no matter where we are, we always get together for those two weeks and go out to the woods and set up a hunting camp. We just get lost and immersed in it."[8.9]

Like Thayer, Czarnopys has been fascinated by the wilderness since childhood, beginning with an interest in taxidermy. Until he enrolled at an art school, nearly all of his drawings were of birds and fish. It was his experience of drawing from a live model in college, juxtaposed with his ritual trips to the woods, that allowed him to find a direction as an adult artist. He recalled: "I wanted the most direct way of working with what was so strong for me and it all came about when I was bow hunting. We were covered with camouflage. You do everything to eliminate the boundary between yourself and that natural world. More than concealment, camouflage is eliminating a boundary. It's like the Guinea mudmen covering themselves with mud. They would, in effect, eliminate the boundary between them and the earth."[8.10]

In the early 1980s, Czarnopys began to

[After failing his U.S. Navy physical, photographer Ralston Crawford] enlisted in the camouflage division of the Army Engineers Corps. His six months in basic training at Fort Meade, Maryland, were psychologically disastrous. For him "the enemy was not Hitler, or Mussolini" but what he considered "those miserable, stupid and sometimes vicious people" who conducted the recruits through basic training "in modern assassination techniques."

—BARBARA HASKELL
Ralston Crawford,
p. 62.

[During World War II, Myron Kozman served for three years in a U.S. Army] camouflage battalion employing skills first developed in a camouflage course initiated at the School of Design in Chicago by György Kepes...

—ADAM J. BOXER
The New Bauhaus,
p. 7.

sculpt life-sized human figures, which were made in polyester resin (or fiberglas) from body casts, then covered with hauntingly natural "skins" of real tree bark and moss. Nearly all of his work from that period is unnerving

◀ **FIGURE 8.C**
Tom Czarnopys
Untitled sculpture (1985).
Collection of
Norman L. Sanderfield.
Photograph courtesy of
Zolla/Lieberman Gallery,
Chicago.

because it undermines our most sacrosanct categories; in particular, it is both persuasively *human* and *not*. He clearly remembers the time and the place when he realized the unsettling path he would take: "Once moving through the woods I saw a birch tree that had fallen over; the inside had rotted out, and what remained was very similar to arms and legs in size. I thought of that as a direct form of camouflage, and that's where this work

[As a captain in the British Camouflage Corps during World War II, theatre set designer Oliver Messel] disguised some pill-boxes as Gothic lodges and others as caravans, haystacks, ruins and wayside cafes, always with his meticulous attention to detail.

—Charles Castle
Oliver Messel: A Biography,
p. 114.

originated."[8.11]

A few years later, Czarnopys became the inadvertent cause of a law enforcement incident when he set up a bark-covered sculpture of a female figure in a remote wooded area in Michigan, tucking it into a blanket of moss. "My intent was just to leave it out and let the seasons take over and start layering things, and integrate it into the landscape. It was sort of an earth mother figure."[8.12]

Once he [American painter Meyer Abel] was even instrumental in getting a young man [graphic designer Noel Martin], who had just been drafted into the army, a spot in a camouflage school where his talent had some outlet or at least some company.

—EVELYN LEVY SHAW
"A Tribute to Meyer Abel"

Unfortunately, the sculpture was discovered by another deer hunter, who thought it was the shrouded corpse of a murder victim. He notified police, who brought in forensic investigators, followed by a television news team. "When they got very close," recalls Czarnopys, "they moved the moss aside and found the fiberglass. They thought they had a real sicko out in the woods. Somebody was murdering people and encasing their bodies in fiberglass."[8.13]

[American graphic designer Gene] Federico was drafted into the U.S. Army, where he served in the Camouflage Corps in the U.S., Europe, and North Africa.

—SAMUEL N. ANTUPIT
"Tribute: Gene Federico"

FIVE: IN 1984, an American ceramic artist named Marilyn Lysohir and her artist husband, Ross Coates, purchased a carved wooden ship model from an antique dealer in Lysohir's hometown of Sharon, Pennsylvania. At the time, they assumed that it must have been made by an untrained folk artist, a primitive or naif, because of the effusive range of colors—red, black, gray, white, green, yellow, and orange—and the seemingly random, desultory way in which they had been arranged.

Lysohir's mother had served in the U.S. Marine Corps during World War II, a factor that prompted the artist to make in 1980 a large ceramic sculpture titled *BAMs*, which is a Marine Corps vulgarity for women recruits (for "Big-Ass-Marines"). That ambitious clay installation consisted of eleven nearly life-sized sculpted figures of women Marines on a platform of tiles.

You see these Greeny-
Browny Blobs?
Well, that's a special kind of
Paint
That makes things look like
What they Ain't.
No fooling, it's the latest
thing—
It's called Disruptured
Patterning.

—GEOFFREY BARKAS
quoted in Hiller (1983).

Later, in the mid-1980s, after Lysohir and Coates had moved to Pullman, Washington, she found that she was still disturbed by the stories she had been told by her mother, her father, and others to whom she had talked about war. She decided to create a large-scale ceramic artwork that would poignantly challenge the legitimacy of warfare, not by depicting battlefield atrocities, but by focusing on its seductive appeal. With that theme in mind, she decided that the work's primary feature might consist of a huge variation on that brightly-colored wooden ship that she had purchased earlier. The resulting 24-foot, two-ton clay battleship (which was roughly modeled on the *U.S.S. Arizona*) would signify war, while its pleasant pastel color scheme would convey the mood of seductiveness.[8.14]

The domestic strawberry disguises certain of its leaves as the ripe fruit; this is the principle of dazzle camouflage [sic].

—IAN HAMILTON FINLAY
quoted in Abrioux,
p. 182.

Because the project was so huge, Lysohir constructed the clay battleship in a storefront studio that she rented in a nearby town. As she worked on it, dozens of curious townspeople walked by, peered in the window, and then came in to watch her work. She kept a daily journal of all the visitors and their comments. One of them was the historian for a local museum, who explained the use of dazzle-painting for ship camouflage in World Wars I and II. At last understanding the origin of the wooden ship model, she decided to formally title her work "The Dark Side of Dazzle."

▶ **FIGURE 8.D**
Marilyn Lysohir
The Dark Side of Dazzle (1986), ceramic installation.

In the finished artwork, the large, central battleship was surrounded by 24 wooden chairs on which viewers could sit as they listened to audio tapes (from speakers housed inside the ship) in which the artist's mother and other veterans of World War II, Korea and Vietnam recalled their wartime experiences, both amusing and horrific.

Named an official war artist [during World War II], he [American artist Paul Gerchik] drew political cartoons and posters to promote the war effort, taught camouflage to military personnel and pioneered art therapy for wounded soldiers in military hospitals.

—Anon
"Paul Gerchik"

In addition to the battleship, two other related components were part of the full installation: One was a life-sized clay figure of a woman, wrapped in a bath towel and walking toward a bathtub in which appeared to be floating a 4-foot clay model of a dazzle-painted battleship. The other was a bathroom sink with a medicine cabinet suspended on the wall above it. The door of the cabinet was partly open, and three small dazzle-painted ships were on the shelves inside.

SIX: Born in Chicago in 1936, American artist David Bower and his family moved out to the country when he was twelve years old. The farmhouse they moved into, remembered Bower, "was one of those old midwestern-style frame buildings which enlarged room by room, bit by bit as the original owner's family grew. Because of this additive building process, these houses seemed to have had more doors than present day houses. One was never quite certain what was beyond a closed door."[8.15]

As a college student, Bower majored in art at the University of Illinois and Northern Illinois University, then studied further for two years in Munich, Germany. When he returned to the U.S., he began to make box-like assemblages of childhood toys, old photographs, souvenirs, and other found objects. "I liked the biographical references in the work," he recalled, "and, through some mysterious and divergent process, it eventually led me to make small room environments."[8.16]

He began to make these miniature rooms (which he refers to as "shelf environments") in the mid 1970s. Most of them look like a cut-

From 1942 to 1945 he [American sculptor Gabriel Kohn] was a camouflage designer in the Army Air Corps.

—Edward Bryant in Kohn entry in Turner (1996).

away view of one wall from a highly-detailed living room from the 1930s or 40s. Constructed on shelves that are hung on the wall or installed on platforms, each of these works is about two feet wide, one foot high, and seven inches deep. The striped wallpapers, wood trim and doors, all of which are precisely crafted are, according to Bower, "somehow reminiscent of my childhood places."

...in 1940 he [French architect Charles Siclis] arrived in New York and tried to sell his inventions in the field of camouflage technology on the American market.

—JEAN-LOUIS COHEN
in Siclis entry
in Turner (1996).

He continues: "The partially opened and closed doors, the cage-like structures, the crawling boards along the floor which move up and over the tables and boxes all seem to come from feelings and thoughts lost somewhere in my subconscious."[8.17]

▲ **FIGURE 8.E**
DAVID BOWER
in his studio (c. 1983).

Like an impish harlequin, one of Bower's intentions is to tease the audience by suggesting while also withholding details, with the purpose of triggering closure. To that end, writes Bower, "I experimented with covering parts of the room with draped canvas and wrapped and tied objects in order to change their appearance."[8.18] In some, he shrewdly hides the names of streets or cities: "Let the viewer try to imagine what is under the drape or behind the curtain. This sort of mischievous attitude about hiding led me to think about camouflage as the ultimate kind of visual hiding."[8.19]

Early in the development of these rooms, while browsing through a military aircraft book, he recalls that he "became intrigued with the variety and richness of camouflage... I began painting the various camouflage patterns and colors directly on the surfaces of the rooms and the objects. I did this long before the trendy use of camouflage pattern in today's clothing fashions. The camouflage had

a rich painterly look about it and the objects in the rooms magically and mysteriously dissolved."[8.20]

▲ FIGURE 8.F
David Bower
Sheep Have No Fear Because of Their Whiteness (1980), mixed media shelf environment.

Sometimes his rooms play up the link between camouflage and psychoanalysis, as when he assigns them such titles as *Room for Sigmund*, *A Jung Room* and *Rollo's Room*. Others are allusions to Surrealist poetry, or to the contents of memorable books. He concludes: "I've always wanted to build places where

During World War II [Australian photographer Max] Dupain worked first in a camouflage unit and then for the Department of Information...

—ROBERT SMITH
in Dupain entry
in Turner (1996).

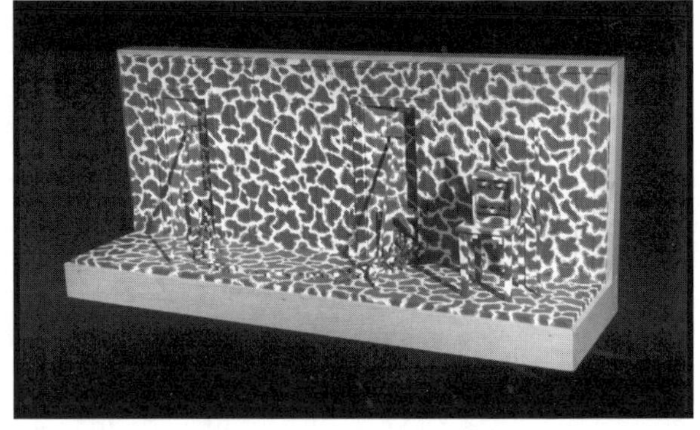

▶ **FIGURES 8.G, 8.H and 8.I**
DAVID BOWER
Mixed media shelf environments, including (from top to bottom) *Room at Himmelstrasse* (1977), *Hide and Seek* (1979), and *A Jung Room* (1977).

things can happen. Like those childhood fantasies when all the lights are turned out and things begin to appear to be what they are not. I've always wanted to quickly turn on the light and witness these strange shapes and mysterious forms in their new reality."[8.21] ✂

Higher and higher we went [on his first airplane flight]. What a cubist painting below, and cubist paintings would appeal, if only they could catch some of the beauty of color and design of all those lovely patches on the canvas beneath us.

—Harry E. Townsend
quoted in Cornebise
(1991b), p. 238.

EXPIRED
1 HOUR
2 HOURS

Chapter Nine

Outraging the Law of the Excluded Middle

Camouflage and Improvisation

TWENTY YEARS AGO, when I wrote a book titled *Art and Camouflage: Concealment and Deception in Nature, Art and War*, it ended with a chapter on "Camouflage and Creativity." More experienced, I believe now it's probably better to say "improvisation" instead of "creativity." Although the terms are used interchangeably, they imply different meanings in the sense that they represent opposite ways of fostering inventive thought.

When art is defined as an activity driven entirely by the needs of self-expression, I become very nervous. The overwhelming history of art, in fact, has been the history of people doing work for a specific purpose, in other words, commissioned work for specific intentions.

—MILTON GLASER
Art Is Work

◀ **FIGURE 9.A**
WALTER HAMADY
Existence Requires Revision of Our Physiognomic Notions (1994). Collage, assemblage, construction, objet trouvé. Private collection.

In current usage, the word "creativity" has become associated almost exclusively with psychic automatism or self-expression, with the goal that a student should learn to "express" himself or herself, to find his or her "true self"—a lifelong legitimate aim to be sure, but one that is rarely attainable at age 18. To often, this is carried out with insufficient regard for the quality and complexity of that expression, so that, as Oscar Wilde remarked, some of the most maudlin, uninteresting art is produced by naive but well-meaning people from the most genuine emotions.

In contrast, the term "improvisation" is associated with design-based problem-solving, whether graphic, interior, product, architectural, or engineering design. In design classrooms, students are rarely expected to bare their inner souls but rather to respond to tasks that have been put to them by someone else, most likely a client or teacher. Unlike "creative" artists, designers are accustomed to working within limits, and, like improvisational actors or comedians, they strain to arrive at a way to respond that is both functional and innovative—and, inevitably, self-expressive.

[In contrast to the "psychic automatism" of the Surrealists, the Swiss painter Paul Klee] favored a mode of "psychic improvisation" whereby the spontaneous gestures of pen or brush are studied, interpreted, even supervised by a purposive, lucid intelligence.

—ROGER CARDINAL in Wintle, p. 206.

An additional problem with the word "creativity" is its tendency to be misleading, in the sense that it often prompts students to make forms that are extraordinarily prosaic, unimaginative and uninventive, the exact opposite of anything fresh or thought-provoking. This happens in part when a person assumes that the verb "to create" means the same thing in art and design as it does in the Old Testament, in which Jehovah made something out of nothing.

[Today, in art schools and university art departments] virtually all our instruction goes into fostering individuality. It's hardly possible to imagine an art classroom at the beginning of the twenty-first century—at least in Europe and America—where students are encouraged *not* to try to find individual voices and styles.

—JAMES ELKINS *Why Art Cannot Be Taught*, p. 21.

As mere human beings, we do not have the option of "creating" things: It is not within our capacity to produce anything out of thin air. Rather, the entire range of human innovation (whether works of art and literature, design solutions, scientific discoveries, or new technologies) has come from the recombination of pre-existing components, by a process that Einstein referred to (in a famous introspective note about his own creative process) as *combinatory play*.[9.1]

I myself discovered this in a roundabout way, over the span of a decade. It took so long not because I lacked determination, but rather because I mistakenly thought that I had to inoculate myself from strong influences to ensure that the work I "created" would be wholly mine. I could not be convinced back then that my ideas were neither unprecedented nor revelatory, that my mind had been marked by a torrent of sorted and unsorted—and sordid—influences since before I had even emerged from the womb. I was not and had never been an innocent eye, a blank slate, a *tabula rasa*. In the end, I decided that I would assuredly grow not by *avoiding* strong, positive role models (in the hope of preserving an unalloyed self) but by *actively seeking* the influence of the widest assortment of strong people, ideas and attitudes.

If I experienced an epiphany, I believe that a lot of the credit belongs to a book I discovered when I was still an undergraduate. First published in 1964 (the year I graduated from high school), it was Arthur Koestler's *The Act of Creation*, a lengthy, elaborate theory of art, scientific discovery and humor: "The originality of genius, in art as in science," wrote Koestler, "consists of a shift of attention to aspects of reality previously ignored, discover-

People often say that this or that person has not yet found himself. But the self is not something that one finds. It is something that one creates.

—Thomas Sasz

One of the illusions people have who don't know about the making of art is that it's an activity that comes out of a creative surge, a genius or passion. What is missed most of the time is how deliberate and how structured the choices that artists make are, and how one can read in works of art the intellectual process that was taking place in the mind of the artist.

—Mira Merriman
quoted in
Deutelbaum, p. 13.

ing hidden connections, seeing familiar objects or events in a new light."[9.2]

I was drawn to that book by its Hungarian author's name, which I recognized from *Darkness at Noon*, his chilling political novel about the show trials and purges in Stalinist Russia. While even the length of this new book was intimidating (my first copy was a 750-page Dell paperback, printed on exceedingly thin paper), I painfully, doggedly tried to embrace its assertions over the next few years, while it gradually altered my thinking and profoundly affected the way that I worked—and still work—as an artist, designer, writer, and teacher.

Jews weren't allowed to carry over a certain amount of cash on the street in Prague...And my father was out on the street one day with what he knew was more than the amount of cash in his pocket that he was supposed to have. And he was stopped and picked up. The cops took him into the police station, and he was supposed to empty his pockets. So he's desperate, but he got this brain wave. He took his handkerchief which he had in his pocket and he wrapped it around the money and pulled it out and blew his nose, and the money was in the handkerchief. Then he cleared his pockets out, and it was okay. They didn't look in his hand, but the money was in his handkerchief. He just stuck it back in his pocket and walked out free.

—MARIANNE ROSS
quoted in Zeitlin, et al., p. 25.

One consequence of this was that I began to think less strictly of human endeavors as inherently contained within rigid conceptual partitions like art, language, psychology, physics, and so on. I began to read and observe more widely, and to regard experience as a cross-section in which previously disparate fields could be linked by such universal form principles as rhyme, analogy, metaphor, montage, and metamorphosis.

I also came to realize the value and significance of humor, the usefulness of accidents and mistakes, and the importance of unconscious ruminating or incubation. Through the writings of Koestler—which I read at the same time as various books by Rudolf Arnheim (*Art and Visual Perception*), E.H. Gombrich (*Art and Illusion*), Lancelot Law Whyte (*Aspects of*

Form), György Kepes (*Language of Vision* and his *Vision + Value* series), Laszlo Moholy-Nagy (*Vision in Motion*), Michel Foucault (*The Order of Things*), Claude Lévi-Strauss (*The Savage Mind*), Edmund Leach (*Culture and Communication*), Gregory Bateson (*Steps to an Ecology of Mind*), Gertrude Stein (*The Autobiography of Alice B. Toklas*), Christopher Alexander (*Notes on the Synthesis of Form*), Morse Peckham (*Man's Rage for Chaos*), Colin Turbayne (*The Myth of Metaphor*), H.G. Barnett (*Innovation: The Basis of Cultural Change*), and Thomas Kuhn (*The Structure of Scientific Revolutions*), among many others—I became deeply interested in human psychology, namely the psychology of perception, psychoanalysis and problem-solving. This eventually merged with my interests in ethology, prestidigitation, ventriloquism, poetry, humor, madness, typography, protective coloration, and military camouflage; and with that, I also then realized that I had followed a tacit, circuitous route that had begun with Koestler's definition of the creative process as "the discovery of hidden similarities" or *bisociation* (perceiving things "in two self-consistent but incompatible frames of reference at the same time"),[9.3] and had come full circle in arriving at Abbott H. Thayer's laws of disguise—figure-ground blending, figure disruption (or dazzle), and coincident disruption—in which two things are seen as one, or one thing looks like two or more.

You could say to him [the poet W.H. Auden]: "Please write me a double ballade on the virtues of a certain brand of toothpaste, which also contains at least ten anagrams on the names of well-known politicians, and of which the refrain is as follows..." Within twenty-four hours your ballade would be ready—and it would be good.

—CHRISTOPHER ISHERWOOD

The blood of the poet is what blood banks call "Rh positive"; his is the two-fold Rh of rhyme and rhythm; together they are his rhapsody, his rhaps + ody, his (in Greek) "ode-stitching." In the ballet of words, rhyme is the *pas de deux* of mated contraries; rhythm is Time in leotards.

—PETER VIERECK
"Strict Wildness: The Biology of Poetry" in *Poets and Writers Magazine* (May/June 1988), p. 8.

At some now long forgotten point, I knew that the passkey to both camouflage and innovation is, as Kenneth Burke had said, a violation of the law of the excluded middle (*A is A and not not-A*). It is (in Arthur Koestler's terms) bisociative thinking, an "unlikely marriage of cabbages and kings—of previously unrelated frames of reference or universes of discourse," whereby we say instead that *A is both A and not-A*.[9.4]

At dinner, Claude Levi-Strauss—very charming toward me. But we didn't talk much. Only in the taxi did I realize I'd taken Levi-Strauss's raincoat by mistake.

—MIRCEA ELIADE
Journal IV 1979-1985
University of Chicago Press, 1990, p. 19.

While in graduate school in Rhode Island, I began to write to Koestler (who was living in London), partly to tell him how much I enjoyed *The Act of Creation*. I had also become an amateur lepidopterist, and with one letter, I sent him a mounted butterfly, inscribed with its Latin name. At the time, he was an outspoken critic of behaviorism, of which the chief proponent was the Harvard psychologist B.F. Skinner. In appreciation of the butterfly, he replied with a humorous holiday card that contained a reproduction of a tapestry of St. George slaying the dragon. Below, beside a hand-drawn arrow pointing to the dragon, he had written *Drakon Skinneris*.

A day sadly spoiled by my growing infirmity—absence of mind. After going to University College Committee, I went to J. Taylor's, to exchange hats, having taken his last night; but he had not mine there. I took an omnibus to Addison Road, drank tea with Paynter, and then went to Taylor's to restore his hat; and then found that I had a second time blundered by bringing Paynter's old hat; and I lost an hour in going to and from Addison Road, and from and to Sheffield House.

—HENRY CRABB ROBINSON
(diary entry April 7, 1847)
in Brett, *The Faber Book of Diaries*, p. 125.

IN *MODERN TIMES*, the silent film star Charlie Chaplin plays a factory worker whose assembly-line assignment is to tighten bolts as they move along a conveyor. Chaplin's character goes berserk from the monotony of his job. He adopts a mechanical rhythm and begins to treat all round things (breasts, noses, buttons) as if they were forms to be tightened.

In another famous Chaplin film, *The Gold Rush*, he plays a prospector who is stranded in

▲ **FIGURE 9.B**
Tom Grothus
Already Scratched (1983).

a cabin in the Yukon. He becomes so hungry that he cooks his shoe in a stew, peels off the shoe leather and tongue, eats the shoe strings like spaghetti, and treats the nails like bones.

These two episodes are among the most memorable and hilarious of any in Chaplin's films. Both were written and produced by the actor, but we might at first suspect that they were written by Karl Duncker, the Gestalt psychologist whose experiments with functional fixedness were discussed in an earlier chapter. In the example we cited, subjects were given a nail, weight and cord, and asked to make a pendulum. Wall space was provided, but no hammer, so that (like Chaplin, and Josef Albers' students at the Bauhaus) they resorted to substituting one thing for another, using commonplace objects in unorthodox and

...I suddenly thought I had got it: I"saw" a book with the odd but promising title *Deceptive Beetles*—obviously some treatise on camouflage. Alas, as I looked more closely the title turned out to read *Decisive Battles*.

—E.H. Gombrich
"Visual Discovery through Art" in J. Hogg, ed., *Psychology and the Visual Arts*. Middlesex, England: Penguin Books, 1969.

inventive ways. It does not take much to imagine Chaplin's sight gags as Duncker-like experiments in problem-solving: Given a shoe and a stew, make them into a meal. Given a wrench and a nose, what can you find to tighten?

On one level these are confusions in which A is naively mistaken for something which it is not, for which Colin Turbayne proposed the term *sort-trespassing*. But on another level they are examples of *sort-crossing* (also his term), which are intentional mock confusions of the type that are found universally in jokes, puns, rhymes, analogies, and other word play.

Sometimes these intentional errors occur when a speaker pretends to have a foreign accent, as Chico Marx invariably did in the films of the Marx Brothers. In one scene, for example, he mistakes the word "taxes" for "Texas," and when "taxes" is defined as "dollars," he continues the error: "Thatsa right—I gotta uncle that lives in Dollahs. Dollahs, Taxes." In other scenes, he says: "You got a haddock? I gotta haddock too. Whatta you take for a haddock?" and "Sturgeon. Sturgeon. Thatsa doctor thatta cuts you up." (The mathematician Norbert Wiener's German grandmother never learned to distinguish the word "kitchen" from "kitten," and friends of mine for whom English is a second language have confused "garbage" with "cabbage," "snakes" with "snacks," "splinter" with "spinster," "condo" with "condom," and "proxy" with "epoxy.")

Starting in September I already began thinking about what snow in Iowa would be like. As autumn wore on and winter came, that promise was approaching . . . until one morning when I woke up I heard a noise at the bedroom window. It sounded like a bird lightly touching the glass. While I was coming fully awake I had memories of similar sounds, such as that of some strange animal rubbing against the glass. And suddenly I remembered the snow, and I jumped out of bed and went to the window. There it was: snow. During the night the whole countryside had changed to white as if by magic. I was so excited that we had to get dressed and run out into the street to feel the light, magical Iowa snow.

—ALFREDO VEIRAVÉ
[Argentine poet]
"Memories of Iowa City and the International Writing Program" in Engle, pp. 195-196.

Inadvertent discoveries come not only from language errors, pretended or otherwise, but just as commonly from other unusual or spurious ways of seeing the world, which may result from youthfulness, lack of training, cultural or temporal displacement, defective vision, mental illness, and so on. Almost daily episodes on radio and television use children's unrehearsed replies to adult-level questions to make them appear to be gurus, poets or stand-up comedians. In one study, a child was overheard to say (as one might expect of an adult poet) that snowflakes are butterflies.

The American architect and inventor R. Buckminster Fuller believed that he became adept at categorical boundary-breaking because he was born cross-eyed: "I could see only large patterns," he recalled, "houses, trees and outlines of people—and all coloring was blurred...Not until I was four years old, in 1899, was it discovered that my cross-eyedness was caused by my being abnormally farsighted. Lenses fully corrected my vision. Despite my new ability to apprehend details, my childhood's spontaneous dependence only upon big patterns has persisted."[9.5] Likewise, because the cartoon character Mister Magoo is so profoundly nearsighted, he mistakes a front-loading washing machine for a television, with the result that he watches a program on clothes.

Did y'hear they crossed a mink with a gorilla? They got a real nice coat but the sleeves were too long.

—HENNY YOUNGMAN

[Laszlo] Moholy-Nagy had a wonderful way of using words as if in error or through not understanding—sometimes, I suspect, on purpose. On one occasion John Betjeman had taken him to a party. As Moholy left he said to the hostess in his strange pronunciation, "Thank you for your hostilities." She was a little taken aback, and when Moholy told John Betjeman what had happened, Betjeman said: "Oh don't worry—she is hostile to everyone."

—JACK PRITCHARD
View From a Long Chair, p. 124.

Years ago, I sometimes used a classroom game in which students were provided with two lists of fifteen kinds of things:

[As a result of poor eyesight] I once entered a bank in Stratford-on-Avon and ordered a drink. I have waved back at people waving at someone else. There was an electric sky sign in All Saints, Manchester, which said UPHOLSTERED FURNITURE and I read as UPROARIOUSLY FUNNY. In the army I failed to salute officers and, fiercely rebuked, then saluted privates. I have spoken to women in the streets I thought I knew and thus got to know them…The myopic eye is not lazy: it is too busy creating meanings out of vague données. Compensation for life-long myopia comes in old age: presbyopia supervenes on the condition and cancels it. I am forced now into perfect sight and I am not sure I like it.

—ANTHONY BURGESS
Little Wilson and Big God: The Autobiography. New York: Wiedenfeld & Nicolson, 1986, pp. 69-70.

A	**Not-A**
peanut butter	tambourine
hat	egg
corkscrew	shoe
Swiss knife	binoculars
stamp	colander
et cetera	*et cetera*

While trying to do "what no one else will think of," each student was instructed to select any object from column A and any from column Not-A, then treat the first as if it were the second, or vice versa.

Most of the hybrids produced by this and similar exercises were silly and innocuous, but it is the same tomfoolery that commonly occurs in art, literature and humor, as well as in problem-solving experiments in psychology. If "weight" is the object I choose (as in Duncker's experiment) and "hammer" the object in the facing column, I can pound nails with weights. Chaplin, on the other hand, might substitute bones for nails, or spaghetti for string, or shoes for food.

This kind of two-list matching game has long been reliably used by comedy writers and other film and television scriptwriters, as is demonstrated by a classroom game I sometimes used as a follow-up to the matching exercise: Having bisociated items from the two lists in the first problem, divide into arbitrarily-assigned groups with other students, and build a short skit with your matches.

Such skits are occasions for nervous laughter, in part because nonsense is likely to cause a certain amount of distress and emotional uneasiness, and laughter (the spasmodic "coordinated contraction of fifteen facial muscles in a stereotyped pattern and accompanied by altered breathing"[9.6]) is a convenient way to alleviate that tension.

ACCORDING TO the mathematician Jacob Bronowski, innovation comes about from "explosions of a hidden likeness" in which the innovator begins with "two aspects of nature and fuses them into one."[9.7] The key ingredient, explains Harry Broudy, is "the rearranging of previously experienced elements into new configurations."[9.8] Or, in the words of Francis A. Cartier: "There is only one way in which a person acquires a new idea: by the combination or association of two or more ideas he already has into a new juxtaposition in such a manner as to discover a relationship among them of which he was not previously aware. An idea is a feat of association."[9.9]

Aside from puns, the best known example of a feat of association is a *metaphor*, with the result that sort-crossing is commonly called a "metaphorical way of knowing." Aristotle said that "the greatest thing by far is to be a

He [his father] loved to call things by the wrong names—or, it may be, the right ones, fantastically the right ones. Either extreme is poetry, of which he had the secret without knowing that he did. It was natural for him to name two lively rams on the place Belshazzar and Nebuchadnezzar... Frank became Fritz Augustus—just why, I never inquired—and I was either Marcus Aurelius or Marco Bozzaris. Guy was Guy Bob, and Carl was Carlo. And Paul, when it came for him to share in the illicit luxuriance, was no other than Wallace P. Poggin—again, I have no faint idea why. My father never discussed his inspirations, any more than he analyzed his spoonerisms, or even admitted that they had fallen from his mouth. He would cough, and appear to apologize by saying: "I have a little throakling in my tit."

—MARK VAN DOREN *The Autobiography of Mark Van Doren* (New York: Greenwood Press, 1968).

master of metaphor"; it is a "sign of genius," he claimed, "since a good metaphor implies an intuitive perception of the similarity in dissimilars."[9.10] Metaphor, William B. Stanford proposed, is "a stereoscope of ideas."[9.11]

Once he [British educator A.S. Neill] visited a school in Stockholm, and was taken in to a geography lesson. He went up to the map on the wall, pointed to Italy, and said: "This is London."

—GRETA SERGEANT quoted in Jonathan Croall, *Neill of Summerhill: The Permanent Rebel.* New York: Pantheon Books, 1983 p. 229.

To understand Stanford's metaphorical definition of metaphor, it is helpful to know that stereoscopic or 3-D vision is a consequence of binocular disparity. Hold an upright pencil at arm's length and view it with one eye at a time in rapid succession—the right, the left, the right and so on. The pencil will appear to move because the eyes are spaced apart, so that, in normal perception, the eyes receive two differing views which the brain then reconciles as one.

In stereo photography, the subject is simultaneously photographed by two cameras, or by one containing two lenses. (Or, more simply, you can make stereo photographs with one camera and a subject that doesn't move by shifting the camera an inch or two to the side before taking the second shot.) Viewed separately, or when both are viewed by both eyes, stereo pictures seem perfectly flat. But when viewed through a stereoscope (a device that enables one image to be seen only by the right eye, the other only by the left), the figure pops out from the background.

As everyone knows, metaphors are not *really* stereoscopes. Yet, they both provide a fusion of disparates, and, in each instance, the paired components must be experienced simultaneously yet, to some extent, separately. Both result in the paradoxical integration of diversities, a perception of the similarity in dissimilars.

To apply this model, imagine for a moment that one lens of a stereoscope belongs to Don Quixote, who, as his creator Miguel de Cervantes explained, was "completely out of his mind." Imagine that the other lens belongs to his loyal if unimaginative companion, Sancho Panza, whose outlook on life is prosaic.

If Don Quixote were a stand-up comedian, Sancho would be his straight man, for the latter knows that *A is A*, that a windmill is simply a windmill. But Don Quixote is deranged (he is "out of contact with reality," says Cervantes) and, in his mind, things are not as they would seem to a person of normal perception. To Don Quixote, *A* and *not-A* are the same, and instead of the windmills that Sancho perceives, he sees only giants.

In Don Quixote's mind, Sancho Panza is a squire, his horse a steed, and a prostitute a lady. When Sancho hears "nothing but the bleating of sheep and lambs," Don Quixote hears "the neighing of steeds, the sound of trumpets and the rattling of drums." In one incident, the maniacal knight dumps curds on his head: "What can this mean?" he wonders, "Methinks my skull is softening, or

A discussion between [British biologist J.B.S.] Haldane and a friend began to take a predictable turn. The friend said with a sigh, "It's no use going on. I know what you will say next, and I know what you will do next." The distinguished scientist promptly sat down on the floor, turned two back somersaults, and returned to his seat. "There," he said with a smile. "That's to prove that you're not always right."

—Clifton Fadiman
The Little, Brown Book of Anecdotes

Having an imagination, it takes you an hour to write a paragraph that, if you were unimaginative, would take only a minute. Or you might not write the paragraph at all.

—Franklin P. Adams

my brains melting, or I sweat from head to foot!" Later, he attacks a bag of wine, mistaking it for a giant with a "head" as large as a wine skin, and when the burgundy wine pours out, he thinks the wine is giant's blood.

By this stereoscopic model, neither Don Quixote nor Sancho Panza can exemplify a metaphor. They are each half-blind; or, in terms that I.A. Richards used, one is *tenor*, the other *vehicle*.[9.12] Viewed separately, they themselves do not make tropes. Instead, the metaphors are made by the author, who makes them happen by presenting simultaneously two divergent points of view, and by those who read the novel, who re-create those sort-crossings in the process of reading.

Man likes to bring two things together into one...He lives by making associations and he is doing well by himself and in himself when he thinks of something in connection with something else that no one ever put with it before. That's what we call a metaphor.

—ROBERT FROST quoted in John Ciardi, *Dialogue with an Audience*. New York: J.P. Lippincott, 1963, p. 172.

A madman, Michel Foucault has said, "takes things for what they are not, and people one for another; he cuts his friends and recognizes complete strangers; he thinks he is unmasking when, in fact, he is putting on a mask...he is unaware of Difference."[9.13]

The moon is a sickle for pruning the stars.

—JANE YOLEN

If Don Quixote is the madman in Cervantes' novel, Magoo is his cartoon counterpart, while Waldo is equal to Sancho. In the same sense, Watson is the pedestrian sidekick of Sherlock Holmes, whose source of extraordinary insight is his irrepressible brilliance, which enables him to unearth clues that Watson and others could never have detected. However, in most inventions, as in most standup comedy, there is no need for a Watson or a

Sancho, since the audience sees through the filters of the straight man.

THE LAW OF IDENTITY tells us that *A is A*; while the law of contradiction says that *Not-A is not A*. The algorithm for translogical or inventive thinking is *A is both A and Not-A*, which is, as earlier mentioned, an outrage of the law of the excluded middle. It is paradoxical or stereoscopic awareness, in which the conventional (Sancho Panza) and the unconventional (Don Quixote) are juxtaposed within one mind.

In your eyes there lives
a green egyptian noise.

—E.E. CUMMINGS

This is the logical structure of puns (*taxes* is and is not *Texas*), similes (*hearts* are like and unlike *pumps*), analogies (*hat* is to *body* as *attic* is to *house*), religious paradoxes (*wine* is and is not *blood*), parables, irony, double entendre, riddles, rhymes, caricature, metamorphoses, allegories, epigrams, alliteration, assonance, hyperbole, impersonation, parodies, witticisms, acronyms, and spoonerisms.

As this book has sought to demonstrate, it is also the logical structure of art, dreams, jokes, magic, poetry, psychoneurotic digressions—and camouflage. ✂

I THINK IT likely that there are no finer galleries of abstract art than the cabinet drawers of the tropical butterfly collector...It is often, I believe, the fascination of this abstract color and design, as much as an interest in biology or a love of nature, that allures the ardent lepidoterist, although all these may be combined; he has his favorite genera and dotes upon his different species of *Vanessa* and *Parnassius*, as the modernist does upon his examples of Matisse or Ben Nicolson.

—ALISTER HARDY
The Living Stream, p. 151.

Notes

Footnotes are the little dogs yapping at the heels of the text.

—William James

1.1 See Wertheimer's paper in Ellis (1939). **1.2** For more on Arnheim's life and work, see Arnheim (1984) and Behrens (1998c) and (1998d). **1.3** Weiss (1971), p. 5. **1.4** Heider (1973). **1.5** Arnheim (1964), p. 1. **1.6** Kepes (1944), p. 46. **1.7** Arnheim in Whyte (1966), p. 201. **1.8** Cary (1965), p. 145. **1.9** Whistler, *The Gentle Art of Making Enemies* (1893). **1.10** Hogarth, *The Analysis of Beauty* (1735). **1.11** Arnheim (1964), p. 1. **1.12** Wright in Kaufmann and Raeburn (1960), pp. 296-297. **1.13** Tafel (1979), p. 91. **1.14** See Behrens (1998b). **1.15** Wright said this, for example, in a television interview with Mike Wallace in 1957. **1.16** Lupton and Miller (1996), p. 62. **1.17** Richter (1965), p. 34. **1.18** For these and other examples, see Richter (1965). **1.19** Lautréamont, quoted in William S. Rubin (1968), p. 19. **1.20** Ernst, quoted in Ghiselin (1955), p. 66. **1.21** See Behrens (2000c). **1.22** Arnheim (1964), p. 1. **1.23** Richter (1985). **1.24** Gombrich (1979), p. 9. **1.25** Arnheim (1954). **1.26** Csikszentmihalyi (1990), p. 52. **1.27** Ibid., p. 53. **1.28** Koestler (1964), p. 338. **1.29** For more on Zeigarnik, see Stroebel, et al. (1980), p. 310. **1.30** Gombrich (1969). **1.31** Koestler (1964), p. 338.

2.1 Keen (1931), p. 202. **2.2** Ibid. **2.3** See A.H. Thayer entry in *National Cyclopedia of American Biography.* **2.4** Faulkner (1973), p. 19. **2.5** White (1951), p. 185. **2.6** Faulkner (1973), p. 20. **2.7** Ibid. **2.8** Kent (1955), p. 109. **2.9** Meryman (1999). **2.10** White (1951), p. 90. **2.11** A.H. Thayer (1902). **2.12** Chapman (1933), p. 78. **2.13** Faulkner (1973), p. 18. **2.14** A.H. Thayer, quoted in White (1951), p. 254. **2.15** White (1951), p. 112. **2.16** Bowditch (1970), p. 188. **2.17** Sumrall (1973). **2.18** A.H. Thayer (1902), p. 597. **2.19** A.H. Thayer (1896), p. 127. **2.20** Ibid. **2.21** White (1951), p. 109. **2.22** Anderson (1982), p. 116. **2.23** A.H. Thayer (1918), p. 494. **2.24** Roosevelt, quoted in Cutright (1956), p. 228. **2.25** Ibid., p. 232. **2.26** Roosevelt, quoted in Allen (1911), p. 472. **2.28** Cortissoz (1923), p. 40. **2.29** Bowditch (1970), p. 151. **2.30** White (1951), p. 190. **2.31** Hobbs (1982), p. 55. **2.32** James, quoted in Faxon (1989), p. 138.

3.1 See Mount (1955), pp. 345-348. **3.2** For more about Fry, see Behrens (1996a). **3.3** Faulkner (1973), p. 85. **3.4** Ibid., p. 87. **3.5** "Wants Camouflage Force" (1917), p. 14. **3.6** "Seeing But Not Seen" (1918), p. 451. **3.7** Faulkner (1973). **3.8** Ibid., p. 88. **3.9** "Seeing But Not Seen" (1918). **3.10** Ibid. **3.11** Faulkner (1973), p. 92. **3.12** E.L. Kahn (1984), p. 14. **3.13** Ibid. 3.14 Ibid. **3.15** Sypher (1960), p. 70. **3.16** Kahn (1984), p. 19. **3.17** Stein (1933). **3.18** Picasso, quoted in J. Richardson (1996), p. 349. **3.19** See Glimcher (1986), pp. 83-87. **3.20** Braque, quoted in Liebermann (1969), p. 143. **3.21** Heider (1973), p. 71. **3.22** Ibid. **3.23** Hartmann (1935), p. 203. **3.24** Köhler (1947), pp. 92-93. **3.25** Koffka (1935), p. 77. **3.26** See Behrens (2000b). **3.27** Metzger, quoted in Ash (1995), p. 385. **3.28** Towle (1917). **3.29** Quoted in E.L. Kahn (1984), p. 98. **3.30** See J. Richardson (1996), p. 352. **3.31** Solomon (1920a). **3.32** Hardy (1965). **3.33** Crowell (1919), pp. 362-363. **3.34** Ibid., p. 362. **3.35** Ibid., p. 364. **3.36** Smith (1917), p. 468. **3.37** Ibid., p. 477. **3.38** Stein (1933).

4.1 See Chapter 2 in Hartcup (1980); and Roskam [English insert] (1987). **4.2** Hartcup (1980). **4.3** Designers will find it of interest to learn that among the Americans who perished on the Lusitania were

Elbert and Alice Hubbard, proprietors of the Roycroft Workshops in East Aurora, New York. **4.4** Hartcup (1980), pp. 35-40. **4.5** Wilkinson (1969), p. 79. **4.6** Wilkinson, "The Dazzle Painting of Ships" (1919), reprinted in *Camouflage* (1988). **4.7** See Wilkinson (1969). **4.8** See B. Wadsworth (1989). **4.9** Wilkinson, "The Dazzle Painting of Ships" in *Camouflage* (1988). **4.10** Quoted in Wilkinson (1969), p. 96. **4.11** See Wilkinson (1969). **4.12** See Behrens (1999). **4.13** Warner (1919a and b). **4.14** Toch (1931). **4.15** Warner, quoted in White (1951), p. 138. **4.16** Roosevelt, quoted in Wilkinson (1969), pp. 90-91. **4.17** Van Buskirk (1919). **4.18** "A Theatre for Studying Camouflaged Ship Models" (1919). **4.19** Warner (1919b). **4.20** Behrens (1999), p. 56. **4.21** See Cork (1994), p. 193, and Adams (1989), p. 86. **4.22** Warner (1919a and b). **4.23** Warner (1919a and b). **4.24** Warner (1919b), p. 108. **4.25** A copy of this unpublished manual was kindly provided to me by Warner's son, Thomas E. Warner. **4.26** Warner (1919), p. 218. **4.27** Hurst (1919), p. 93. **4.28** Quoted in Roskam (1987), DeKay (1918), and "Camouflage" (1939). **4.29** Quoted in Wilkinson (1969), p. 92. **4.30** D.R.E. Brown (1963), p. 2. **4.31** Ibid. **4.32** See G.H. Thayer (1909), illustration facing page 152. **4.33** Kerr (1919), pp. 204-205. **4.34** Wilkinson (1919), pp. 304-305. **4.35** Wilkinson, "The Dazzle Painting of Ships" in *Camouflage* (1988). **4.36** Fusscass (1992). **4.37** Ibid. **4.38** Ibid., p. 36.

5.1 For more on Mahler and Gropius, see Hochman (1997). **5.2** Ibid., p. 11. **5.3** Gropius, quoted in Wingler (1969), p. 31. **5.4** See Hochman (1997). **5.5** Arnheim (1997). **5.6** See Tilmann Buddensieg, ed., *Architecture and Design*. New York: Cooper-Hewitt Museum, 1987, p. 30. **5.7** See Teuber (1976). **5.8** Beckmann, quoted in Neumann (1993), p. 209). **5.9** Kranz, quoted in Neumann (1993), p. 276. **5.10** See M.E. Chevreul, *The Principles of Harmony and Contrast of Colors*. New York: Garland, 1980. **5.11** Watts (1969), p. 19. **5.12** Bateson (1972). **5.13** Source unknown. **5.14** See Fritjof Capra, *The Tao of Physics*. Berkeley, California: Shambhala, 1975. **5.15** See Behrens (2000b). **5.16** See J.L. Locher, ed., *The World of M.C. Escher*. New York: Harry N. Abrams, 1971. **5.17** Watts (1969). **5.18** A. Conan Doyle in "The Boscombe Valley Mystery" in *The Adventures of Sherlock Holmes* (1892). **5.19** Kierkegaard (1959), p. 32. **5.20** See Harris (1987). **5.21** Albers, quoted in Harold Osborne, ed., *The Oxford Companion to Twentieth-Century Art*. New York: Oxford University Press, 1981, p. 12. **5.22** Albers (1963). **5.23** See Karl Duncker, "On Problem-Solving" in J.F. Dashiell, ed., *Psychological Monographs* 58:5 (1945). **5.24** Dearstyne (1986), pp. 90-91. **5.25** Ibid., p. 92. **5.26** Ibid. **5.27** For more on Froebel's influence, see Lupton and Miller (1991), and Brosterman (1997). **5.28** Schlemmer (1972), p. 378. **5.29** See S. Moholy-Nagy (1969) and Kostelanetz (1970). **5.30** S. Moholy-Nagy, quoted in Kostelanetz (1970), p. 24. **5.31** Ibid. **5.32** Ibid. **5.33** Ibid., p. 179. **5.34** Kepes (1944), p. 45. **5.35** Ibid., p. 4.

6.1 Weiss (1971). **6.2** Gombrich in Renier and Rubinstein (1986). **6.3** Ibid., pp. 75-76. **6.4** For more on chance images, see Janson (1973) and Behrens (2000b). **6.5** See Gombrich (1969), p. 105-109. **6.6** Ibid., p. 188. **6.7** Gombrich (1969). **6.8** Rodari (1988). **6.9** Janson (1973), p. 352. **6.10** Behrens (2000b), **6.11** Köhler (1947), pp. 92-93. **6.12** Sloane (1942). **6.13** Cott (1940), p. 70. **6.14** See Behrens (1998c). **6.15** Jastrow, quoted in Gibson (1969), p. 38. **6.16** See Alastair Brotchie, ed., *A Book of Surrealist Games*. Boston: Shambhala Publications, 1995. **6.17** Jackson, quoted in "Freud on Dreams" entry in R.L. Gregory, ed., *The Oxford Companion to the Mind*. New York: Oxford University Press, 1987 p. 274. **6.18** Fallico (1962). **6.19** Dali, quoted in Romm and Slap (1983). **6.20** Ibid. 6.21 Freud, quoted in Rose (1987), p. 8. See also Behrens (2000c). **6.22** See Luis Buñuel, *My Last Sigh*. New York: Vintage Books, 1984. **6.23** Dali, quoted in Wintle (1984), p. 85. **6.24** Reik (1949). **6.25** Ibid. **6.26** Osborne in *The Oxford Companion to Twentieth-Century Art* (1981), p. 231. **6.27** Gorky, quoted in Schwabacher (1957), p. 81. **6.28** Ibid., p. 82. **6.29** Ibid., p. 82. **6.30** Spender (1999). **6.31** Levy (1972), p. 8.

7.1 Rose (1983). **7.2** Rawson (1938). **7.3** See Maskelyne (1949), and Fisher (1983). **7.4** Maskelyne (1949), p. 17. **7.5** For Cott's exquisite drawings, see Cott (1940). **7.6** Trevelyan (1957), p. 113. **7.7** Ibid., p. 112. **7.8** Ibid., p. 130. **7.9** Penrose (1941). **7.10** Trevelyan (1957), p. 117. **7.11** Penrose (1981), p. 130. **7.12** Goodman (1978), pp. 154-155. **7.13** Trevelyan (1957), p. 118. **7.14** Maskelyne (1949), p. 14. **7.15** Ibid. **7.16** Maskelyne (1949), p. 59. **7.17** Steinkraus (1979), p. 23. **7.18** Ibid., p. 25. **7.19** Dessoir, quoted in Steinkraus

(1979), p. 19. **7.20** Barzun (1984), p. 7. **7.21** Schiffman (1997), p. 367. **7.22** Cott (1938), p. 508. **7.23** Ibid., 508-509. **7.24** Sun Tzu, The Art of War. **7.25** Sypher (1960), p. 270. **7.26** Gablik (1992). **7.27** Ibid., p. 182. **7.28** See Milbourne Christopher, *The Illustrated History of Magic*. New York: Thomas Y. Crowell (1973), p. 161. **7.29** Fisher (1973), pp. 14-15. **7.30** Gardner (1960), pp. 10-11. **7.31** Fisher (1973), p. 11. **7.32** Florence Becker Lennon, in Phillips (1971), p. 72.

8.1 Frederic Fox, quoted in Goossen (1973), p. 12. **8.2** See Solomon (1920a). **8.3** See Goossen (1973), p. 35. **8.4** Bob Colacello in Richardson (1998), p. 8. **8.5** See Richardson (1998), pp. 21-22. **8.6** Warner (1919a). **8.7** Veruschka in Lehndorff and Trulzsch (1970), p. 145. **8.8** Ibid., p. 146. **8.9** Czarnopys, quoted in Kamholtz (1988), p. 12. **8.10** Ibid. **8.11** Czarnopys, quoted in Komac (1987), p. 10. **8.12** Czarnopys, quoted in Kamholtz (1988), p. 15. **8.13** Ibid., p. 16. **8.14** See Lysohir (1988). **8.15** Bower in *David Bower: Painted Wood Constructions* (1986). **8.16** Ibid. **8.17** Bower in *David Bower* (1980). **8.18** Quoted in *Bower* (1986). **8.19** Quoted in *Bower* (1980). **8.20** Quoted in *Bower* (1986). **8.21** Quoted in *Bower* (1980).

9.1 Einstein, quoted in Jacques Hadamard, *The Psychology Invention in the Mathematical Field*. Princeton, New Jersey: Princeton University Press, 1949. **9.2** Koestler (1964). **9.3** Ibid., p. 35. **9.4** Ibid., p. 201. **9.5** R. Buckminster Fuller, *I Seem To Be A Verb*. New York: Bantam Books, 1970, p. 1. **9.6** Koestler (1964), p. 29. **9.7** Bronowski, *Science and Human Values*. New York: Harper and Row, 1956, pp. 30-31. **9.8** Broudy, quoted in George F. Kneller, *The Art and Science of Creativity*. New York: Holt, Rinehart and Winston, 1965, p. 12. **9.9** Cartier, quoted in W. Sparke and C. McKowen, *Montage: Investigations in Language*. New York: Macmillan, 1970, p. 2. **9.10** Aristotle, quoted in Shibles (1974). **9.11** Stanford, quoted in Shibles (1974). **9.12** See I.A. Richards, *Practical Criticism*. New York: Harcourt Brace, 1954. **9.13** Michael Foucault, *Madness and Civilization*. New York: Vintage Books, 1965.

Acknowledgments

THE RESEARCH FOR this book took place over a period of more than thirty years. A great number and variety of people, agencies, and institutions have contributed to it. As I was preparing this book, for example, I was receiving mail and e-mail weekly from sources all over the world, alerting me to new publications, new examples, stories of first-hand military service, and so on. There have been so many contributors to this project that to list everyone of them would require an additional small book. I am sincerely grateful to them all.

THE ILLUSTRATIONS published here represent only a fraction of the hundreds of historic photographs, cartoons, paintings, and other images that might have been used. In some cases, the sources for these were a challenge to find. Among the known illustration sources are Dover Publications [from various volumes of the Dover Pictorial Archives] (1.K, 2.B, 2.D, 2.E, 2.G, 4.J, 4.O, 4.S, 6.J, 6.K, 6.L, 7.A, 7.G, and 7.J); Oxford University Press (1.G); Uncle Goose Toys (5.N); Time Warner Trade Publishing (8.C); various graphic design students at the Art Academy of Cincinnati and the University of Northern Iowa (1.B, 5.F, 5.G, 5.H, 5.L, 5.M, 6.I, 6.N, 7.D, and 7.F); individual artists and designers [as listed by specific works] (1.A, 1.E, 7.E, 7.I, 8.A, 8.D, 8.E, 8.F, 8.G, 8.H, 8.I, 8.J, 9.A, and 9.B); the State Historical Society of Iowa (cover, frontispiece, 3.A, 3.C, 3.H, 3.N, and 7.B); and, over many years, a variety of U.S. Government sources of public domain images, among them the U.S. Marine Corps, U.S. Department of the Navy, National Archives, and Smithsonian Institution. In preparing this book, an extensive effort was made to identify the copyright holders of illustrations and to obtain their permission. If brought to the attention of the publisher, any credits that are listed incorrectly or were omitted inadvertently will gladly be corrected in subsequent printings. ✂

THIS BOOK IS dedicated to my brilliant and beautiful wife without whom I would be nothing. She always comforts and consoles, never complains or interferes, asks nothing and endures all. She also writes my dedications.

—ALBERT MALVINO

Bibliography

Art, Design and Modern Camouflage

Yves Abrioux (1992) *Ian Hamilton Finlay: A Visual Primer*. Cambridge, Massachusetts: MIT Press.
Carl W. Ackerman (1930) *George Eastman*. Boston: Houghton Mifflin.
Henry Adams (1989) *Thomas Hart Benton: An American Original*. New York: Alfred A. Knopf.
"Air Raid Protection" (1940) in *Architectural Forum* (November), pp. 429-436.
Josef Albers (1963) *Interaction of Color*. New Haven, Connecticut: Yale University Press.
Christopher Alexander (1964) *Notes on the Synthesis of Form*. Cambridge, Massachusetts: Harvard University Press.
Francis H. Allen (1912) "Remarks on the Case of Roosevelt vs. Thayer, with a Few Independent Suggestions on the Concealing Coloration Question" in *Auk* 29 (October), pp. 489-507.
J.A. Allen (1910) "Thayer on Concealing Coloration in Animals" in *Auk* 27 (April), pp. 222-225.
_________ (1911) "Roosevelt's 'Revealing and Concealing Coloration in Birds and Animals'" in *Auk* 28 (October), pp. 472-480.
William Rodney Allen, ed. (1988) *Conversations with Kurt Vonnegut*. Jackson: University Press of Mississippi.
"American 'Camouflage'" (1917) in *Literary Digest* (May 12), pp. 1411-1412.
Ross Anderson (1982) *Abbott Handerson Thayer*. Exhibition catalog. Syracuse, New York: Everson Museum.
Annual Report of the Secretary of the Navy (1918). Washington DC: U.S. Government Printing Office.
Samuel N. Antupit (2000) "Tribute: Gene Federico, 1918-1999" in *Print* 54(1) (January/February), pp. 22-24.
Stanley Applebaum (1974) *Bizarries and Fantasies of Grandville*. Mineola, New York: Dover Publications.
Rudolf Arnheim (1954) *Art and Visual Perception: A Psychology of the Creative Eye*. Berkeley: University of California Press (New version, 1974).
_________ (1964) *Entropy and Art*. Berkeley: University of California Press.
_________ (1966) "Gestalt Psychology and Artistic Form" in Whyte.
_________ (1971) *Visual Thinking*. Berkeley: University of California Press.
_________ (1989) *Parables of Sun Light*. Berkeley: University of California Press.
_________ (1984) "My Life in the Art World." Printed transcript of a talk delivered at the School of Art, University of Michigan, Ann Arbor, on February 8.
_________ (1997) "Bauhaus in Dessau" in *Print* (November/December), pp. 60-61.
Arthur B. Carles (1970). Exhibition catalog. Philadelphia: Philadelphia Museum of Art.
Mitchell Ash (1995) *Gestalt Psychology in German Culture, 1890-1967*. Cambridge, England: Cambridge University Press.
Paul Atterbury (1975) "Dazzle Painting in the First World War" in *Antique Collector* 46 (April), pp. 25-28.
Barbara Babcock-Abrahams (1975) "Why Frogs are Good to Think and Dirt is Good To Reflect On" in *Soundings* (Summer), pp. 167-181.
Bruce Bairnsfather (1919) *From Mud to Mufti*. New York: G.P. Putnam.
Betty Ballantine, ed. (1990) *The Art of Bev Doolittle*. New York: Bantam Books.
Martha Banta (1987) *Imaging American Women: Idea and Ideals in Cultural History*. New York: Columbia University Press.
Geoffrey Barkas (1952) *The Camouflage Story (From Aintree to Alamein)*. London: Cassell.
H.G. Barnett (1953) *Innovation: The Basis of Cultural Change*. New York: McGraw-Hill.
Ursula Barry (1943) "Mother Nature and Camouflage" in *School Arts* (September), pp. 32-33.

Jacques Barzun (1984) *A Stroll with William James*. Chicago: University of Chicago Press.

Gregory Bateson (1972) *Steps to an Ecology of Mind*. New York: Ballantine Books.

_________ (1979) *Mind and Nature*. New York: E.P. Dutton.

John I.H. Bauer (1982) *The Inlander: Life and Work of Charles Burchfield*. Newark: University of Delaware Press.

Cecilia Beaux (1930) *Background with Figures*. Boston: Houghton Mifflin.

Roy R. Behrens (1974) "On Creativity and Humor: An Analysis of Easy Street" in *Journal of Creative Behavior* (4th quarter), pp. 227-238.

_________ (1977) "Camouflage, Cubism and Creativity: The Dissolution of Boundaries" in *Journal of Creative Behavior* (2nd quarter), pp. 91-97.

_________ (1978) "On Visual Art and Camouflage" in *Leonardo*, pp. 203-204.

_________ (1981) *Art and Camouflage: Concealment and Deception in Nature, Art and War*. Cedar Falls, Iowa: University of Northern Iowa / North American Review.

_________ (1984) *Design in the Visual Arts*. Englewood Cliffs, New Jersey: Prentice Hall.

_________ (1986) *Illustration as an Art*. Englewood Cliffs, New Jersey: Prentice Hall.

_________ (1987) "The Art of Dazzle Camouflage" in *Defense Analysis* 3 (3), pp. 233-243.

_________ (1988) "The Theories of Abbott H. Thayer: Father of Camouflage" in *Leonardo* 21(3), pp. 291-296.

_________ (1991) "Blend and Dazzle: The Art of Camouflage" in *Print* 45 (January/February), pp. 92-98.

_________ (1996a) "Among the Dazzle Painters: Sherry Fry and the Invention of American Camouflage" in *Tractor: Iowa Arts and Culture* (Fall), pp. 26-28.

_________ (1996b) "Camouflage" entry in Turner.

_________ (1997) "Iowa's Contribution to Camouflage" in *Iowa Heritage Illustrated* 78(3), pp. 98-109.

_________ (1998a) "On Max Wertheimer and Pablo Picasso: Gestalt Theory, Cubism and Camouflage" in *Gestalt Theory* 20(2) (June), pp. 111-118.

_________ (1998b) "Little Houses on the Prairie: Grant Wood and Frank Lloyd Wright" in *Tractor: Iowa Arts and Culture* (Summer), pp. 4-6.

_________ (1998c) "Art, Design and Gestalt Theory" in *Leonardo* 31(4), pp. 299-303.

_________ (1998d) "Rudolf Arnheim: The Little Owl on the Shoulder of Athene" in *Leonardo* 31(3), pp. 231-233.

_________ (1999) "The Role of Artists in Ship Camouflage During World War I" in *Leonardo* 32(1), pp. 53-59.

_________ (2000a) "Legs, Logos and Ethology: So Just How Graphic Is Graphic Design?" in Steven Heller, ed., *Graphic Design and Sex Appeal*. New York: Allworth Press.

_________ (2000b) "Revisiting Gottschaldt: Embedded Figures in Art, Architecture and Design" in *Gestalt Theory* 22(2) (June), pp. 97-106.

_________ (2000c) "Fields of Dreams: When Salvador Dali Crossed Paths with Freud and Iowa" in *Ballast Quarterly Review* 16(2) (Winter), pp. 3-8.

_________ and Paul D. Whitson (1976) "Mimicry, Metaphor and Mistake" in *Journal of Aesthetic Education* (1st quarter), pp. 45-60.

Norman Bel Geddes (1960) *Miracle in the Evening: An Autobiography*. Garden City, New York: Doubleday.

Chloe Bennett (1996) *Colin Moss: Life Observed*. Ipswich, England: Malthouse Press.

Henry Berry (1978) *Make the Kaiser Dance*. Garden City, New York: Doubleday.

Piet Bess (1993) "Infrared Surveillance and Concealment" in *Military Illustrated Past and Present* (July and August).

Jehangir Bhownagary (1972) "Creativity and the Magician" in *Leonardo* 5, pp. 31-35.

Charles Bittinger (1940) "Naval Camouflage" in *U.S. Naval Institute Proceedings* (October), pp. 1394-1398.

Louis Bouché (c1960) Unpublished autobiographical notes in the Archives of American Art, Smithsonian Institution, available on microfilm rolls 688-689.

Nancy Douglas Bowditch (1970) *George de Forest Brush*. Peterborough, New Hampshire: William L. Bauhan.

David Bower (1980). Exhibition brochure. Muncie, Indiana: Art Gallery, Ball State University.

David Bower: Painted Wood Constructions (1986). Exhibition brochure. Maitland, Florida: Maitland Art Center.

Adam J. Boxer, ed. (1993) *The New Bauhaus School of Design in Chicago: Photographs 1937-1944*. Exhibition catalog. New York: Banning + Associates.

Rutherford Boyd (1918) "Camouflage—In the Year One and 1918" in *Everybody's Magazine* (March), pp. 45-47.

Alexandre Bracke-Desrousseaux (1916) "Le Rire de la Semaine" in *Le Rire* (August 3).
Carolyn Bradley (1944) "A Department of Fine Arts Integrates with War" in *School Arts* (March), pp. 219-220.
Stewart Brand (1974) *Cybernetic Frontiers*. New York: Random House.
Robert Breckenridge (1942) *Modern Camouflage*. New York: Farrar and Rinehart.
Simon Brett, ed. (1987) *The Faber Book of Diaries*. London: Faber and Faber.
British War Artists (1989). Exhibition catalog. New York: Guillaume Gallozzi Gallery.
Norman Brosterman (1997) *Inventing Kindergarten*. New York: Harry N. Abrams.
D.R.E. Brown (1963) *Ships Concealment Camouflage Instructions*. Washington D.C.: Bureau of Ships, U.S. Navy Department.
Robert Brown (1974), Oral history interview with Nancy Bowditch, at Peterborough, New Hampshire (January 30), in the Archives of American Art, Smithsonian Institution, Washington, D.C.
Lillian Browse (1978) *Forain: The Painter 1852-1931*. London: Paul Elek.
Jerome S. Bruner, et al. (1956) *A Study of Thinking*. New York: John Wiley and Sons.
Gerome Brush and Abbott H. Thayer (1902) "Process of Treating the Outsides of Ships for Making Them Less Visible." U.S. Patent No. 715,013 (filed December 2).
Robert Lee Bullard (1925) *Personalities and Reminiscences of the War*. Garden City, New York: Doubleday.
Charles Burchfield (1965) *His Golden Year: A Retrospective Exhibition of Watercolors, Oils and Graphics by Charles E. Burchfield*. Exhibition catalog. Tucson: University of Arizona Press.
Kenneth Burke (1965) *Permanence and Change*. Indianapolis: Bobbs-Merrill.
Pierre Cabanne (1977) *Pablo Picasso: His Life and Times*. New York: William Morrow.
"Call for 'Fakers' to Fool Germans" (1917) in *New York Times* (September 4), p. 7.
"Camouflage" entry in *Encyclopedia Britannica* (1922) (12th edition).
"Camouflage" (1939) in *Time* (September 25), p. 42.
"Camouflage" (1942) in *Architectural Forum* (January), pp. 14-25.
Camouflage (1988). Exhibition catalog. Edinburgh, Scotland: Scottish Arts Council.
"Camouflage Against U-Boats: The Art of Dazzle-Painting" (1919) in *Illustrated London News* (January 4), pp. 20-22.
"Camouflage: Art's Aid in Modern Warfare" (1917) in *Current Opinion* 63 (July), pp. 50-51.
"Camouflaged Roads of the War" (1918) in *Scientific American* 119 (August 17), p. 121.
"Camouflage in Modern Warfare" (1940) in *Nature* (June 22), pp. 949-951.
"Camouflage in Nature" (1927) in *Science* (August 12), p. xii.
"Camouflage School" (1940) in *Time* (October 28), p. 32.
Joyce Cary (1965) *The Horse's Mouth*. New York: Time Life Books [1944].
Charles Castle (1986) *Oliver Messel: A Biography*. London: Thames and Hudson.
Frank M. Chapman (1933) *Autobiography of a Bird Lover*. New York: Appleton Century.
Nicholas Cherkasoff (1941) *Basic Principles in Camouflage*. New York: Saxon Printing.
C.H.R. Chesney (1941) *The Art of Camouflage*. London: R. Hale.
C.H. Claudy (1918) "Gun Camouflage" in *Scientific American* (December 7), pp. 460ff.
"Color-Blind Flyers" (1941) in *Scientific American* (February), pp. 103-104.
"Color-Blindness and Camouflage" (1940) in *Nature* 146 (August 17), p. 226.
"Color Photographs at Night Penetrate Camouflage" (1940) in *Science News Letter* (October 26), p. 270.
"Company A: American Camoufleurs" (1917) in *Literary Digest* (October 13), pp. 32-33.
"Completing Military Camouflage with Camouflage Robes" (1917) in *Scientific American* (September 29), p. 225.
Michele Cone (1975) *The Roots and Routes of Art in the 20th Century*. New York: Horizon Press.
M. Cordier (1980) "Louis Guingot (1864-1948)" in *Le Pays Lorrain* 61(3), pp. 173-174 [as translated for the author by Jackie Stockdale-DeLay].
Richard Cork (1976) *Vorticism and Abstract Art*. Berkeley: University of California Press.
_________ (1994) *A Bitter Truth: Avant-Garde Art and the Great War*. New Haven, Connecticut: Yale University Press.
Alfred E. Cornebise (1991a) *Art From the Trenches: America's Uniformed Artists in World War I*. College Station: Texas A&M University.
_________, ed. (1991b) *War Diary of a Combat Artist* [Harry E. Townsend]. Niwat, Colorado: University Press of Colorado.
Royal Cortissoz (1923) *American Artists*. New York: Charles Scribner's Sons.

Hugh B. Cott (1938) "Camouflage in Nature and War" in *Royal Engineers Journal* (December), pp. 501-517.

_________ (1940) *Adaptive Coloration in Animals*. London: Methuen.

Cornelia C. Coulter (1918) "Ancient Camouflage" in *Nation* (June 22), p. 738.

Benedict Crowell (1919) *America's Munitions 1917-1918*. Washington DC: U.S. Government Printing Office.

Charles Cruickshank (1979) *Deception in World War II*. Oxford, England: Oxford University Press.

C.R.M.F. Cruttwell (1936) *A History of the Great War 1914-1918*. Oxford, England: Oxford University Press.

Mihaly Csikszentmihalyi (1990) *Flow: The Psychology of Optimal Experience*. New York: Harper and Row.

Paul Russell Cutright (1956) *Theodore Roosevelt, the Naturalist*. New York: Harper and Brothers.

Magdalena Dabrowski, et al. (1998) *Aleksandr Rodchenko*. New York: Museum of Modern Art.

Roger Dean and Martyn Dean (1984) *Magnetic Storm*. New York: Harmony Books.

Howard Dearstyne (1986) *Inside the Bauhaus*. New York: Rizzoli International Publications.

"Decoy Blackouts" (1942) in *Scientific American* (January), p. 8.

Charles DeKay (1918) "Ships That Fade Away" in *Nation* (July 27), pp. 105-107.

Danielle Delouche (1993) "Cubisme et Camouflage" in *Guerres Mondiales et Conflits Contemporains* 43(171), pp. 123-137 [as translated for the author by Jackie Stockdale-DeLay].

Richard DeMeis (1987) "Visual Stealth" in *Aerospace America* 25(7) (July), pp. 12-15.

_________ (1988) "Now You See It Now You Don't" in *Wings* 18(4) (August), pp. 18-33.

"Detect Camouflage" (1942) in *Science News Letter* (November 28), p. 342.

Wendy Deutelbaum (1998) "The Art of Teaching: Interviews with Three Masters" in *The Iowa Review* 28(1).

John Dewey (1958) *Art as Experience*. New York: Capricorn Books.

William G. Dooley, Jr. (1969) *Great Weapons of World War I*. New York: Army Times Publishing.

Arthur Wesley Dow (1997) *Composition*. Berkeley: University of California Press [1899].

Andre Ducasse, et al. (1962) *Vie et Mort des Francais 1914-1918*. Paris: Hachette.

James E. Edmonds, ed. (1932) *History of the Great War: Military Operations; France and Belgium 1916*. Vol. I. London: Macmillan.

Edward Wadsworth 1889-1949 (1974). Exhibition catalog. London: P&D Colnaghi and Company.

Anton Ehrenzweig (1971) *The Hidden Order of Art*. Berkeley: University of California Press.

Joost Elffers (1997) *Tangram: The Ancient Chinese Puzzle*. New York: Stewart Tabori and Chang.

W.D. Ellis, ed. (1939) *A Source Book of Gestalt Psychology*. New York: Harcourt, Brace and Company.

Aymar Embury II (1917) "Architects and the Camouflage Service" in *Architectural Forum* 27 (November), pp. 137-138.

Paul Engle, et al., ed. (1987) *The World Comes to Iowa*. Ames: Iowa State University Press.

Arthur B. Fallico (1962) *Art and Existentialism*. Englewood Cliffs, New Jersey: Prentice-Hall.

Barry Faulkner (c1957) Transcripts of broadcasts on radio station WKNE, Keane, New Hampshire.

_________ (1973) *Sketches from an Artist's Life*. Dublin, New Hampshire: William L. Bauhan.

Susan Faxon (1989) "Frank Weston Benson, Abbott Thayer, and Dublin, New Hampshire" in *Frank W. Benson: A Retrospective*. Exhibition catalog. New York: Berry-Hill Galleries, pp. 134-143.

Keith Ferris (1976) "The Keith Ferris Deceptive Aircraft Paint" in *Topgun Journal* 1(2) (Spring), pp, 11-17.

David Fisher (1983) *The War Magician*. New York: Coward and McCann.

John Fisher, ed. (1973) *The Magic of Lewis Carroll*. New York: Bramhall House.

"Fooling the Enemy's Eye" (1917) in *Literary Digest* (December 22), pp. 21-22.

Michel Foucault (1973a) *The Order of Things*. New York: Vintage Books.

Michel Foucault (1973b) *Madness and Civilization*. New York: Vintage Books.

Milton Fox (1942) "Camouflage" in *School Arts* (April), pp. 136ff.

_________ (1943) "Camouflage" in *School Arts*.

Herbert Friedmann (1942) *The Natural History Background of Camouflage*. War Background Studies No. 5. Washington DC: Smithsonian Institution.

"French Artists Remobilized" (1916) in *Literary Digest* (August 19), p. 411.

Michel Frizot (1998) *A New History of Photography*. Koln: Konemann.

Thomas G. Frothingham (1971) *The Naval History of the World War: The United States in the War*. Freeport, New York: Books for Libraries Press.

Sherry Edmundson Fry (1917) "An American Corps for Camouflage" in *American Architect* 112 (July 25), p. 68.

Grace Hadley Fuller, ed. (1940) *Camouflage: A List of References*. Washington DC: Library of Congress, Division of Bibliography.

_________, ed. (1942) *A List of References on Camouflage*. Washington DC.: Library of Congress,

Division of Bibliography.
Helen K. Fusscas (1992) *A World Observed: The Art of Everett Longley Warner 1877-1963*. Exhibition catalog. Old Lyme, Connecticut: Florence Griswold Museum.
Suzi Gablik (1992) *Magritte*. London: Thames and Hudson.
Richard Gale (1968) *Call to Arms*. London: Hutchinson.
Martin Gardner, ed. (1960) *The Annotated Alice*. New York: New American Library.
John Garraty and Mark Carnes, eds. (1999). *American National Biography*. New York: Oxford University Press.
Darrell Garwood (1944) *Artist in Iowa: A Life of Grant Wood*. New York: W.W. Norton.
William Gaunt (1949) *The March of the Moderns*. London: Jonathan Cape.
Brewster Ghislen, ed. (1955) *The Creative Process*. New York: Mentor Books.
Walter Gibson (1969) *Dreams*. New York: Constellation International.
Rosamond Gilder (1944) "'You Bet Your Life': Report on a Camouflage Show" in *Theatre Arts* (September), pp. 521-527.
Francoise Gilot (1964) *Life with Picasso*. New York: McGraw-Hill.
Rene Gimpel (1966) *Diary of an Art Dealer*. New York: Farrar Straus and Giroux.
Daniele Giraudy (1971) "Correspondance Henri Matisse - Charles Camoin" in *Revue de l'Art* 12, pp. 7-33.
Milton Glaser (2001) *Art as Work*. Woodstock, New York: Overlook Press.
John Goldsmith, ed. (1986) *Stephen Spender: Journals 1939-1983*. New York: Random House.
E.H. Gombrich (1969) *Art and Illusion: A Study of the Psychology of Pictorial Representation*. Princeton, New Jersey: Princeton University Press.
__________ (1979) *The Sense of Order*. Ithaca, New York: Cornell University Press.
__________, et al. (1972) *Art, Perception and Reality*. Baltimore, Maryland: Johns Hopkins University Press.
"Good Camouflage or None" (1942) in *Science News Letter* (December 26), p. 410.
Jean Goodman (1978) *Edward Seago: The Other Side of the Canvas*. London: Collins.
Nelson Goodman (1960) "The Way the World Is" in *Review of Metaphysics* (September), pp. 48-56.
E.C. Goossen (1973) *Ellsworth Kelly*. New York: Museum of Modern Art.
Arshile Gorky (1962) Description of camouflage course at Grand Central School of Art reprinted in Rosenberg.
Kurt Gottschaldt (1966) "The Influence of Past Experience on the Perception of Figures" [1926] in Vernon.
Stephen Jay Gould (1985) "Red Wings in the Sunset" in *Natural History* (May), pp. 12-24.
Nan Wood Graham (1993) *My Brother, Grant Wood*. Iowa City: State Historical Society of Iowa.
Richard L. Gregory (1966) *Eye and Brain: The Psychology of Seeing*. New York: McGraw-Hill.
__________ (1970) *The Intelligent Eye*. New York: McGraw-Hill.
__________, ed. (1987) *The Oxford Companion to the Mind*. New York: Oxford University Press.
__________ and E.H. Gombrich, eds. (1973) *Illusion in Nature and Art*. New York: Charles Scribner's Sons.
James G. Harbord (1925) *Leaves from a War Diary*. New york: Dodd, Mean and Company.
David A. Hanks (1999) *The Decorative Designs of Frank Lloyd Wright*. Mineola, New York: Dover Publications.
Rudy de Harak (1988) "Gyorgy Kepes Revisits the Visual Landscape" in *AIGA Journal of Graphic Design* 6(3), pp. 8-9ff.
Alister Hardy (1965) *The Living Stream*. New York: Harper and Row.
Meirion and Susie Harries (1983) *The War Artists: British Official War Art of the 20th Century*. London: Michael Joseph.
Anne Harrington (1999) *Reenchanted Science: Holism in German Culture from Wilhelm II to Hitler*. Princeton, New Jersey: Princeton University Press.
Mary Emma Harris (1987) *The Arts at Black Mountain College*. Cambridge, Massachusetts: MIT Press.
Guy Hartcup (1980) *Camouflage: A History of Concealment and Deception in War*. New York: Charles Scribner's Sons.
George W. Hartmann (1935) *Gestalt Psychology*. New York: Ronald Press.
Barbara Haskell (1985) *Ralston Crawford*. Exhibition catalog. New York: Whitney Museum of Art.
George R. Havens (1969) *Frederick J. Waugh: American Marine Painter*. Orono, Maine: University of Maine Press.
Henry Hay, ed. (1975) *Cyclopedia of Magic*. New York: Dover Publications.
Robert R. Hays (19xx) Correspondence with the author.
Fritz Heider (1973) "Gestalt Theory: Early History and Reminiscences" in Henle.

_________ (1983) *The Life of a Psychologist: An Autobiography*. Lawrence: University Press of Kansas.

Mary Henle, et al., eds. (1973) *Historical Conceptions of Psychology*. New York: Springer.

_________, ed. (1976) *Vision and Artifact*. New York: Springer.

"Hiding a Big Gun in the Open with a Coated of Spotted Camouflage Paint" (1917) in *Scientific American* 117 (November 10), p. 349.

Bevis Hiller (1975) *Austerity Binge*. London: Studio Vista.

_________ (1983) *The Style of the Century 1900-1980*. London: Herbert Press.

Susan Hobbs (1982) "Nature Into Art: The Landscapes of Abbott Handerson Thayer" in *American Art Journal* 14 (Summer), pp. 5-55.

Brad Holland (2000) "Express Yourself—It's Later Than You Think" in Steven Heller and Marshall Arisman, eds., *The Education of an Illustrator*. New York: Allworth Press.

Alissair Home (1964) *The Price of Glory: Verdun 1916*. Middlesex, England: Penguin.

Kay Hong and Judy Hughes (1994) "The Concept of Concealment: Mimicry in Nature and Hidden Images in Art" in *Wildlife Art News* 13(4) (July-August), pp. 58-64.

"How an Artist Discovered a Natural Law" (1911) in *Scientific American* (January 7), p. 3.

Patrick Hreachmack (1999) *The Painter's Guide to World War Two Naval Camouflage*. Phoenixville, Pennsylvania: Clash of Arms.

Morton Hunt (1993) *The Story of Psychology*. New York: Doubleday.

Hugh Hurst (1919) "Dazzle-painting in War-time" in *International Studio* (September), pp. 93-99.

"Ideas in Camouflage from Dame Nature" (1918) in *Current Opinion* (October), p. 240.

Horst W. Janson (1973) "Chance Images" in Philip P. Wiener, ed., *Dictionary of the History of Ideas*. Vol. I. New York: Charles Scribner's Sons.

Arthur B. Jensen (1919) *The Jensen System of Modeling*. Chicago: Jensen Modeling Device Company, pp. 3-5.

Even Hebbe Johnsrud (1994) "Randbemerkninger: Kust og Kamuflasjekunst" in *Kust og Kulture* 77(3), pp. 171-176.

Jon Gnagy: An Exhibition of Paintings and Litho Drawings (1964). Exhibition catalog. Idyllwild, California.

Barbara Jones and Bill Howell (1972) *Popular Arts of the First World War*. New York: McGraw-Hill.

R.V. Jones (1973) "The Theory of Practical Joking—Its Relevance to Physics" in R.L. Weber, ed., *A Random Walk in Science*. New York: Crane, Russak and Company.

E.J. Kahn, Jr (1988) *Year of Change: More About The New Yorker and Me*. Nw York: Viking.

Elizabeth Louise Kahn (1984) *The Neglected Majority: "Les Camoufleurs," Art History, and World War I*. Lanham, Maryland: University Press of America.

Richard Kalina (1999) "Andy Warhol at Gagosian" in *Art in America* (June), pp. 115-116.

Jonathan Kamholtz (1988) "Sited and Unsighted Figures: The Sculpture of Tom Czarnopys" in *Dialogue* 11(6), pp. 12-16.

Edgar Kaufmann and Ben Raeburn, eds. (1960) *Frank Lloyd Wright: Writings and Buildings*. New York: Meridian Books.

Angeline Myra Keen (1932) "Protective Coloration in the Light of Gestalt Theory" in *Journal of General Psychology*, pp. 200-203.

Rockwell Kent (1955) *It's Me, O Lord*. New York: Dodd, Mead and Company.

György Kepes (1944) *Language of Vision*. Chicago: Paul Theobald.

_________ (1956) *The New Landscape in Art and Science*. Chicago: Paul Theobald.

John Graham Kerr (1919) "Camouflage of Ships in War" in *Nature* (May 15), pp. 204-205.

_________ (1941a) "Camouflage in Warfare" in *Nature* 147 (June 21), pp. 758-760.

_________ (1941b) "Use of Paint in Camouflage" in *Nature* (November 1), p. 527.

Soren Kierkegaard (1959) "The Rotation Method" in R. Bretall, *A Kierkegaard Anthology*. New York: Modern Library, pp. 21-33.

Gregory A. Kimble and Michael Wertheimer, eds. (1998) *Portraits of Pioneers in Psychology: Volume III*. Mahwah, New Jersey: Lawrence Erlbaum Associates.

Adrian Klein and J.C. Mottram (1919) "Military Camouflage" in *Nature* (July 10), p. 364.

Arthur Koestler (1964) *The Act of Creation: A Study of the Conscious and Unconscious in Science and Art*. New York: Macmillan.

_________ (1978) *Janus: A Summing Up*. New York: Random House.

_________ and J.R. Smythies, eds. (1971) *Beyond Reductionism*. Boston: Beacon Press.

Kurt Koffka (1935) *Principles of Gestalt Psychology*. New York: Harcourt, Brace and World.

Wolfgang Köhler (1947) *Gestalt Psychology*. New York: New American Library.

_________ (1956) *The Mentality of Apes*. New York: Vintage Books.

Dennis L. Komac (1987) *Passion of Nature / Nature of Passion: Recent Figurative Sculpture by Tom Czarnopys*. Exhibition brochure. Grand Rapids, Michigan: Grand Rapids Art Museum.

Richard Kostelanetz (1970) *Moholy-Nagy*. New York: Praeger.

Katharine Kuh (1969) *Break-Up: The Core of Modern Art*. Greenwich, Connecticut: New York Graphic Arts Society.

Thomas S. Kuhn (1970) *The Structure of Scientific Revolutions*. Chicago: University of Chicago Press.

Edmund Leach (1976) *Culture and Communication*. Cambridge, England: Cambridge University Press.

Vera Lehndorff and Holger Trulzsch (1986) *Veruschka: Trans-figurations*. New York: New York Graphic Arts Society / Little Brown and Company.

Julien Levy (1972) Foreword in William C. Seitz, ed., *Arshile Gorky*. New York: Museum of Modern Art / Arno Press.

Miriam A. Lewin (1998) "Kurt Lewin: His Psychology and a Daughter's Recollections" in Kimble and Wertheimer.

Alexander Liberman (1969) *The Artist in His Studio*. New York: Viking Press.

David Lodge (1985) *Small World*. New York: Macmillan.

Amy Lowell (1918) "Camouflaged Troop-Ship" in *The Dial*, p. 403.

Matthew Luckiesh (1919) "The Principles of Camouflage" in *Scientific American* (January 25, and February 8 and 22).

_________ (1965) *Visual Illusions: Their Causes, Characteristics and Applications*. Mineola, New York: Dover Publications.

Ellen Lupton and J.A. Miller, eds. (1993) *The ABCs of Triangle Circle Square: The Bauhaus and Design Theory*. New York: Princeton Architectural Press.

_________ (1996) *Design Writing Research: Writing on Graphic Design*. New York: Princeton Architectural Press.

Marilyn Lysohir (1988) "The Dark Side of Dazzle" in *Ceramic Monthly* 36(6) (June/July/August), pp. 44-47.

Fiona MacCarthy (1972) *All Things Bright and Beautiful*. Toronto, Canada: University of Toronto Press.

Carol Orsag Madigan and Ann Elwood (1983) *Brainstorms and Thunderbolts: How Creative Genius Works*. New York: Macmillan.

Frederich George Marcham, ed. (1971) *Louis Agassiz Fuertes and the Singular Beauty of Birds*. New York: Harper and Row.

Julia Markus (1989) "Two Years After His Death, the Curtain Rises" in *Smithsonian Magazine* (February), pp. 63-75.

Edward Marsh (1939) *A Number of People*. New York: Harper and Brothers.

Jasper Maskelyne (1949) *Magic: Top Secret*. London: Stanley Paul.

Abraham Maslow (1968) *Toward a Psychology of Being*. New York: Van Nostrand.

E. Armitage McCann (1931) "Dazzle-Painting a Model" in *Popular Mechanics* (April), p. 89.

Ken McCormick and Hamilton Darby Perry, eds. (1990) *Images of War: The Artist's Vision of World War II*. New York: Orion Books.

Kynaston McShine, ed. (1989) *Andy Warhol: A Retrospective*. Exhibition catalog. New York: Museum of Modern Art.

T.R. Merton (1940) "Camouflage in Modern Warfare" in *Nature* (September 28), p. 429.

Richard Meryman (1999) "A Painter of Angels Became the Father of Camouflage" in *Smithsonian Magazine* (April), pp. 116-128.

Wolfgang Metzger (1975) *Gesetze des Sehens*. Frankfurt am Main: Verlag Waldemar Kramer.

Leonard Meyer (1956) *Emotion and Meaning in Music*. Chicago: University of Chicago Press.

Michael Lekakis: A Retrospective Exhibition (1987). Exhibition Catalog. New York: Camillos Kouros Gallery.

Katherine Michaelsen and Nehama Guralnik (1986) *Alexander Archipenko: A Centennial Tribute*. Washington DC: National Gallery of Art.

Peter Mitchell (1984) Article on "Dazzle-Painting" in Peter Young, ed., *The Marshall Cavendish Illustrated Encyclopedia of World War I*. Vol. 9. New York: Marshall Cavendish.

William Mitchell (1960) *Memoirs of World War I*. New York: Random House.

Laszlo Moholy-Nagy (1947a) *The New Vision and Abstract of an Artist*. New York: George Wittenborn.

_________ (1947b) *Vision in Motion*. Chicago: Paul Theobald.

Sibyl Moholy-Nagy (1969) *Moholy-Nagy: An Experiment in Totality*. Cambridge, Massachusetts: MIT Press.

Elting Morison, ed. (1954) *The Letters of Theodore Roosevelt*. Cambridge, Massachusetts: Harvard University Press.
A. Reynolds Morse (1973) *Salvador Dali - Pablo Picasso: A Preliminary Study in Their Similarities and Contrasts*. Cleveland, Ohio: Salvador Dali Museum.
Charles Merrill Mount (1955) *John Singer Sargent: A Biography*. New York: W.W. Norton.
National Cyclopedia of American Biography (1892-). New York: J.T. White.
"Natural and Artificial Camouflage" (1919) in *Nature* (January 23), p. 408.
"Natural Camouflage" (1941) in *Time* (August 4).
Ron Naverson (1989) *The Scenographer as Camoufleur*. PhD Dissertation. Carbondale: Southern Illinois University.
Alexander Nemerov (1997) "Vanishing Americans: Abbott Thayer, Theodore Roosevelt, and the Attraction of Camouflage" in *American Art* (Summer), pp. 51-81.
Eckhard Neumann, ed. (1993) *Bauhaus and Bauhaus People*. New York: Van Nostand Reinhold.
Tim Newark, Quentin Newark and J.F. Borsarello (1996) *Brassey's Book of Camouflage*. London: Brassey's Ltd.
Margot Norris (1985) *Beasts of the Modern Imagination*. Baltimore, Maryland: Johns Hopkins University Press.
Kevin Nute (1993) *Frank Lloyd Wright and Japan*. New York: Van Nostrand Reinhold.
Stanley Olson (1986) *John Singer Sargent: His Portrait*. New York: St. Martin's Press.
Alex Osborn (1963) *Applied Imagination*. New York: Charles Scribner's Sons.
Edwards Park (1985) "A Phantom Division Played a Role in Germany's Defeat" in *Smithsonian Magazine* (April), pp. 138-147.
"Paul Gerchik; Artist, Army Camouflage Expert" (1998) in *Los Angeles Times* (August 20) [obituary page].
Morse Peckham (1967) *Man's Rage for Chaos: Biology, Behavior and the Arts*. New York: Schocken.
_________ (1978) "Perceptual and Semiotic Discontinuity in Art" in *Poetics*, pp. 217-230.
Roland Penrose (1941) *Home Guard Manual of Camouflage*. London: G. Routledge and Sons.
_________ (1973) *Picasso: His Life and Work*. New York: Harper and Row.
_________ (1981) *Scrapbook 1900-1981*. London: Thames and Hudson.
Ernest Peixotto (1917) "Special Service for Artists in War Time" in *Scribner's Magazine* 62(1) (July), pp. 1-10.
Walter A.R. Pertuck (1943) "Camouflage" in *Wilson Library Bulletin* (February), pp. 473 and 480.
Robert Phillips, ed. (1971) *Aspects of Alice*. New York: Vintage Books.
William Plomer, ed. (1960) *Kilvert's Diary: Selections from the Diary of Rev. Francis Kilvert*. London: Jonathan Cape.
_________ (1976) *The Autobiography of William Polmer*. New York: Taplinger.
Adolf Portmann (1959) *Animal Camouflage*. Ann Arbor: University of Michigan Press.
_________ (1967) *Animal Forms and Patterns*. New York: Schocken Books.
Stephen Potter (1978) *The Complete Upmanship*. New York: New American Library.
Edward B. Poulton (1902) "The Meaning of the White Under Sides of Animals" in *Nature* (April 24), p. 596.
_________ (1921) "Natural Camouflage" in *Nature* 107 (May 12), pp. 338-340.
E. Alexander Powell (1917) *Italy at War*. New York: Charles Scribner's Sons.
Lucien Price, ed. (1954) *Dialogues of Alfred North Whitehead*. New York: Mentor.
Jack Pritchard (1984) *View from a Long Chair*. London: Routledge & Kegan Paul.
"Progress of Camouflage" (1940) in *Nature* 146 (October 12), pp. 482-483.
"Protective Coloration of Fleets" (1916) in *Literary Digest* (August 26), p. 458.
Paul Raabe, ed. (1985) *The Era of German Expressionism*. Woodstock, New York: Overlook Press.
Clayton Rawson (1938) *Death From a Top Hat: A Merlini Mystery*. New York: G.P. Putnam's Sons.
Paul Regusis (1990) Letters to the author dated August 21 and August 30.
Theodore Reik (1949) *Listening with the Third Ear: The Inner Experience of a Psychoanalyst*. New York: Farrar Straus.
Seymour Reit (1978) *Masquerade: The Amazing Camouflage Deceptions of World War II*. New York: Hawthorn Books.
"Remarkable Example of Camouflage" (1919) in *Scientific American* (May 10), p. 491.
R. Roger Remington and Barbara J. Hodik (1989) *Nine Pioneers in American Graphic Design*. Cambridge, Massachusetts: MIT Press.

O. Renier and V. Rubinstein (1986) *Assigned to Listen: The Evesham Experience 1939-1943*. London: British Broadcasting Corporation.

Brenda Richardson (1998) *Andy Warhol: Camouflage*. Exhibition catalog. New York: Gagosian Gallery.

John Richardson (1991) *A Life of Picasso. Volume I: 1881-1906*. New York: Random House.

_________ (1996) *A Life of Picasso. Volume II: 1907-1917*. New York: Random House.

John Adkins Richardson (1971) *Modern Art and Scientific Thought*. Urbana: University of Illinois Press.

Hans Richter (1965) *Dada: Art and Anti-Art*. New York: McGraw-Hill.

Florian Rodari, et al. (1998) *Shadows of a Hand: The Drawings of Victor Hugo*. New York and London: The Drawing Center and Merrell Holbertson.

Peter Rodyenko (1941) "Camouflage" in *Life* (January 13), pp. 39-42.

Sharon Romm and Joseph William Slap (1983) "Freud and Dali: Personal Moments" in *American Imago* 10(4) (Winter), pp. 344-345.

Theodore Roosevelt (1919) *African Game Trails*. New York: Charles Scribner's Sons.

Gilbert Rose (1987) *Trauma and Mastery in Life and Art*. New Haven: Yale University Press.

Phyllis Rose (1983) *Parallel Lives: Five Victorian Marriages*. New York: Afred A. Knopf.

Harold Rosenberg (1962) *Arshile Gorky: The Man. The Time. The Idea*. New York: Horizon Press.

Robert Rosenblum (1961) *Cubism and Twentieth-Century Art*. New york: Harry N. Abrams.

Albert Roskam (1987) *Dazzle Painting: Kunst Als Camouflage: Camouflage Als Kunst*. Exhibition catalog. Rotterdam, The Netherlands: Stichting Kunstprojecten en Uitgevergij Van Spijik.

Alan Ross (1983) *Colors of War*. London: Jonathan Cape.

Brenda Warner Rotzoll (2000) "Obituaries: Jo Mead, 81, Interior Design Artist" in *Chicago Sun-Times* (August 14), p. 52.

F. Roussanne (1994) "Chronique de l'Institut d'Histoire des Conflits Contemporain" in *Guerres Mondiales et Conflits Contemporains* 44(175), pp. 147-150 [as translated for the author by Jackie Stockdale-DeLay].

C.H. Rowe (1940) "Camouflage in Wartime" in *Nature* (August 3), p. 168.

Harry Rubin (1943) "The Art of Camouflage" in *School Arts* (September), pp. 9-13.

William S. Rubin (1968) *Dada, Surrealism and Their Heritage*. New York: Museum of Modern Art.

Homer Saint-Gaudens (1919) "Camouflage and Art" in *International Studio* (August), pp. 2-7.

_________ (1933) "Camouflage Reminiscences" in *Military Engineer* (May-June), pp. 242-248.

_________ (1941a) "Present Day Camouflage" in *Reserve Officer* (May), pp. 10-13.

_________ (1941b) "We're the Men of the Fantasy Forces: Military Camouflage" in *Christian Science Monitor Magazine* (June 21), p. 6.

_________ (1941c) *The American Artist and His Times*. New York: Dodd, Mead and Company.

Maurice de Sausmarez (1964) *Basic Design: The Dynamics of Visual Form*. New York: Reinhold.

Nathan Schiffman (1997) *Abracadabra!: Secret Methods Magaician and Others Use to Deceive Their Audience*. Amherst, New York: Prometheus Books.

Tut Schlemmer, ed. (1972) *The Letters and Diaries of Oskar Schlemmer*. Middletown, Connecticut: Wesleyan University Press.

Ethel Schwabacher (1957) *Arshile Gorky*. New York: Macmillan.

Hillel Schwartz (1996) *The Culture of the Copy: Striking Likenesses, Unreasonable Facsimiles*. New York: Zone Books.

Peter Scott (1961) *The Eye of the Wind*. Boston: Houghton Mifflin.

"Seeing But Not Seen" (1918) in *Scientific American* 118 (May 18), pp. 451 and 464.

Andre Dunoyer de Segonzac (1970) *Dessins 1900-1970*. Geneve: Pierre Cailler.

Theda Shapiro (1976) *Painters and Politics*. New York: Elsevier.

Evelyn Levy Shaw (1985) "A Tribute to Meyer Abel" in *Art Academy News* (May). Cincinnati, Ohio: Art Academy of Cincinnati.

Warren Shibles (1971) *Metaphor: An Annotated Bibliography and History*. Whitewater, Wisconsin: Language Press.

_________ (1974) "The Metaphorical Method" in *Journal of Aesthetic Education* (April), pp. 25-36.

Eric Sloane (1942) *Camouflage Simplified*. New York: Devin-Adair.

Preston Slosson (1931) *The Great Crusade and After*. New York: Macmillan.

Corinna Lindon Smith (1962) *Interesting People*. Norman: University of Oklahoma Press.

Cyril H. Smith (n.d.) *Camouflage Simply Explained*. London: Sir Issac Pitman and Sons.

J. Andre Smith (1917) "Notes on Camouflage" in *Architectural Record* (November), pp. 468-477.

Roberta Smith (1998) "Warhol's 15 Minutes Tick On, in Abstraction Shows" in *New York Times* (December 4), p. B31.
Solomon J. Solomon (1920a) *Strategic Camouflage*. London: John Murray.
_________ (1920b) "The Secret of German Camouflage" in *World's Work* (April), pp. 453-458.
"Some Thoughts on Camouflage" (1939) in *Action Francaise* (July 15) [as translated by U.S. military].
Chris Staerck, ed. (1998) *Allied Photo Reconnaissance of World War II*. San Diego, California: Thunder Bay Press.
Roy M. Stanley II (1998) *To Fool a Glass Eye: Camouflage Versus Photoreconnaissance in World War II*. Washington, D.C.: Smithsonian Press.
Francis Steegmuller (1968) *Cocteau: A Biography*. Boston: Nonpareil Books.
Gertrude Stein (1933) *The Autobiography of Alice B. Toklas*. New York: Random House.
_________ (1945) *Wars I Have Seen*. New York: Random House.
Warren Steinkraus (1979) "The Art of Conjuring" in *Journal of Aesthetic Education*.
"Striped Suits and Papier Mache Carcasses as Camouflage" (1918) in *Scientific American* (January 26), p. 31.
Leslie Stroebel, et al. (1980) *Visual Concepts for Photographers*. New York: Focal Press.
Robert Sumrall (1971) "Ship Camouflage (WWI): Deceptive Art" in *U.S. Naval Institute Proceedings* 97 (July), pp. 57-77.
_________ (1973) "Ship Camouflage (WWII): Deceptive Art" in *U.S. Naval Institute Proceedings* 99 (February), pp. 67-81.
_________ (1973) Comments and Discussion regarding "Ship Camouflage (WWI): Deceptive Art" in *U.S. Naval Institute Proceedings* 99 (February), pp. 90-91.
Remar Sutton and Mary Abbott Waite, eds. (1992) *The Common Ground Book: A Circle of Friends*. Latham, New York: British American Publishing.
Steven Sykes (1990) *Deceivers Ever: Memoirs of a Camouflage Officer 1939-1945*. Kent, England: Spellmount.
Wylie Sypher (1960) *Rococo to Cubism in Art and Literature*. New York: Vintage Books.
_________ (1962) *The Loss of Self in Modern Art and Literature*. New York: Random House.
Edgar Tafel (1979) *Apprentice to Genius: Years With Frank Lloyd Wright*. New York: McGraw-Hill.
_________, ed. (1993) *About Wright*. New York: John Wiley and Sons.
Harlan Tarbel (1924) *How to Chalk Talk*. Chicago: T.S. Denison.
Marianne L. Teuber (1976) "Blue Night by Paul Klee" in Henle, pp. 131-151.
Abbott H. Thayer (1896a) "The Law Which Underlies Protective Coloration" in *Auk* (April), pp. 124-129.
_________ (1896b) "Further Remarks on the Law Which Underlies Protective Coloration" in *Auk* 13 (October), pp. 318-320.
_________ (1902) "The Meaning of the White Undersides of Animals" in *Nature* (April 24), p. 597.
_________ (1911) "Concealing-Coloration: A Demand for Investigation of My Tests of the Effacive Power of Patterns" in *Auk* 28 (October), pp. 46-464.
_________ (1918) "Camouflage" in *Scientific Monthly* (December), pp. 481-494.
Gerald H. Thayer (1909) *Concealing Coloration in the Animal Kingdom; An Exposition of the Laws of Disguise Through Color and Pattern; Being a Summary of Abbott H. Thayer's Discoveries*. New York: Macmillan (Second Edition, 1918).
"Theatre for Studying Camouflaged Ship Models" (1919) in *Scientific American Supplement* (December 13), pp. 348-349.
Frank Thone (1941) "For Better Camouflage" in *Science News Letter* (March 1), p. 142.
_________ (1944) "Cloaks of Invisibility" in *Science News Letter* (February 5), pp. 90-92.
Niko Tinbergen (1968) *Curious Naturalists*. Garden City, New York: Anchor Books.
Maximilan Toch (1931) "Adventures in Camouflage" in *The Military Engineer* 23 (July/August), pp. 307-309.
Oleta Stewart Toliver, ed. (1994) *An Artist at War: The Journal of John Gaitha Browning*. Denton: University of North Texas Press.
H. Ledyard Towle (1917) "What the American 'Camouflage' Signifies" in *New York Times* (June 3), p. 14.
Julian Trevelyan (1957) *Indigo Days*. London: MacGibbon and Kee.
"Tricks of the War-Trade" (1915) in *Literary Digest* (July 3), pp. 33-34.
Colin M. Turbayne (1971) *The Myth of Metaphor*. Columbia: University of South Carolina Press.
Jane Turner, ed. (1996) *The Dictionary of Art*. London and New York: Grove Dictionaries.
Diane Upright (1987) *Ellsworth Kelly: Works on Paper*. New York: Harry N. Abrams.
"Use of Paint in Camouflage" (1941) in *Nature* (November 1), p. 527.
"Value of Dazzle-Painting" (1919) in *Literary Digest* (July 19), p. 31.

Harold Van Buskirk (1919) "Camouflage" in *Transactions of the Illuminating Engineering Society* 14 (July 21), pp. 225-232.

M.D. Vernon, ed. (1966) *Experiments in Visual Perception*. Baltimore, Maryland: Penguin Books.

Clare M. Verstegen (1990) "Camouflage: A Master's Thesis" in *Surface Design Journal* (Fall), pp. 15-17.

Kurt Vonnegut (1988) *Bluebeard*. New York: Dell.

Barbara Wadsworth (1989) *Edward Wadsworth: A Painter's Life*. Salisbury, UK: Michael Russell Ltd.

Emily Duane Wallace (1942) "Camouflage Exhibit at the Franklin Institute" in *Scientific Monthly* 54 (May), pp. 484-487.

"Wants Camouflage Force" (1917) in *New York Times* (August 30), p. 14.

"War and the Art Schools" (1940) in *Art Digest* 15(1), p. 28.

Everett L. Warner (1919) "The Science of Marine Camouflage Design" in *Transactions of the Illuminating Engineering Society* 14 (5), pp. 215-219.

_________ (1919) "Fooling the Iron Fish: The Inside Story of Marine Camouflage" in *Everybody's Magazine* (November), pp. 102-109.

_________ (1944) *Ship Camouflage Manual for Pattern Design Application*. Washington DC: Bureau of Ships (unpublished typescript).

Thomas E. Warner (c1998) Correspondence with the author and various other materials pertaining to the role of Everett L. Warner in U.S. naval camouflage.

Lynne Warren (1988) *Tom Czarnopys*. Exhibition brochure. Chicago: Museum of Contemporary Art.

Alan Watts (1969) *The Two Hands of God*. New York: Collier Books.

Herta Wecher (1971) *Collage*. Robert E. Wolf, trans. New York: Harry N. Abrams.

Judith Wechsler (1978) *György Kepes: The MIT Years 1945-1977*. Cambridge: MIT Press.

William R. Weigler (1920) "Camouflaging Airplanes" in *Literary Digest* (June 12), pp. 34-35.

Louis Weinberg (1927) *Color in Everyday Life*. New York: Dodd, Mead and Company.

Paul Weiss (1971) "The Living System: Determinism Stratified" in Koestler and Smythies.

Max Wertheimer (1939) "Laws of Organization in Perceptual Forms" in Ellis.

Don Wharton (1942) "Fooling Enemy Airmen" in *Reader's Digest* (May), pp. 33-35.

Nelson C. White (1951) *Abbott H. Thayer: Painter and Naturalist*. Hartford: Connecticut Printers.

Frank Whitford (1984) *Bauhaus*. New York: Thames and Hudson.

Lancelot Law Whyte, ed. (1966) *Aspects of Form*. Bloomington: Indiana University Press.

Wolfgang Wickler (1968) *Mimicry in Plants and Animals*. New York: McGraw-Hill.

Eliot Wigginson (1979) *Foxfire 5*. Garden City, New York: Anchor Books.

Norman Wilkinson (1969) *A Brush with Life*. London: Seeley Service.

_________ (1919) "Camouflage of Ships in War" in *Nature* 32 (June 19), pp. 304-305.

David Williams (1989) *Liners in Battledress: Wartime Camouflage and Color Schemes for Passenger Ships*. St. Catharines, Ontario: Vanwell.

Hans Wingler (1969) *Bauhaus*. Cambridge, Massachusetts: MIT Press.

Justin Wintle, ed. (1984) *Dictionary of Modern Culture*. London: Arc Paperbacks.

Barbara A. Wolanin (1983) *Arthur B. Carles: Painting with Color*. Exhibition catalog. Philadelphia: Pennsylvania Academy of the Fine Arts.

Natacha Wolinski (1998) "Art et Camouflage: Les Grandes Manoevres" in *Beaux Arts Magazine* 58(169) (June), pp. 58ff.

Joan Wyndham (1986) *Love Lessons: A Wartime Diary*. London: Flamingo/Fontana.

Edward Yardley (1996) "Passion for the Sea [Frank Henry Mason]" in *Antique Dealer and Collectors Guide* 49(12) (July), pp. 36-39.

Richard D. Zakia (1979) *Perception and Photography*. Rochester NY: Light Impressions.

_________ (1997) *Perception and Imaging*. Newton, Massachusetts: Focal Press.

Steven J. Zeitlin, et al. (1982) *A Celebration of American Family Folklore*. New York: Pantheon Books.

Leonard Zusne (1970) *Visual Perception of Form*. New York: Academic Press.